BUCKET
~ TO ~
GREECE

Volume 9

V.D. BUCKET

Editor: James Scraper

Proofreader: Alan Wood

Cover: German Creative

Interior Format: The Book Khaleesi

Other Books in the
Bucket to Greece Series

Chapter 1

A Touch of Daffodil

What on earth, Barry? Is this a deliberate ploy to kill off Violet Burke's few remaining brain cells?"

My nose twitched involuntarily, the distinctive smell of toxic paint fumes assailing my olfactory senses the moment I stepped into the *apothiki*. I attempted to suppress a surge of irritation at the sight of my brother-in-law wielding a paintbrush. As far as I was concerned, all work on the conversion had been completed in readiness for my mother's arrival the next day, yet here we were once again knee-deep in dust sheets. I doubted Violet Burke would welcome the pervasive whiff of enamel paint. Having only popped in to stash another pair of Marigolds and a carton of Vim under the kitchen sink, I was taken aback by Barry's burst of activity.

"Don't blame me, this is down to Marigold," Barry protested. "Mind you, she had a point; you were the one that insisted on buying the cheapest MDF kitchen cabinets and they did look a bit dreary."

"They were a perfectly serviceable brown," I contended, picking up the tin of paint and reading the label aloud, "*Pikralida*. If only it did smell of daffodils."

Reaching into my pocket, I retrieved my sunglasses to protect my eyes from the dazzle of the now glossy and vibrant yellow kitchen cabinets.

"Marigold thought that a touch of daffodil would cheer the place up. I think it's very thoughtful of her to go to so much effort to make your mother feel at home," Barry said.

The irony of Barry's words appeared to be lost on him: it seemed to have escaped his notice that he was the one putting in all the effort whilst Marigold was off swanning around the shops in town with Athena.

"Anyway, the aroma of paint will soon be disguised by the smell of your mother's chip pan. I doubt she will be able to go a day without frying," Barry assured me. I did hope that Marigold remembered to buy a suitable chip pan since it was the convenient excuse she'd used for taking off for the day. I rather suspected she was actually on a mission to buy some new frocks for her imminent trip to Manchester. "You could give me a hand now that you're here."

I was a tad bewildered by Barry's request. He usually goes out of his way to dissuade me from getting involved in DIY, insisting I am incapable of completing a job without botching it. "If I must. Do you have another paintbrush?"

"Don't be daft, Victor. Marigold will kill me if I let you loose on the paint job. You can help out by going and fetching a fan to blow the smell out," Barry chortled.

"I can do better than that. I will halve an onion and leave it out to absorb the fumes..."

"You just happen to be walking round with an onion in your pocket," Barry scoffed as I deftly cut an onion in two.

"I have a bag full of them amongst my shopping. I have people coming for dinner this evening. I thought I'd knock up a pan of *Elliniki kremmydosoupa*, it should be perfect to counter the nip of a November evening," I said.

Rubbing his chin as he mentally translated my words, Barry carelessly daubed a vibrant streak of daffodil across his day-old stubble: it gave him a rather dissolute jaundiced air. "Greek onion soup. I thought onion soup was French."

"I will give it a Greek twist by adding a dash of *ouzo* and some grated *feta*," I explained.

"Mmm, sounds tasty. Is it one of the recipes you've cooked up for your culinary classes?"

"Perish the thought. I don't want a bunch of weepy expats flooding my kitchen."

"Weepy?"

"Onions, Barry, onions."

"Oh, yes, I get it now. I wish I could think of a tactful way of persuading Cynthia to attend your cookery school. She tends to lack imagination in the kitchen."

"Surely not," I said diplomatically. I didn't want it getting back to Cynthia that I had disparaged her cooking, even though it was pretty tasteless.

BUCKET TO GREECE (VOL.9)

"As soon as the weather turned, she cooked up toad-in-the-hole three nights on the trot. Those cheap German sausages in a jar that she got from Lidl are no substitute for a British banger," Barry sighed.

"There's nothing to stop you attending my classes, Barry, we're in the twenty-first century now. Some would consider it sexist to send your wife along to improve her kitchen skills rather than enrolling yourself," I chided, recalling my brother-in-law's own culinary prowess only extended to opening tins and burning toast.

"As if I've got the time to take off mid-day with my workload," Barry scoffed. To be fair he does put in long hours on the job and all that manual labour must be tiring. "Have a word with Cyn for me, Victor. Turn on that old Bucket charm."

"I'll see what I can do," I promised. Barry's suggestion would at least spare me from choking down the stodgy offerings that comprised Cynthia's limited winter repertoire. The thought of Marigold dragging me along to be force-fed the amateur offerings of the expat dining club was enough to persuade me that it would be in my own interest to sign up as many of the British contingent as possible: they were in desperate need of being schooled in the art of producing a decent meal.

"So who are you feeding this evening?" Barry asked.

"Spiros and a potential buyer for the house he inherited from his Uncle Leo."

"I didn't think anyone was biting."

"A likely buyer fell into my hands this afternoon, it was a stroke of luck really as I was meant to knock off at lunchtime," I confided.

My six weeks of helping out in the village shop had dragged on rather longer than expected. Now in my eighth week, I had curtailed my hours to just four mornings a week: since I was about to commence teaching cookery classes in my kitchen, I would need more free time to prepare. Tina was by now back in the shop some of the time, but still at the beck and call of her wart-faced old hag of a mother, Despina, now in residence above the shop whilst she recuperated from her knee op. I suspected Despina of being an attention seeking malingerer, playing up the sympathy card so that her daughter wouldn't send her home to fend for herself. Even though Tina truly has the patience of a saint, her halo is beginning to look a tad tarnished as she reaches the end of her tether.

"So tell me how you ran across a house hunter," Barry urged.

"As I said, it was a stroke of luck. Kyria Kompogiannopoulou was late to relieve me and this English bloke wandered into the shop and we got chatting. He'd flown over to look at property but hadn't been sold on anything he'd seen. He asked if I knew of any houses for sale in the area. I didn't like to bother Spiros as he was off burying someone so I popped round to yours to borrow Sampaguita's keys. I must say that he seemed very keen on the house so I invited him to dinner to meet Spiros."

"It's a solid house with air conditioning. Old Leo didn't scrimp when it came to maintaining the property in excellent condition," Barry said.

"He was certainly one for his home comforts," I agreed, fondly remembering Leo propped up in his bed, a glass of *Metaxa* in hand, Tesco the kitten curled up on his chest. "Gordon Strange seemed quite impressed when I showed him round."

"I suppose Spiros will be bunging you a brown envelope stuffed with cash if you can persuade this fellow to buy it…hang on; did you say he was called Strange?" A wide grin creased Barry's face.

"I certainly did but there didn't appear to be anything strange about him, beyond the fact that he was a stranger. Despite his strange name, he seemed perfectly normal."

"Fancy that. And Spiros will give you some money if he buys?" Barry persisted.

"A commission was mentioned," I confirmed, thinking a cash injection would come in very handy considering the eye-watering amount I had shelled out on the *apothiki* conversion.

The once dusty storage area was now transformed. The welcoming living room conveniently overlooked the street, ensuring Violet Burke would be able to keep a beady eye on everyone's comings and goings. Spiros had claimed the old wooden barrel that held 500 kilos of olive oil, its removal allowing the space to install a bathroom. Although Marigold had been loath to part with this most traditional of features, she agreed that a bathroom was crucial and the oil barrel was in the way. I was quite jealous since we'd installed a bathtub for Violet Burke; a deal breaker as far as my mother was concerned. In turn the new bath required the addition of a second back-up water tank due to the extremely precarious water supply in the village. Unfortunately, my own outdoor spa would be pretty much useless in winter unless I wished to risk freezing my extremities. A kitchen and bedroom completed the conversion.

Admittedly corners had been cut on the cheap kitchen but otherwise Marigold had spared no expense, flashing my credit card on a comfortable sofa and bed in the new IKEA store that had recently opened in Athens. Naturally my wife had managed to turn our shopping expedition into a luxury mini-break in the Greek capital. Neither of us had been tempted to follow Ashley's recommendation of squeezing in a visit to the Andreas Syggros Museum with its extensive collection of moulage depicting deformities caused by VD: even being dragged round Marks and Sparks by my wife was preferable to viewing the grotesqueries on display there.

"I must say that you and Vangelis have done an excellent job on the *apothiki*," I said.

"I think your mother will be comfortable down here, but aren't you worried that she's going to get under your feet?"

"Only in the literal sense," I quipped. "I'm sure that once she gets settled she will be pretty independent and not too reliant on me for company. I was pleasantly surprised when she didn't kick up a stink about having to catch the bus from Athens when she flies in tomorrow."

"None of her usual bellyaching about having to squash her swollen feet onto the bus?" Barry whistled.

"Not a murmur." I had taken the precaution of holding the phone at arm's length when breaking the news to Violet Burke that I wouldn't be able to make it to Athens to collect her because I needed to cover for Tina in the shop: she had to take Despina for a hospital check-up. Perchance the blow was somewhat softened when I assured Violet Burke that I would be waiting for her at the bus station in town to chauffeur her home in the Punto.

"At least you'll have company whilst Marigold is back in Manchester," Barry said. "I expect you'll feel lost without her."

"Nonsense, we aren't joined at the hip. Anyway, she's only going back for a week. I have plenty to occupy my time," I bristled. In truth, I was quite looking forward to having the house to myself; it would certainly be a novelty. I would be able to blast Puccini without my wife complaining about my preference for opera being pretentious. I also hoped to carve out some peaceful time to work on the sequel to my moving abroad book without Marigold hovering over my shoulder, pestering me to add superfluous exclamation marks.

"Ah, here's Marigold now," I said, noting the Punto pull up outside. Not too surprisingly, my wife was laden down with numerous bags as she emerged. As I rushed out to help with her packages, she breezed by me.

"There's still so much to do before your mother can move in," Marigold cried, casting a critical eye around the *apothiki*.

"It looks ready to me," I retorted.

"And to me, Sis," Barry agreed.

"That's just the sort of typical response I would expect from you two. It still needs the vital finishing touches to make it homely. I need to hang the lace edged curtains at the windows, anyone walking by can see right in, and make the bed up…"

"This deep fat fryer won't do at all," I interrupted, spotting the fryer amongst Marigold's purchases. "Violet Burke will expect a proper chip pan, not some fancy gadget."

"Nonsense, she's sure to appreciate an upgrade," Marigold blustered.

"I wouldn't be so sure of that," I muttered under my breath.

"Now, Victor, I bought some lovely new sheets for your mother. Come and give me a hand to make up her bed…"

"You'll have a job," Barry interrupted. "I've been so busy painting that I haven't had time to assemble it yet."

"Really, Barry, all I asked you to do was put the flat-pack bed together…"

"But then you told me to paint all these cupboards. I've only got one pair of hands."

"Then you should have told Victor to assemble the bed…"

"Are you having a laugh, Sis? If Victor tries to put it together, it will likely collapse the moment Violet Burke puts her considerable bulk on it."

"Surely he can help by passing you the widgets or whatever it is that holds it together," Marigold suggested.

"I'll sort it out when I've finished painting," Barry promised.

"I'll have to pop down again later to add the finishing touches then. Victor, there are some pot plants in the boot. Could you dig them out and arrange them artfully on the outside windowsill?"

"Why did you waste money on pot plants

when you could have taken cuttings from the garden?" I asked.

"You know how persuasive Lefteris can be..." Marigold simpered.

"I certainly do," I agreed. One flex of his leather clad tattooed muscles and Marigold was putty in the young man's hands.

"Pot plants, Victor," Marigold snapped.

"I haven't got time to be faffing about with pot plants, dear. We have guests arriving for dinner this evening," I said.

"Surely you don't expect me to knock up a three-course dinner at such short notice," Marigold clucked. "I'm rather worn out from traipsing around town."

"Leave the cooking to me, dear. I must pop upstairs and get started."

The dulcet tones of Marigold exclaiming, "Guests. You never warned me..." reverberated in my ears as I flounced away with my onions.

Chapter 2

A Culinary Stumbling Block

Marigold clattered up the stairs, demanding to know why I hadn't consulted her before deciding to throw a dinner party on a whim. Up to my elbows in flour, I retorted, "It isn't a dinner party, it's just Spiros and an English chap who seems keen on buying Leo's old house."

Marigold's rapid blinking hinted that she was processing the meaning of my words. As the penny dropped that if I played my cards right, I might earn a nice little commission, my wife changed her tune. Peering over my shoulder, she cooed, "What are you cooking, darling?"

"I thought we'd start with a warming *Elliniki kremmydosoupa* and follow it with a homemade potato, olive and sun-dried tomato quiche. The tomatoes from the garden that I dried in the sun turned out superbly, if I do say so myself."

"It's a pity the same can't be said for your pastry, dear." Marigold's attempt to be tactful was incredibly kind considering the sticky and lumpy mess clinging to my rolling pin. "It would have been easier to just defrost that last batch of rabbit *stifado* from the freezer, not to mention far less messy. Don't you think it's a bit risky attempting shortcrust after those mangled Cornish Pasties you turned out the other week?"

"Whilst it is true that they turned out a tad malformed, they tasted perfectly fine. Well, according to Barry, at least."

"A tad malformed is a bit of an understatement," Marigold jeered. "You know full well that Barry would dust off and devour a week-old sausage roll that he'd dropped in the cement mixer if he was hungry enough."

Marigold certainly had a point; pastry remains my culinary stumbling block. I considered it absolutely crucial that I master the technique if I was going to successfully sell my skills as a competent instructor in the fine art of cooking: after all, so many Greek dishes are wrapped in the wretched stuff. The filo pastry required for *spanakopita* is especially tricky. My Greek neighbours have a head start on me in mastering *filo kroustas,* hardly surprising since they have benefited from five centuries of practice to get it right. Rumour has it that the Ancient Greeks were a dab hand at producing wafer thin sheets of filo, the very name derived from the Greek word for leaf, *fyllo.*

"I don't know why you don't just buy frozen pastry," Marigold suggested. "I'm sure that no one would cotton on."

"You wouldn't have caught Fanny Craddock using frozen."

"Fanny Craddock, you're so old-fashioned, Victor," Marigold scoffed. "These days it's all that foul-mouthed Gordon Ramsay."

Shocked that my wife would countenance such subterfuge, I rubbed my fingers to dislodge the clumps of soggy pastry gluing them together. There again, Marigold isn't above cheating when it comes to dousing shop bought *kourabiedes* in icing sugar and passing them off as her own home baked almond biscuits.

"Well, some Greeks must use frozen or Tina wouldn't sell it," Marigold argued. Rushing to my rescue, she admonished, "You're far too heavy-handed with the rolling pin. And your hands are much too warm for handling pastry, it likes a cold touch. Here, hold them under the cold water tap. Drat, there's barely a trickle. I dread to think what the supply will be like once Violet Burke starts wallowing in that tub downstairs."

"There's no water pressure. It's probably just a temporary blip because the back-up tank is full. Mother will never be able to fill the tub unless the pressure increases," I laughed as Marigold scraped the gunk from my fingers.

"What's so funny?"

"You've got a dusting of flour on your nose. It's quite attractive," I said.

"Let's hope the water pressure picks up so that I can shower the flour off before our guests arrive." Marigold blushed at my compliment. "Perhaps I'll try and smuggle some proper Cornish pasties back from England for Barry."

"Only another day before you leave. Are

you looking forward to the trip?" I asked, relinquishing the rolling pin to Marigold as she attempted to make my stubborn shortcrust more pliable.

"I'm certainly not looking forward to the Manchester weather. Geraldine tells me it's damp and cold. I think I've rather become acclimatised to the lovely Greek sunshine."

"If it makes you feel better, we've rain forecast here," I consoled her. "The garden could certainly do with a downpour. I expect that Geraldine is excited about your visit."

"I think that she'll certainly appreciate a friendly shoulder to lean on. She's got herself in quite a tizzy worrying that Ashley is about to propose." A hint of concern crept into Marigold's tone.

"I can imagine it must feel overwhelming. She certainly kissed enough frogs before her prince came along."

"That's the thing, it turns out that Ashley is just another in a long line of ill-matched frogs." Marigold shook her head as she spoke. "Poor Geraldine isn't convinced that he's the one after all, but she doesn't feel she can just trade him in for a more suitable model after that pathetic business about him ditched at the altar. She thinks he may end up a broken man if he's jilted again. Geraldine couldn't bear to have that on her conscience."

The secret that Ashley had confided in me was now general gossip. No sooner had Ashley poured his heart out to Geraldine, than Geraldine indiscreetly blabbed everything to Marigold. However, it was news to me that things weren't going smoothly between Geraldine and her nylon haired suitor. Although neither of us had exactly taken to Ashley, we had accepted that Geraldine was desperate enough to settle for him. For as long as I've known her, Geraldine has been in hot pursuit of any likely candidate to bag as a husband, becoming increasingly less fussy as the years slip by.

"She says that now she's really got to know him, she finds him dull and boring…"

"But he's tall," I protested, feeling that I ought to put up a bit of a defence in male solidarity. "And he keeps his hairpieces in pristine order."

"Victor, you know as well as I do that he's an insufferable bore. And would you want his hands all over you after what he's been handling in that lab all day?"

It struck me as rather redundant to bother

replying to such an outrageous question, my mind otherwise occupied with the unwelcome image of curdled cauliflower cheese that always popped into my head whenever I thought of Ashley investigating his sexually infected samples under a microscope.

"I don't know how Geraldine could stomach it, to be honest," Marigold continued.

"I must say that I'm surprised. I thought that Geraldine was desperate enough to settle for anyone that would have her."

"Well, it turns out that she has a few standards after all and Ashley just doesn't live up to them. There's no doubt that she's got herself into a bit of a pickle if he proposes."

"Surely she won't go through with it just to spare his feelings?"

"Oh no, she couldn't endure it. She says that now it's so cold in England, he keeps his socks on in bed whenever he stays over; it's a terrible passion killer," Marigold shuddered.

"I struggle to get my head around the notion of Ashley being passionate in the first place: he had too much of a dead fish about him," I pointed out.

"I prefer not to speculate," Marigold shuddered again. "I think that I'll advise Geraldine to try and come up with some ingenious way to put Ashley off her, so that he'll be the one to do the dumping. What would you find most off-putting in a woman, Victor? Hypothetically."

"I'm quite repulsed by women who aren't too scrupulous about their personal hygiene and dress up like tarts," I admitted.

"Once I'm in Manchester, I could drag Geraldine along to Top Shop and kit her out in a new wardrobe of transparently provocative skin tight mini-dresses..." Marigold piped up.

"I don't think she's quite got the figure to carry that off."

"That's the whole point; we'll go for the mutton dressed as lamb look. I'm sure that Geraldine could be persuaded to stop bathing if she thought the pong might put Ashley off."

"Well, I just hope you know what you're doing. Your interference may well backfire," I warned.

The wonderful scent of caramelised onions filled the kitchen as I prepared the soup. Once it was sweating away on a low heat, I popped down to the garden to pick some sage leaves to use as a decorative feature for the quiche, surprised to discover it was already dark outside.

The nights drew in so quickly at this time of year. I shivered slightly at the unexpected chill in the air. No matter how much warmth we basked in during the late autumn days, the temperature swiftly plummeted as soon as the sun went down.

Crouching over the sage bush, I felt something brush up against my arm. The smell of stale sweat vied with the subtle scent of sage, alerting me to Guzim's presence: the Albanian shed dweller is a consummate master of creeping around in the dark.

After dispensing with the usual greetings, Guzim shuffled around on the spot before announcing, "*I gynaika mou einai enkyos xana.*"

The darkness made it impossible to read Guzim's indistinct features. Moreover, his muttered words gave no intimation whether I should offer my congratulations or commiserations at the news that his wife was pregnant again. Deciding to hedge my bets, I asked if he was happy about it, "*Eisai charoumenos gi afto?*"

"*Eimai charoumenos an einai agori,*" Guzim replied. His tone lacked any excitement as he told me he was happy if it was a boy.

Since he had presumably managed to impregnate Luljeta in the pink palace of love during her recent visit to Greece, I calculated that it would be a good seven months before Guzim made a decision if the news was good or not. Personally, I blamed Marigold for Luljeta's condition: by interfering and transforming Guzim's hovel, she had set the scene for a romantic encounter. No sane woman would have allowed herself to be sweet talked into bed if the shed had been left in its original state of festering squalor.

"*Echete akousei kati gia to Besnik?*" I said, asking if he had heard anything about Besnik.

"*Tipota, echei exafanistie.*" Guzim's response of 'Nothing, he has vanished,' was the same reply he had uttered ever since the Albanian building foreman disappeared, abandoning Luljeta in Greece. Fortunately Spiros and Nikos had whisked Luljeta back over the border in the hearse without incident. Pragmatically, my two sage friends were of the opinion that it was better all-round if Besnik remained a missing person, unable to embroil any more innocents in his criminal schemes. We remained none the wiser if Besnik had acted under his own initiative or if he had merely been a pawn doing the bidding of the scheming criminals he had become entangled with.

At least Guzim and Luljeta were now able to stay in touch without the use of an intermediary. When Marigold had finally heard what had happened, she had been most concerned about Luljeta: my wife had grown very fond of the young woman. Marigold came up trumps by flashing my credit card to purchase a pair of cheap mobile phones for the Albanian couple. I just hoped that Guzim would earn enough to pay for any calls. His regular work on the coast had dried up since Besnik's disappearance and there was only so much gardening work that I could put his way as winter approached. Fortunately, he still had the chickens to keep him busy.

"*Vrikes douleia?*" I asked if he had found any work.

"*Nai, tha kano tis elies me ton Niko.*" A note of pride inflected Guzim's tone when he informed me that he would be doing the olives with Nikos. That was certainly a turn up for the books, Guzim usually complaining that Nikos was a miserly slave-driver who only paid a pittance. Clearly Nikos' selfless altruism in helping Luljeta return to Albania had made Guzim view him in a new light.

"*Bravo, afto einai exairetiko.*" Thumping

Guzim on the back supportively, I told him that was excellent. The news was indeed music to my ears as it would hopefully get Nikos off my back: he had already started dropping heavy hints that I should give him a hand with his olive harvest this year. I had no desire to undertake such back-breaking work under the direction of a slave-driver who only paid a pittance.

This was the third year in succession that Nikos had tried to sell me on the ridiculous notion that picking olives was some romantic idyll that I should undertake to feel at one with the changing Greek seasons. Although I must confess to quite fancying having a go, I was sure that a half-day in the olive groves would be quite sufficient to satisfy my curiosity. I knew full well that a meagre few hours of my time would never satisfy Nikos: he expects nothing less than to see me toiling from dawn to dusk for six weeks straight without so much as a single day off. Since Dimitris is the very antithesis of a hard taskmaster, I may offer to give him a hand for a couple of hours in order to experience olive picking first-hand. I must make him promise not to tell Nikos.

My teeth were beginning to chatter in the cold, yet Guzim remained seemingly impervious to it. Fortunately, Marigold rescued me from any further shivering chat with Guzim by calling out that Barry had finally assembled Violet Burke's new bed and she needed me to give her a hand to make it up.

"I've dinner to see to, why can't Barry help you?" I complained as we trailed back to the *apothiki*.

"I don't want him getting paint all over the new bedding. Anyway, he's gone home; he couldn't wait to see his beautiful baby. Now, I think this new electric blanket goes under the sheet..."

"I can't see Violet Burke wanting to sleep on something that might electrocute her. You should have bought her a hot water bottle instead," I grumbled.

"Nonsense, Victor, it will be a treat for your mother to be all toasty and warm."

"Guzim has some news," I confided. "It seems that Luljeta is pregnant again but he'll only be happy about it if she produces a boy."

"How on earth did that happen?" Marigold exclaimed.

"In the usual way, I should imagine."

"Yes, but she was only here for...what was it, one night or two?"

"It only takes once. Anyway, what did you

expect would happen after you turned that flea-pit hovel of his into a love nest?"

"I don't like your tone, Victor. One doesn't like to think of that kind of thing going on in the shed, even if it had been given a makeover."

Marigold's aloof tone let me know that she absolved herself of all responsibility but I found that her highfalutin manner rather amused me. Firing what I imagined was a rather saucy wink at my wife, I pointed out that she needn't come over all proper at the thought of a dalliance taking place in the shed.

"At least his shed has a bed. I don't recall you having a fit of the vapours when it came to the backseat of my old Ford Cortina back in the day."

"Victor, you'll make me blush," Marigold simpered, dropping her imperious tone and turning as red as a beetroot.

"Ouch." A stab of pain shot through my finger as it encountered something sharp, impaling it on the base of the new bed. Pulling my finger free, drops of blood sprayed freely all over my mother's pristine new bedding.

"Oh, Victor, really. Must you be so careless? This duvet cover is brand new," Marigold cried as the crimson stain spread on the sky blue cover. It was typical of my wife to have her priorities upside down, quite happy to disregard the fact that I may be bleeding to death as long as I didn't make a mess on the bedding.

"I'm sure that Violet Burke will come armed with some hideous candlewick thing she can throw over the bed," I retorted, stomping off in search of a plaster.

Chapter 3

Boors, Bores and Boars

A tentative tap on the front door heralded the arrival of our first guest.

"If that's your house buyer then he's thirty minutes early, it's terribly impolite of him not to stick to the invited time. I haven't even changed yet: I must look a total fright," Mari gold hissed. Dashing off to the bedroom to change, she reminded me, "You haven't even put the quiche in the oven to bake yet. Do you want everyone to come down with food poisoning from eating raw pastry?"

"I haven't given anyone salmonella yet," I countered. "Besides, it's too soon to put the quiche in the oven. Spiros is sure to be on Greek time which means he'll be at least thirty minutes late."

Having said that, I was rather taken aback to discover Spiros, rather than the potential house buyer, lurking on the doorstep. Grabbing me by the collar, Spiros pulled me outside, whispering, "Is he to here yet? I want to know if he is the serious to buy the house."

"Come inside, Spiro," I invited. "He hasn't arrived yet."

"Good. Tell to me what he said," Spiros insisted, sprawling untidily on the sofa.

"I told you on the phone. I showed him around the house and he seemed very keen. He told me that he and his wife are looking for a house in the area. They don't want anything on the coast, too touristy, he said. They want something in the hills where it's quieter."

"The house of the Uncle Leo is the quiet. Did you to tell to him he can to hear the quiet? You must to the persuade him to buy it, Victor. The sooner it is the sold, the sooner the fragrant Sampaguita have no the excuse not to move in with the me."

"I thought you had to sell the house to pay your tax bill."

"I get the new, how you to say in the English, the *logistis*?"

"An accountant…"

"Yes, the accountant. He have the clever way to make me pay the less tax. But it is the stupid to pay the electric on the two houses; it will be the cheaper to have the Sampaguita live with the me."

I certainly couldn't fault Spiros' logic. Paying for the upkeep of two households seemed a profligate waste of money in my opinion. The only thing holding Sampaguita back from moving in with Spiros before they married was an out-dated sense of shame about their living in sin.

"And you to say he is the English?" Spiros continued.

"Yes, indeed."

"I like the English very the much, the most of them to make the good neighbour. I trust in the you, Victor, that you will not to sell the house to another like the Harold," Spiros chuckled.

"Heavens, no. We don't want any more riff-raff like Harold and Joan blighting the village."

"Riff-raff?" Spiros queried.

"Drunken boors," I clarified.

"Ah, you have to hear there are the *agriogourounoi* in the village," Spiros said, greedily gulping his glass of *ouzo*.

Running the tongue twister of the Greek word through my brain, I came up blank. "I'm afraid I don't know that word," I admitted.

Finger-combing his busy eyebrows, Spiros gave me a quizzical look.

"Victor, you are the confusion. You have just to said that word in the English…"

Now I was really confused by the odd turn of the conversation.

"The *agriogourounoi* is the wild boars, they get into the garden of the Doreen and make the trample of the plant. And in the field of the Panos, they make the dig up the many onion."

A light bulb clicked in my brain. "Spiro, I was talking about boors, not boars."

"*Ti?*" It was Spiros' turn to look flummoxed. I suppose I couldn't blame him, it was hard for his Greek brain to master the complexities of the many homophones that pepper the English language. I decided it would be prudent to give Spiros a short lesson to clarify the language mix up.

"We are speaking at cross purposes, Spiro. A peculiar quirk of the English language means that certain words can be confusing for non-native speakers. In English we have the words bore, boor and boar, which whilst sounding exactly the same each have different meanings. Such words are known as homophones."

"I tell to you many the time, Victor, that we the Greek invent the homosexual."

"Not homosexual, homophones," I groaned, thinking we could well end up going round in circles all evening.

"*Kalispera, Spiro*," Marigold trilled, floating into the kitchen in some strange sort of kaftan dress that appeared to be a new and rather unflattering addition to her wardrobe. As she rushed over to exchange double kisses with our guest, I took a close look to see if I could spot a tell-tale price tag dangling below her back neckline.

"Spiros was just saying that wild boars have got into Doreen's garden and trampled her plants," I said.

"Oh, how dreadful, Doreen takes such pride in her garden," Marigold sympathised. "Are the creatures likely to get into ours too, do you think?"

"I expect that Kostis is keeping a keen eye out. He'll soon hunt out any intruders," I said. Casting an eye over Catastrophe, sprawled out on the sofa next to Spiros, reminded me that Kostis loved nothing more than firing off random pot-shots at anything that moved. It was a wonder the feline had ever recovered its sense of balance considering the trauma Kostis had inflicted on its tail.

Whilst not wishing to worry my wife, I found the idea of wild boars on the loose in Meli very disturbing. Although clueless if they posed a threat to my livestock, I rather doubted that my chickens would be brave enough to stand up to any invading swine, plucky little creatures though they are.

"The Kostis will to hunt the *agriogourounoi*," Spiros assured us. "Perhaps if he to kill them, the Eleni will to believe he hunt the *agriogourounoi* and not the woman. If he to shoot one, she might to return to the husband."

"You've lost me, Spiro," Marigold said. "Are you saying that Eleni has left Kostis?"

"Yes, you not to hear? It is the talk of the village. The Nikos and the Dina are the furious with the Kostis. The Eleni go back to the parent and take the Nikoleta with the her, she say the

Kostis is the *achristos anoito…*"

Clearly unsure of Nikos' meaning, Marigold looked to me to offer a translation.

"A useless fool," I duly interpreted.

"Eleni say the Kostis is the bad husband, he stay away the night after the night and say he the hunting, but she think he to hunting the woman."

"Well, he does have a reputation for it," I conceded.

"And anyone can see that Kostis is a complete waste of space as a husband," Marigold chimed in. "He treats poor Eleni like a servant and much as I like Nikos and Dina, they have Eleni running around at their beck and call too."

"It is the Greek way for the *nyfi* to help the parent of the husband," Spiros defended.

"I appreciate that but it doesn't excuse Kostis' behaviour," Marigold countered, climbing up on her high-horse. "When was the last time that Kostis took Eleni out for a romantic evening or took his turn with the childcare?"

"Eleni have the Dina to help with the child but you to make the good point, Marigold. The man should to *romantikos* the woman, yes," Spiros agreed. "I tell to you, I am the happy to eat the here tonight. The Nikos put the black cloud over the taverna with his temper."

"You're welcome anytime," Marigold assured him. "Perhaps you could come and keep Victor company whilst I'm in England. I expect he'll be lost without me."

"Spiros doesn't want me cramping his style, playing gooseberry on his romantic evenings with Sampaguita," I said before repeating for the umpteenth time, "And I am more than capable of fending for myself and have plenty to keep me occupied."

The sound of a horn blasting on the street outside interrupted our conversation. Peering through the balcony doors, I spotted a car outside. "I think that must be Gordon Strange now. I'll go down and meet him. He may come a cropper if he attempts the outside stairs in the dark."

"I hope I'm not too early, I allowed plenty of time to drive up in the dark from the coast. The road is a bit of a challenge with its myriad of twists and turns," Gordon said once the introductions were dispensed with.

"Not at all, do come and have a seat in the grand salon and let me pour you some wine," Marigold invited.

"Just a soft drink, I don't want to drink and

drive," Gordon responded.

"Considering his name is Strange, there doesn't appear to be anything strange about him. He seems perfectly normal," Marigold whispered as she returned to the kitchen to pour him a glass of orange juice.

Marigold's observation was on point. I would hazard a guess that Gordon Strange was about my age and appeared to be perfectly normal. His sensible attire of a pair of grey slacks and a button down appeared to reassure Marigold that Gordon wasn't another Harold type, blotting the landscape in some gaudy Hawaiian shirt paired with indecent budgie smugglers. Whilst showing Gordon around Leo's house earlier, I had already discovered that he wasn't a one dimensional bore like Norman. A spot of subtle interrogation had uncovered that he had no literary leanings towards porn like Milton. Gordon had told me that whilst he was semi-retired, he kept busy by doing the odd bit of consultancy work in computing. He could turn out to be a handy neighbour if our WiFi went down.

After popping the quiche in the oven, I joined the others in the grand salon, catching the conversation between Marigold and Gordon. "So you're staying down on the coast."

"Yes. We made an appointment to view property with a local estate agent who suggested we base ourselves there. Unfortunately, my wife Moira had to postpone at the last moment, she had a booking. She flies into Athens tomorrow and plans to catch the bus through to town. I will drive up in the hire car and meet her in the afternoon."

"Oh, Victor's mother may well be on the same bus from Athens as your wife, he's driving up to the bus station tomorrow afternoon to collect her. Perhaps you could go with Victor since you aren't so used to the local roads," Marigold suggested.

"I'm afraid that my mother will be weighed down with so much luggage that there won't be any room in the car for any additional passengers," I said apologetically, thinking it would be prudent to keep Violet Burke well away from the potential house buyer. "My mother is flying over to spend the winter in Greece."

"And she's staying with you?" Gordon asked.

"In a manner of speaking. We've had the *apothiki* downstairs converted into a separate abode for her," I said.

"She's very independent, she wouldn't

want us cramping her style," Marigold revealed. After hearing Spiros' stated opinion that it was a daughter-in-law's duty to help out her mother-in-law, Marigold remained tight-lipped about her intention to put Violet Burke to work as our cleaner. It certainly turned the traditional Greek way of doing things on its head. Still, I expected that Mother would find the pocket money quite handy: she seemed to be in a constant state of penury.

Frowning anxiously, Spiros tapped Gordon on the shoulder to get his attention. "You to say you to meet the estate agent." Clearly Spiros was worried that the potential buyer might be lured away by a professional agent before any deal was sealed. As Spiros closed in on our guest's personal space, I noticed Gordon subtly recoil, no doubt repelled by a whiff of stale embalming fluid.

"Yes, but I'm afraid to say that he was pretty useless. Some Norwegian chap, he spent two days showing me houses that were completely unsuitable, new builds near the coast. I told him we wanted something in the hills but all he seemed to have on his books was a pile of overgrown ruins in need of complete renovation jobs. We don't want to undertake a massive project like that," Gordon explained. "It was a stroke of luck meeting Victor and the house which he showed me earlier definitely ticked all our boxes. It has been very well maintained and the views are to die for. The air conditioning is certainly a bonus; I expect it will take us a while to acclimatise to the heat over here."

The way that Gordon fanned himself vigorously with a stray magazine as he spoke gave me second thoughts about putting a match to the fire laid in the hearth. His comfort was paramount until he had signed on the dotted line.

Catching my eye, Marigold suppressed a giggle. We both recalled the Norwegian agent that had tried to sell us a bridge, so to speak, when he'd shown us around more than two years ago. It seemed he still wasn't having much luck attempting to flog his motley collection of modern Mani towers and old wrecks to gullible foreigners.

"The house he belong to the Uncle, he leave him to the me," Spiros volunteered, hastily adding, "The Uncle not to die in him, he die in the hospital."

I remembered Spiros using the same line on us when he'd first shown us the house he'd inherited from his Uncle Pedros. Technically it was true since the uncle had been scraped up from the pavement outside after plummeting to his death from the roof terrace.

"So your wife will be joining you tomorrow, Gordon," Marigold said, keen to move on to less maudlin subjects. "You mentioned that she had a booking, I take it she still works in England then."

"Yes, the agency rang with a modelling job; it was too good for Moira to turn down. Unfortunately the bookings are not as frequent as they used to be, one of the downsides of ageing."

"Your the wife is the model." Spiros' eyes hung out on stalks. His years of making *kamaki* with any beautiful tourist woman had become a habit too ingrained to be easily discarded, even though he was now engaged. It was evident that Spiros was impressed by Gordon's wife being a model; Marigold not so much.

I couldn't help but notice the way my wife's eyes narrowed at the prospect of a model moving into the village. She has become accustomed to being the most attractive woman in Meli, excepting Poppy who is so gorgeous and leggy that I had believed the rumours she was a supermodel. Of course, Poppy isn't technically a village resident, just an overnighter when she stays with Giannis. Her model looks don't worry Marigold since she's of a different generation, but I could understand that Marigold's nose might be put out of joint if a newcomer was to outshine her in the pending pensioner age range.

"And do you and Moira enjoy cooking?" I asked, testing the waters to see if either of them would be likely candidates for my culinary classes.

"Oh yes, we both enjoy experimenting in the kitchen. I suppose we'll have to get to grips with Greek dishes if we buy the house in the village. It would make sense to master the local specialities."

His answer was music to my ears. If I could enrol the Stranges along with Cynthia, the classes may well prove quite lucrative. I already had Doreen and Norman, Edna and Milton, and Sherry, all signed up. To be precise, although Edna and Milton were both signed up, they would take it turns to attend alternate classes. Pleading poverty, Milton had proposed that I accept both of them onto the course for the price of one as a pensioner special, but I rejected his proposal out of hand since I had no intention of running a charity. If I made an exception for the

Hancocks, who knew where it could all end.

Ushering our guests through to the kitchen, I turned on my persuasive charm, ladling out the *Elliniki kremmydosoupa* whilst launching my practiced sales spiel.

Chapter 4

A Surprise Candlelit Dinner

T his soup is absolutely superb," Gordon enthused.

"*Einai nostimo,*" Spiros raved, confirming it was delicious. "I am the happy you learn to cook the *Elliniko fagito* instead of the foreigns curry." Spiros grimaced, recalling his first encounter with a spicy Indian.

Turning to Gordon, Marigold offered a translation, saying, "Spiros is pleased that Victor has cooked Greek food. He didn't quite take to the Indian curry that Victor served up. Most

Greeks seem to prefer Greek food."

"The Greek he is the best food in the world," Spiros boomed.

"I thought that Sampaguita's influence was rubbing off and you were becoming more cosmopolitan in your taste," I laughed.

"I try to persuade the Sampaguita to cook more the Greek food," Spiros admitted.

"Well, at least you won't have to suffer fried grasshoppers at this time of the year," Marigold chortled.

"Yes, you're lucky that they are a seasonal delicacy," I guffawed.

"I noticed that there was a very neat vegetable garden at the house that I viewed..." Gordon began.

"The Sampaguita plant the carrot and the broccoli, she like to use the fresh," Spiros interrupted.

"I'd quite like to grow our own if we buy the house but it would only make sense if we decide to make the move a permanent one," Gordon continued.

"Where do you live in England," Marigold asked.

"Salisbury."

"The cathedral town. How lovely. So Leo's

house would be a holiday home?" Marigold persisted. Although she appeared quite adept at squirreling information out of our guest, she was still a novice when compared to our Greek neighbours. Athena would be demanding to know how much modelling paid whilst Kyria Maria would be jotting down Gordon Strange's inside leg measurement.

"We are thinking of spending three months at a time in Greece, at least to start with," Gordon said. "The local airport will be convenient for Moira to fly back from in summer if she gets any modelling jobs."

"But your wife hasn't even seen the property yet," Marigold said. I must confess that the point she made was one that I found worrying: in my experience it is invariably the woman who makes the decision when it comes to choosing a home.

"Moira is more than happy to leave that kind of thing to me. Her remit is something quiet in the hills."

"Since so many British prefer to live by the coast, the mountains retain their tranquillity. You will find that Meli is peace personified," I said. Crossing my fingers behind my back, I hoped that Panos' ferocious guard dog didn't kick off with its regular round of raucous barking until our guest had left. Fortunately Gordon wasn't staying the night so he wouldn't be woken at dawn by the rousing early morning cacophony of crowing roosters. "You will find that Meli is a most welcoming community."

"And there's a lively circle of expats," Marigold disclosed. I considered her remark a tad hyperbolic: I would hardly describe the likes of Norman and Milton as lively. "I'm sure that you would enjoy the regular get-togethers of the expat dining club."

"If the standard of food is as good as this delicious soup, I'm sure that we will," Gordon replied enthusiastically.

Opening my mouth to make a quip about dismal slop, I intercepted the withering look that Marigold fired in my direction. Left gaping like a goldfish, I read my wife's look as a warning to keep schtum that I found most of the food served up by the club to be inedible. Perchance Marigold's unspoken caution was unnecessary: the quality of food would be sure to improve once I had knocked some standards into my expat pupils during my cookery classes.

"So you to want to see the house the again the tomorrow?" Spiros said to Gordon.

"I think it would be better to wait until the day after," I advised. "The bus from Athens doesn't arrive until mid-afternoon so it would be nearly dark by the time they got up to Meli."

Sending a quizzical look in my direction, Spiros' bushy eyebrows furrowed to form a single monobrow. Clearly he thought I was trying to sabotage the sale or leave Gordon ripe to be plucked by the grasping hands of another unscrupulous estate agent. Fortunately Marigold caught on, backing me up by saying, "Victor is quite right. It was the wonderful views that sold me on living in Meli and your wife won't be able to appreciate the glorious views in the dark."

"The morning *methavrio* then," Spiros confirmed. Satisfied that the buyer was still on the hook, Spiros excused himself. "Marigold, I go to the balcony for the cigarette."

No sooner had Spiros left the room than Gordon Strange put a proposition to me. "If Moira likes the house as much as I do, then we'll put in an offer for sure. I'd really feel more comfortable having you on our side to act as a go-between; you strike me as someone that would keep everything above board. I'd be willing to pay you a commission to have a fellow Brit on side to navigate through the uncharted course of the Greek way of doing things."

Gordon's offer made me feel quite nostalgic when I thought back to how trusting Marigold and I had been when first dealing with Spiros, never thinking to employ an intermediary. We hadn't hesitated for a moment in putting our trust in the local undertaker: the instant rapport we had formed had developed into a true friendship. Still, I was happy to accept a commission from both the seller and the buyer if it would put the Stranges at ease to have a fellow Brit in their corner.

"I'd be happy to guide you through the Greek system, it can be a tad daunting when everything is conducted in a foreign language. I have some experience beyond my own as I held my brother-in-law's hand when he purchased a house in the village," I said. Spiros had already asked me if I would tag along on the necessary trips to the notary and lawyer to facilitate the smooth running of the buying process and to keep the conversation flowing during the numerous pit stops to drink Greek coffee and eat cheese pies.

Our hushed conversation came to a halt when Spiros returned, the smell of tobacco thankfully watering down the lingering whiff of embalming fluid. Clearing the soup bowls away, I served the quiche and salad, hoping that the pastry wouldn't be a complete disaster.

"This is excellent fare, Victor. I quite forgot to mention that I've been experimenting with vegetarianism when you invited me to dinner, yet you have served up a top-notch meatless meal. I take it you must be a fellow vegetarian..."

Marigold snorted and Spiros nearly choked on his quiche, repeating the word vegetarian in Greek, "*Chortofagos*," as though it described some alien condition. I was very relieved that I had gone to the trouble to make something fresh rather than defrosting the last batch of rabbit *stifado* from the freezer. Our vegetarian guest may have fled Meli never to return if I'd served him a plate of bunny.

"Although we aren't technically vegetarians, we often enjoy meat free meals without even noticing. The local vegetables are just so fresh and bountiful," I boasted.

"Well this quiche surpasses the ones we buy from Marks and Sparks," Gordon enthused. Spiros had gone very quiet, examining the food on his plate suspiciously as though I had tricked him into becoming an unwitting herbivore.

"Victor could write a cookery book on a hundred and one things to do with a courgette. I never realised he was so imaginative until we had a glut of the things," Marigold said. "So, Gordon, is your wife a vegetarian too?"

"Oh no, Moira will eat anything. She's particularly partial to tucking into a Fray Bentos while I graze on a salad."

Marigold arched her eyebrows, no doubt surprised that his model wife didn't starve herself on the latest popular fad diet.

"I may well revert back to a diet that includes meat once we are in Greece on a regular basis. I only gave it up after contracting a debilitating dose of campylobacter from some chicken I ate. It rather knocked the stuffing out of me," Gordon sighed. "I'm sure the restaurant served up some inferior bird from a supermarket rather than the free range variety their menu promised."

"Campylobacter can certainly be a nasty condition to contract," I sympathised, thinking I had spared half the population of Manchester from coming down with the same ailment due to my vigilant eye. My rigid insistence that thermometers were stuffed inside chickens had prevented the serving of birds with dangerously raw pink bits.

"There will be no the need to holiday in the tent if you to buy the house," Spiros piped up. The undertaker continued to shovel quiche into his mouth as though he hadn't eaten for a week, oblivious that three pairs of eyes were regarding him rather askance. The penny dropped and I realised that Spiros had mistaken a dose of campylobacter with a camping holiday.

"I imagine there are some splendid walks in the area for Waffles to enjoy," Gordon said, rather adeptly changing the subject.

"Waffles?"

"Waffles is our goldendoodle, a new addition to the family."

"*Ti?*" Spiros spluttered. There was no point in my Greek friend looking at me to translate. I had no clue what Gordon was talking about either.

"He's a cross between a golden retriever and a poodle. During the summer, Moira spotted one on the cover of Life magazine and just had to have one," Gordon explained.

"*O skylos poodle*," I said for Spiros' benefit, pronouncing poodle with a Greek accent, before adding the word gold for good measure. "*O chrysos poodle*."

The gold poodle part would have to suffice since I had no idea what different dog breeds were known as in Greek.

"A designer dog," Marigold clarified.

"*Enas skylos fylakas*?" Spiros asked me if it was a guard dog. I shrugged to indicate I didn't know, though I imagined a yapping poodle would scare most things away.

"That reminds me," Gordon said. "Moira said I must be sure to ask if there are any grooming parlours in the area. If Waffles is going to adjust to the heat, he'll need to have his curls trimmed regularly."

"The Apostolos cut the hair but he to give the lopsided neckline," Spiros volunteered.

Sending Spiros a withering look, Marigold said, "Apostolos doesn't do dogs. Gordon, there is a dog grooming parlour in the centre of town. Our friend Lefteris takes Fufu there for grooming and she always looks very chic."

"Fufu?" Spiros questioned.

"A pampered poodle decked out in pink ribbons," I clarified, shrugging again when Spiros expected me to come up with a translation.

"That will be music to Moira's ears. It was a bit of deal breaker, she's quite vain where Waffles is concerned." Gordon sighed in relief.

"Waffles is sure to enjoy walks in the hills. We have a holiday home just inland from the coast in Devon but he hasn't taken to the beaches there at all. He seems to have a real aversion to sand."

I wondered if perchance the pampered pet had manicured toenails and worried they may be sandpapered if they came into contact with the beach. I reflected that in addition to owning a home in Salisbury and a holiday home in Devon, the Stranges were about to snap up a lovely house in Greece. It struck me that with three homes to their name plus enough spare cash to splash out on a designer dog, they must be rolling in it. The slight feeling of guilt I had about accepting Gordon's offer to pay me a commission, receded. We would be the poor neighbours next to the Stranges.

"Do you happen to know if there are any caves in the local area?" Gordon asked. "I'd be particularly keen to explore any."

"There's plenty along the coastline. Nearer to home we discovered an interesting looking one in Nektar, the next village along," I replied.

"I don't suppose I could prevail upon you to give me a tour of the one in Nektar," Gordon requested.

"Oh, I think we could arrange something," I agreed. The cave that we had stumbled across in Nektar had looked quite fascinating. Unfortunately, Marigold's fear that a plague of bats would attempt to mate with her hair had rather put the lid on my exploring inside.

"Can I tempt you to another slice of quiche?" I offered. No sooner had I picked up the knife than the kitchen was plunged into darkness. I cursed under my breath: the power going off in the village on a regular basis was hardly a convincing selling point.

"Victor, find some candles," Marigold cried. Belatedly coming to the same conclusion that I had already reached about frequent power outages being off-putting, she added in an up-beat tone, "I always think that candlelit dinners are so romantic."

"I have the light," Spiros announced, flicking his cigarette lighter into action.

"Allow me," I said, snatching the lighter from Spiros in case the naked flame ignited any embalming fluid still clinging to him. Within minutes the kitchen and grand salon were pleasantly illuminated by a lavish selection of Marigold's posh scented candles.

As Marigold continued to extract personal

information out of our guest, my mind wandered to a recent trip on Pegasus when I had stood in for Cynthia during one of *Kapetainos* Vasos' moonlit cruises. The tourist trip left in the late afternoon, incorporating a stop at an old town where I gave a guided tour. The holidaymakers were then free to wander at leisure or eat in one of the many fine tavernas that the town boasted before meeting up in the town square to make our way back to Pegasus as a group. Anchor ahoy was at 10pm for the cruise back in the moonlight.

After duly showing the tourists around the ancient part of the town, I had caught up with Vasos and Sami, joining them for a pizza in a quaint taverna with a wood-fired oven. Disaster struck later as we led our group back to the harbour: the power went out, plunging the town into absolute blackness. Considering we were supposed to be on a moonlit trip, the moon wasn't playing ball, the darkness so thick that it was impossible to even discern a hand held up in front of one's face.

I worried that I may lose some of the tourists or that more than a few of them may trip over and break something vital, necessitating a tedious trip to the nearest hospital. I had never been so relieved in all my days of repping to have my trusty whistle around my neck. Blasting out a rallying call on said whistle and flicking my torch on, I herded the group together, instructing them not to move an inch.

Vasos and Sami went ahead to Pegasus to start the engine to power up the lights. Returning, they arranged the tourists in a conga line to blindly fumble their way back towards the dimly lit boat. Progress was painstakingly slow, the way ahead punctuated with groans of pain as toes were stubbed. Cries of fear permeated the night air as the tourists mistook random cats for something more ominous and there were outraged squeals as Vasos' helping hands may have accidentally goosed a few of the female tourists.

The shuffling conga line finally reached our embarkation spot on the harbour. Although the group were naturally anxious about traversing the gangplank in such impenetrable blackness, the tension was relieved by Vasos personally helping everyone across individually, depositing each person safely on deck with a cheery, "Beautiful towel," or an exuberant, "I love you."

I was quite touched when, with everyone across, Vasos came back for me. It took a brave man indeed to cross a wobbly plank in pitch darkness when one wrong move could result in a moonless swim in the inky water below. Vasos' irrepressible banter calmed the whole party and once on-board he ordered Sami to serve shots of ouzo all round to steady the nerves. There was a resounding cheer from the whole group when the lights on the coast we were approaching finally flickered into life, illuminating our arrival just as Vasos negotiated Pegasus back into dock.

The frantic barking of dogs accompanied by the strident sound of distressed squawks reverberating from the garden shocked me back to reality. Alarm coursed through my veins as the cumulative din assaulted my ears. Grabbing a torch and bravely disregarding my personal safety, I grabbed hold of Spiros' shirt-tail and legged it down to the garden, the others following in hot pursuit.

Chapter 5

Moonlit Carnage

My torch cast a spectral glow in the darkness, the chilly night air echoing with the eerie hoot of owls, the outraged screeches of cats and an angry chorus of barking. Clueless what type of foe may be lurking in the garden, I found myself reluctant to leave the shadows of the outdoor staircase. After Spiros' earlier talk of wild boars, it wasn't an enormous leap to suppose that a passel of savage hogs may be on the loose in my garden. I didn't consider it cowardly to suffer from palpitations at the prospect of being trampled underfoot.

The sound of my Greek neighbours leaning out of their windows, hollering their annoyance at the disturbance whilst ironically adding to it, reached my ears. It was shocking to hear a man of the cloth come out with the sort of vulgar expletives that I could hear drifting down from Papas Andreas' bedroom window.

"*Ela, Victor.*" Grabbing a garden rake as a likely weapon, Spiros urged me to follow him across the garden as he strode fearlessly towards the apparent source of the ruckus, the chicken coop. Not wishing to throw myself into harm's way without protection, I snatched the esoteric back scratcher from the outdoor bathtub. I imagined it might prove pretty useless as a defence against a marauding wild boar unless said boar had a particular itch that it needed scratching.

The silvery orb of the moon drifted out from the cover of clouds, flooding the garden with moonlight. The sudden illumination highlighted a shadowy figure hurling itself through the hole in the fence. A streaking flash of Christmas trees caught my attention, revealing Guzim sprawled flat on his face in the mud, tripping over the too-long legs of the hideous sleep suit which Barry had gifted me.

"What the...?" Gordon exclaimed, no doubt baffled by the appearance of a shifty looking character clad in a giant babygrow.

The moonlight disappeared as quickly as it had emerged, replaced with the guttural swearing of the Albanian shed dweller, bi-lingually switching between Greek and Albanian obscenities. Spiros' cry of "The Guzim he run away," indicated that the undertaker was blessed with superior night vision since I couldn't make out any movement. The distinctive sound of water being sprayed was accompanied by Guzim yelling, "*Parte afto, omi.*" It seemed that rather than fleeing in a moment of cowardice, he had only turned tail to grab the hosepipe, using it as an improvised water cannon.

"What's he shouting?" Marigold called in a quivering voice, huddled in terror at the bottom of the stairs.

"Take that, you brute," I translated, hastily adding, "Not you, darling. It seems that Guzim is trying to drown whatever has invaded the garden. I'll ask him what it is. Guzim, *ti einai afto?*"

"*Mia alepou,*" Guzim shouted back. My

heart sank. No one who keeps chickens ever wants to hear the word fox bandied about.

The moon reappeared, the brilliant rays allowing me to distinguish a fox speedily slinking away, one of my chickens clamped between its teeth. Slinging the hosepipe aside, Guzim fell to his knees in the mud, bemoaning that a fox had dug its way under the wire fence and invaded the coop: "*Mia alepou echei skapsei kato apo to syrmatoplegma kai eisevale sto kotetsi.*"

I followed fast on Spiros' heels as he rushed forward, opening the gate and flinging himself into the chicken coop. Our torches illuminated a scene of barbaric destruction, a headless, bloody chicken wantonly tossed aside amidst a thick carpet of chicken feathers, enough to stuff a duvet.

"*I alepou efyge me ena.*" Guzim wailed that the fox had got away with one. I already knew that, having seen the crafty thief steal a chicken away from under my nose.

"*Poio kotopoulo?*" A lump formed in my throat as I called out, "Which chicken?" Although I am admittedly fond of all my brood, poor lame Raki with the gammy leg holds a special place in my affections. It would be devastating if the fox had beheaded my favourite pet or made off with it under the cover of darkness. I am not ashamed to admit that tears blurred my vision as I scanned the chicken coop, trying to identify the survivors amid the mass of feathers.

"*Nomizo oti i alepou apogeiothike me ton Ouzo,*" Guzim spat, his guttural accent choked with emotion as he said he thought that the fox had made off with Ouzo.

"*Kai to akefalo ptoma?*" I cried, asking about the headless corpse. I couldn't bring myself to examine its bloody body too closely in case my fears were confirmed that it was Raki.

"*Moiazei me Mavrodafni.*" Bending over the featherless cadaver, Guzim announced that it looked like Mavrodafni, adding, "*Choris to kefali tou, den boro na eimai sigouros.*" Without its head, he couldn't be sure.

"It is the nature for the fox to kill the chicken, Victor," Spiros sagely commiserated, refusing to get sentimental over the natural order of things.

Confident she was no longer in danger of falling victim to a wild boar, Marigold joined me in the chicken coop, exclaiming, "What a grisly mess." Nudging the headless remains of Mavrodafni with her shoe, she pondered the outrageous notion, "Do you think there's enough of the body left to make a decent roast dinner? You know how Violet Burke loves a nicely done chicken."

Unable to believe my wife could be so callous, I turned away, stalking the perimeter of the fence in a desperate search for my beloved Raki, hoping against hope that it had survived the brutal carnage. Spotting a trembling form sheltering next to the hen house, I scooped up the hapless bird, relieved beyond measure to discover my most treasured chicken was still alive.

"Raki, you survived," I cried, joyfully depositing kisses on its beak and squeezing the creature so hard that Spiros warned me that I might hug the life out of it. Loosening my grip, my tears dripped onto the blood embellishing Raki's feathers.

"There's blood, it could be hurt," I shouted across to Guzim, switching to Greek when I remembered that he didn't understand English. "*Yparchei aima, bori na pligothei.*"

Dashing to my side, Guzim grabbed Raki. Running his hands over the still quivering chicken, he attested that the bird was fine, its feathers merely splattered with the blood of the other victims. Telling me that he would conduct a chicken head count, Guzim took stock of the rest of the flock. Returning to my side, he muttered that he thought there were only two casualties, the deceased Mavrodaphni and the snatched Ouzo.

"It could have been the much the worse if the Guzim had not reacted so the quickly," Spiros said. "It was the clever thinking to turn the water on the fox."

"I can't believe that you're making an exhibition of yourself over a chicken, Victor. What will Gordon think?" Marigold hissed in heartless mockery. "It's not as though you haven't enjoyed your fair share of chicken dinners."

"Yes, but they weren't my pets. You wouldn't be so unfeeling if you discovered the cat curry you were about to tuck into was made out of Clawsome."

"What a stupid comparison. I would never eat cat, the very idea is repugnant," Marigold snapped.

"That's what you think," I sneered. "Do you think I don't know that you sometimes indulged in a takeaway from that grubby little place, the Spicy Grill, when I was working late in Manchester? Why do you think they were closed down?"

"You don't mean…"

"Yes, I do mean exactly that, Marigold. They were caught red-handed cooking up cat in the kitchen."

My petty argument with Marigold was interrupted by the sound of Guzim gnashing his few remaining teeth and wailing. His voice dripped with pitiful desperation as he lamented, *"Doruntina, to kouneli mou."* Reduced to hysterics, it struck me that the Albanian's pet rabbit must have been another victim of the intrusive fox. After having come so close to losing my own beloved chicken, my heart went out to Guzim in his moment of agony, the loss of his rabbit a shared common bond between us.

The thud of a door banging drew my attention to the neighbouring garden. It took me a moment to recognise the figure wrapped in a voluminous pink dressing gown as Kyria Maria. I had only ever seen her clad in customary Greek widow's weeds, but there she was, a vision in pink and clearly on the warpath. Perchance all the racket from my garden had disturbed her slumbers and made her ill-tempered.

"Eisai ilithios Alvanos, ela kai pareis to kouneli sou," Maria screeched. *"To aidiastiko pragma prospathei na kanei sex me to chelona mou."*

Sidling up next to me, Gordon croaked, "What is that?"

I had no intention of letting him know that Maria had shouted, "You stupid Albanian, come and get your rabbit. The disgusting thing is trying to make sex with my tortoise." It wouldn't do at all for Gordon to get a bad impression of his potential neighbours until he had signed on the dotted line and I had pocketed my commission.

"It's just my sweet elderly neighbour, Kyria Maria. She's such a dear. I expect that she's just stepped outside for a breath of night air," I fibbed, watching in disbelief as Guzim vaulted over the wall.

"I could have sworn she said something about sex," Gordon muttered.

"Good grief, no. The very idea that a dear old pensioner would speak of such things," I laughed. "Some Greek words can sound quite inappropriate in translation. For instance, if a Greek offers you a drink, the word could be mistaken for penis. And the Greek word for where sounds like juvenile toilet humour?"

"Why?" Gordon queried.

"Because it's *pou*," I replied.

"Ah, that will be it then," Gordon said in

relief. "Pity about your chickens, you'll need to get the fence reinforced."

"I'll get my brother-in-law onto it first thing in the morning," I replied.

A light appeared in our upstairs window, the power seemingly restored. As Marigold led Gordon back inside, Guzim clambered back over the garden wall. Clutching his rabbit to his chest, he joined me, tears of joy soaking Doruntina's fur. Placing a firm hand on my shoulder, Guzim said, "*Avrio to proi echoume mia kideia gia Mavrodafni.*"

Touched beyond measure by Guzim's kind suggestion that we hold a funeral for the decapitated chicken the next morning, I agreed. It would be a far more suitable send off than tossing the bird in the oven.

Chapter 6

Not Just any Admirer

The mid-afternoon sunshine dazzled, forcing me to squint behind my sunglasses as I drove up to the bus station in town to collect my mother. I felt a tad weary: a busy morning in the shop dealing with demanding and cantankerous customers had followed a very early start, necessitated by the need to bury Mavrodafni in a secluded corner of the garden before I headed off to work. I felt beyond grateful for the emotional support that I had received from a contrite Marigold and a tearful Guzim.

My wife had tipped out of bed at the crack of dawn, most unlike her, full of remorse for her tactless suggestion that we bung my ravaged pet in the oven. I had been extremely touched when Papas Andreas, after spotting Guzim digging a hole from his bedroom window, stopped by to say a few words over the grave. I appreciated his selfless gesture, particularly since he had been under no obligation, my late chicken not being of the orthodox persuasion. The Papas also offered a prayer for Ouzo, its status missing but presumed dead. It seemed unlikely that poor Ouzo had survived being so cruelly kidnapped by the fox.

Full of the joys of spring on her return from the hospital, Tina confided that despite her mother's protestations to the contrary, the doctor had given Despina the all clear to return to her own home.

"He say it will be good for the *mama* to be back in her own home. When she stay with me, she sit in the chair and bark out the orders. She not to get off the, how to say in English, the *piso plevra*?

"Her backside," I translated.

"Yes, she not to get off her backside to

exercise the knee," Tina beamed.

"Does that mean that my services are no longer required?" I asked hopefully.

"Can we to make the Sunday the last day, Victor? I will drive my mother home and settle her in on Sunday."

Happy to hang up my grocer's hat, I had readily agreed to accept my metaphorical P45. Considering that I had commenced working in the shop immediately after the repping season had finished, I was well overdue a break. Even if I would be technically unemployed, my new business venture of cookery classes would keep me busy and ease the cash flow.

Despite Marigold's thoughtfulness in attending the burial, I couldn't persuade her to join me for the trip up to town. She claimed that she couldn't face the drive on top of the one she would be making the next day. Fortunately, the Lycra clad Frank and his wife Julie were sparing me from driving Marigold to Athens to catch her plane to Manchester the next day; the couple also returning to England on the same flight. The cycling pair from Nektar had conveniently offered Marigold a lift to the airport in their hire car having decided it was too far to peddle on their bicycles.

Unfortunately, their return to England ruled them out as likely candidates for my cookery classes. That was the problem with part time expats; one could never pin them down to anything concrete. Much as I would have enjoyed Marigold's company, I didn't press her. In addition to the pile of packing she needed to tackle, she had offered to cook a welcome home dinner for my mother. Out of respect for the trauma I had suffered the previous evening, Marigold promised that chicken would most definitely be off the menu.

I made excellent time, the road for once free of dawdling tourists and pesky camper vans travelling in convoy. I slammed on my brakes half way up the mountain, stopping for a hitch-hiking pensioner waving me down with his walking stick. Luckily my kind act did not delay me because he indicated he wanted dropping off at the side of the road, thus sparing me an unnecessary detour. Alas, I was not able to practice my Greek conversation skills since my passenger remained as mute as Sami, only grunting at me to stop when we reached his destination.

Stopping for a top-up of unleaded fuel on the outskirts of town, I managed to outsmart the swindling scammer operating a fiddle at the petrol station. Inserting his nozzle, he made a great show of sniffing around my bonnet before pronouncing that I was in dire need of fresh engine oil. After encouraging him to pontificate on the dangers the Punto faced if I didn't allow my vehicle to succumb to an immediate oil injection, I smugly informed him that the car had been treated to a full oil change during its service only two days prior. His jaw fell when he realised that I was onto his con: he had stupidly assumed that I was a foreign mug who would fall for his greedy trick to boost his coffers by flogging unnecessary oil. To be fair, if it had not been for Vangelis' prior warning that the chap was running a fiddle, I would likely have been taken in. Plastering a smug expression on my face as I drove away, I made a mental note to avoid the place in future and instead refuel at the Shell garage.

The sea looked an inviting blue as I hit the beach road in town. If it wasn't for my failure to slip on a pair of swim shorts beneath my trousers, I would have been tempted to stop for a dip. I particularly enjoy swimming out of season when the beaches are more or less deserted, the sand clear of rows of sunbeds and matching parasols. My Greek neighbours see nothing too peculiar about my occasional indulgence in a November dip, concurring it can be a bracing and healthy practice. Perish the thought that one should be caught frolicking in the sea in April though: such insanity came with dire warnings about contracting pneumonia. Whilst not yet ruled by typical Greek habits, I was painfully aware that I stuck out like a sore thumb if I wandered around town in shorts at this time of year when everyone else had switched to winter garb. With that in mind, I had dressed in long trousers for my trip to town, a decision I now regretted in the warm afternoon sunshine.

With plenty of time to spare, I parked up on the road by the bus station. When the helpful chap in the kiosk informed me the bus from Athens was running behind schedule, I mosied over to the coffee shop opposite. Grabbing a seat from which I could keep an eagle eye out for Violet Burke's arrival, I ordered a *sketos kafes* to perk me up.

With a good forty minutes to kill, I needed something to occupy my time. There was nothing for it but to resort to thumbing through the copy of Scarlett Bottom's 'Delicious Desire.' Milton had accosted me in my car a couple of days earlier, thrusting a copy of his book on me as a gift for Violet Burke. I was as yet undecided how to deliver Milton's gift to my mother: it hardly seemed appropriate to peddle porn to a pensioner, particularly one that I was so closely related to Fortunately I had a brown paper bag in the car which I fashioned into a makeshift cover: it served to keep my reading material hidden from prying eyes as I sipped my coffee. Milton's attempt at erotica was as dire as I'd expected, crammed with overly long dirgeful sentences heavy on smut. Even without Marigold's assistance, Milton had managed to attach an exclamation mark to the end of every saucy sentence.

"Reading anything good?" Turning puce at the prospect of being discovered flicking through porn in a public place, the book slipped through my fingers as I stood up to greet Gordon Strange. Bending down, he retrieved the book, raising his eyebrows as the brown paper bag slipped to reveal the risqué cover. Since conjuring up a convincing lie when put on the spot has never been my forte, I rather landed Marigold in it by claiming the book belonged to her. It struck me that Gordon was far too much of a gentleman to crassly comment to my wife's face about her questionable taste in literature.

Inviting Gordon to join me, I informed him that the bus was running late.

"Yes, Moira phoned me from the bus to let me know," he said.

"My mother will likely be hopping mad at the delay," I told him. "She doesn't enjoy the bus ride one bit. Being on the rather bulbous side, she finds the seats a tad tight and complains there is nowhere to stuff her swollen feet."

"Moira didn't mind the delay at all. She said she was having a marvellous time chatting to a lovely woman in the next seat."

I was relieved to hear that it sounded as if Gordon's wife had managed to avoid being stuck anywhere near Violet Burke. I was sure that the ear-splitting carping of my mother's bellyaching would drown out any chance of pleasant chatter by anyone unfortunate enough to be seated in close proximity to her. If I was able to persuade the Stranges to go ahead with the house purchase, it was imperative that I keep them well away from any negative influences such as Violet Burke.

With the arrival of Gordon's coffee, the table wobbled, threatening to spill the contents of his cup. Grabbing hold of Milton's book, I discovered that porn served very well as a piece of padding to shove under the wonky table leg.

As Gordon and I chatted it appeared that the house sale was almost certainly a done deal unless his wife found some unfathomable reason to hate the property or the village. Inviting Gordon to dinner had greased the wheels nicely, the rumpus in the garden bizarrely giving him a taste for country living: despite the moonlit carnage, he seemed keen on the idea of keeping chickens. Gordon was now chomping at the bit to add Uncle Leo's house to his property empire, meaning my commission was riding on Moira Strange falling in love with the place the next day.

My chat with Gordon was interrupted by my mobile ringing.

"*Yassou, Victor. Ti kaneis file mou*?" The familiar voice booming down the phone, saying, "Hello, how are you my friend?" left me in no doubt that the caller was the ever affable *Kapetainos* Vasos. No one else conducted their telephone conversations at such a deafening decibel level, a hangover from Vasos' navy days when he had to compete against the noise of the ship's engines.

After dispensing with the formalities, Vasos

invited me to join him for coffee at the marina where he was hard at work painting his boat. Curious as to how he knew I happened to be in town, I was quite gobsmacked when he informed me, "*O Sami mou eipe oti se eide konta sto stathmo ton leoforein.*" I expect my readers will be as amazed as I was to hear that Sami had told Vasos he had seen me near the bus station. Considering Sami's permanent state of muteness, I had no idea how he had managed to relay the information unless he had mimed it.

"*Alli fora, Vaso. Tora perimeno to leoforeio tis miteras mou,*" I replied, telling Vasos another time, I was waiting for my mother's bus.

"*I Violet. Agapo ti mitera sou,*" Vasos blasted down the phone, nearly shattering my eardrums as he declared that he loved my mother. Without pausing for breath, Vasos extended an invitation for me to bring my mother along too, saying he would treat her to cocktails. "*Fere kai ti mitera sou, tha agoraso ta kokteil tis.*"

"*Nomizo oti i mitera mou tha einai poly kourasmeni meta to makry taxidi tis apo tin Anglia.*" Telling Vasos that I thought my mother would be too tired after her long journey from England, the Greek words I used were nowhere near as grammatically correct as they appear in the retelling. Still, Vasos understood my meaning, immediately adopting a wheedling tone, insisting Violet would have a wonderful time drinking cocktails with him. We volleyed back and forth, Vasos trying to persuade me to bring Violet Burke for cocktails whilst I argued she would surely be too exhausted.

Finally worn down, I agreed to meet Vasos at the marina if my mother was up for it. Since I knew from experience that Violet Burke's swollen feet wouldn't entertain the notion of anything more taxing than a good soaking in my washing up bowl, I hoped that Vasos wouldn't be too disappointed when we failed to show up.

As I terminated the call, Vasos boomed, "I love you, Victor," his words clearly audible to anyone in the near vicinity.

Tilting his head to one side, Gordon Strange couldn't contain the snort that trumped from his nose.

"It's none of my business I know, but fancy you having a male admirer," he sniggered.

Loathe to defend myself yet again against spurious charges that I was a homosexual, I simply replied, "Not just any admirer: this one has a huge boat."

Chapter 7

A Strange Sort of Model

A flurry of activity across the road heralded the arrival of the bus from Athens. As Gordon scampered over to meet his wife, I followed at a more sedate pace. The significance of the moment really struck home as it dawned on me that I was about to be stuck with Violet Burke for the foreseeable. Although mother had said she would try out *apothiki* living in Meli for three months to start with, there was always the chance that she may become so enamoured with the Greek lifestyle that she may extend her visit, or perish the thought, never return to England. It was a sobering thought. Nevertheless, I plastered a smile on my face as I joined Gordon.

"Moira, you made it," he said, extending a hand to help his wife off the bus. In light of Gordon's incessant boasting that he was married to a model, I expected to see a woman with show-stopping looks alight. I was thus rather taken aback when he greeted a perfectly pleasant looking middle aged woman with nothing apparently exceptional about her appearance. Moira struck me as the epitome of what one would describe as about average in the looks department, rather than a great beauty: she lacked any of the glamour one associates with the type making a living posing for photographers or tripping up catwalks. She certainly posed no competition for Marigold in the beauty stakes. I found it all very strange.

"How was the trip?" Gordon asked his wife.

"Quite marvellous, such splendid scenery. It's hard to believe how wonderfully hot it is, it was practically glacial back in England," Moira trilled, shrugging off a shapeless cardigan to reveal a perfectly average figure, neither overly thin nor fat, clad in slacks and a floral blouse.

Flashing a pleasant smile in my direction when her husband introduced us, Moira said, "Gordon tells me that he lucked out meeting you. He says that I will simply love the house you showed him. It's all terribly exciting."

"You'll see it for yourself tomorrow. It would be too dark for you to appreciate the views if you came up to Meli today," I replied.

"I can't wait," Moira said, adding, "It's very good of you to come up with Gordon to meet the bus."

"I didn't, I came up to meet my mother," I confessed, craning my neck to see if there was any sign of Violet Burke shifting her sizeable bulk from the bus. "Ah, there she is now," I added, spotting the familiar sight of my mother's feet making their descent down the steps of the bus, rolls of bulging flesh strangulated by wrinkled nylon threatening to explode from the top of her drab lace-up shoes.

As Violet Burke came into view, Moira exclaimed in surprise. "Violet is your mother." With not even the slightest trace of sarcasm, she continued, "We've enjoyed such a lovely natter on the journey. Having such an interesting companion to sit next to made the time just fly by. Your mother is a real character."

"Here, Victor. Give me a hand, my feet are that puffed up they'll likely explode any minute," my mother complained as her swollen feet hit solid ground. "I'm bursting to use the lavatory. I didn't trust that toilet on the bus; I doubt a splash of bleach had been down it in months."

"Violet, my husband is here with your son. Isn't it a wonderful coincidence that they've already met?" Moira called out to Vi.

"Victor will be tickled when I tell him what you do for a living," my mother chuckled. "You'll never guess, Victor. Moira here has the strangest job, which is a hoot because her surname is Strange."

"A strange job," I parroted. "I thought that Moira was a model."

"An ear model," Vi blurted. "Did you ever hear of such a thing?"

"An ear model," I repeated, my eyes instantly drawn to Moira's ears. They were certainly aesthetically pleasing: perfectly proportioned, the auricles almost elfin like and the lobes delicately rounded.

"I still manage to get the odd booking to advertise earrings but most of the jobs I land these days are for TV ears or for drops that unclog waxed up lugholes," Moira revealed, her eyes creasing in a smile. "I expect that before long the only bookings I'll be offered will be for hearing aids."

"I told Moira to have a word with her agent to see if there's any call for swollen ankles. They could use mine in the before shot for remedies that reduce unsightly puffiness," Vi said.

"I can see by the way that your ankles are on the point of exploding that you neglected to wear compression socks on the flight again, Mother," I said, annoyed that she hadn't bothered to stick her feet in the pair that I'd ordered to be delivered to her in Warrington.

"I gave them a go, lad, but I didn't get on with them. By the time I got to Passport Control at Manchester, they were that tight they were stopping the blood from flowing to my head. I had to rip them off," Vi countered.

"You're meant to wear them on the flight, not on the way to the airport, Mother," I admonished, struggling to hide my exasperation.

"Well, never mind that now, Victor. Just point me in the direction of the nearest lav and make sure that no one makes off with my suitcases when they start chucking the luggage around."

BUCKET TO GREECE (VOL.9)

As my mother waddled off in search of the loo, I bid goodbye to Gordon and Moira, arranging to meet them in Meli at noon the next day. The bus driver began to unload the luggage and I made a grab for Violet Burke's cases as they emerged from the bowels of the bus, nearly giving myself a hernia in the process. By the weight of them, I hazarded a guess that mother had stuffed every last inch of space with tins of Spam and Fray Bentos. I crossed my fingers that the Punto would take the extra strain of two heavy cases combined with the excess weight of my mother.

Mother emerged from the bus station, her crinkled nose conveying her displeasure at the facilities. I made a mental note to steer her well clear from the toilets at the market if she was ever caught short in town. I dreaded to think how she would react to the basic hole in the floor conveniences which were the only inconvenient toilets the market offered.

"Where's that wife of yours, Victor? Couldn't be bothered to come up and meet her mother-in-law?" Violet Burke griped.

"Marigold is up to her neck in packing. I told you that she's flying to England tomorrow for a week to stay with her pal Geraldine," I reminded her.

"I remember Geraldine," Vi said, dislike evident in her tone. "The man mad harpy that can't land herself a decent husband while I had them coming out of my ears."

"Well it appears that she may have landed herself one now, Mother."

I had no idea why I leapt to Geraldine's defence, particularly since she was now apparently desperate to ditch Ashley, but something in Mother's condescending tone riled me. Knowing full well that Violet Burke had caught herself four husbands, I thought it rather crass of her to rub it in at the expense of a woman yet to net her first one.

Squashing her considerable bulk into the Punto's passenger seat, Violet Burke left it to me to stow her luggage. With a weary sigh, she complained, "I'm that knackered. All I want to do is shove my swollen feet in a bath. You did have a bath put in for me downstairs like you promised?"

"Yes, mother, a top of the range tub complete with all mod cons. It even boasts running water and a plug," I assured her. Since plugs were actually quite a novelty in these parts, I hoped she would appreciate the efforts I had made to secure one.

"That's grand lad, I thought you might try to palm me off with that outside tub of yours and a washing up bowl for my feet. I'm that done in that I'm fair fit for nothing but tucking into a Fray Bentos and sinking into a bath. In fact, I'm that exhausted that I might eat the pie in the bath."

"Marigold is preparing you a welcome home dinner," I said.

"I'm in no mood for oily salad. I need some proper food," my mother grimaced ungraciously. "I couldn't touch that slop they tried to pass off as food on the flight. I'm that starving I could eat a scabby horse on mouldy bread."

"Well, let's get you back to Meli," I sighed, checking her seatbelt was tightly secured. "It's a pity that you're in such a hurry to get back though. Captain Vasos just phoned, he wants to treat you to a cocktail to two at the marina."

"A cocktail, you say, with Captain Vasos. He's such a hoot. It would look that rude to stand him up," Violet Burke immediately perked up, all thought of her swollen feet instantly forgotten. "'Appen I could manage a nice cocktail with him. The bath can wait, lad."

Chapter 8

Mucky Fat

Sited in a secluded cove of the Messinian Gulf not too distant from the harbour, the marina is an oasis of peace compared to the bustle of town. Arriving at our destination, I slowed down to a suitably sedate pace, having no desire to test the Punto's suspension by flying over the speed bumps at the entrance. Violet Burke gasped in surprise at the sight of opulent yachts and luxury boats berthed on floating or permanent pontoons.

"There's some money parked here, Victor,

and no mistake," Vi stated. Rather than being impressed, her tone oozed disapproval at such a flagrant display of wealth.

"The marina is where the moneyed moor their boats. They also bring them here for refuelling or repairs," I explained, wondering if I had perchance misunderstood Captain Vasos when he told me to meet him here. Pegasus would surely stand out as conspicuous in the wrong way amongst such superior boats. I imagined the type of people to own luxury yachts might be rather inclined to look down their noses at Vasos' vessel. Pegasus, commonly stuffed to the gills with paying passengers, might be considered vulgar in comparison; Pegasus passengers possibly labelled the hoi polloi by the snobbish yachting fraternity.

The marina certainly didn't strike me as a natural hangout for the unsophisticated *Kapetainos*. Recalling our earlier conversation, I was certain he told me to meet him here. Despite my acknowledged incompetence with telephone Greek, there could be no mistaking the meeting place since the Greek word for marina is conveniently the same in translation, albeit with the addition or an accented stress in the middle.

"I shall drive around slowly. Keep your

eyes peeled, Mother, and see if you can spot Pegasus," I instructed.

"Rightio, lad. We won't miss it if it's here, it would stick out like a sore thumb next to all these posh boats."

"Vasos said he was painting it…"

"A new coat of paint won't have shrunk it. Vasos' boat is bigger than any of these," my mother pointed out as though size was everything.

My eyes were drawn to the expanse of sea beyond the marina on the off chance that Pegasus had dropped anchor just outside the section allocated for parking up boats. Heavy grey clouds tinged with black undertones loomed above Taygetos in the distance, casting dark shadows and hinting we may be caught in a downpour on the drive home. After circuiting the road with no sign of Pegasus, I pulled over in the car park behind the couple of restaurants offering prime views of the collected yachts. I needed to telephone Vasos to pinpoint his location.

"Vaso, eimaste sti marina alla den boro na do ton Pegasus. Pou eisai," I said, dispensing with the pleasantries.

"What are you saying to him? Speak English,

Victor," Violet Burke demanded.

"I told Vasos we are at the marina but can't see Pegasus. I asked him where he is," I duly translated, attempting to listen to Vasos with one ear whilst my mother bleated away in the other.

"*Zografizo to psarovarka mou, ochi to Pegasus,*" Vasos boomed down the phone, telling me was painting his fishing boat, not Pegasus. It was news to me that Vasos even owned a second boat. Continuing to blast my eardrums, he told me to drive around again and he would wave when he saw the car.

Following Vasos' instructions, I drove around the marina for a second time, slamming my brakes on when Violet Burke shrieked, "There he is."

Following her gaze, I spotted Vasos perched atop the hull of an upended fishing boat by the side of the water, paint brush in hand. The old wooden boat, weather-beaten and tatty, much like its owner, struck me as being decidedly out of place amongst the luxury fibreglass vessels maintained in pristine condition. As we piled out of the car, a typical toff attired all in linen and flashing an expensive Rolex stepped off one of the more ostentatious yachts. Doffing his starched cap, he exchanged a cheery greeting in Greek with Vasos, before continuing on his way. Although his Greek was rather mangled by his heavy foreign accent, he was clearly familiar with the irrepressible boat captain.

"*Rosika, polla chrimata*," Vasos called out to me, telling me the man was Russian and had plenty of money. As if to drive home his point that the man was wealthy, Vasos ran his thumb over his fingers in what I suppose is a universal gesture to indicate loaded. Cringing inwardly, I hoped that the Russian's mastery of Greek extended to no more than the basic greetings: he may not wish to have word of his wealth bandied about even though his yacht was a bit of a giveaway.

Jumping down from the boat, Vasos landed quite nimbly. Hoisting his sweat stiffened tee-shirt up under his armpits to wipe his dripping brow, he shamelessly exposed his rotund stomach. His legs protruded like sticks from his shorts, a pair of flip flops held together with masking tape flapping from his surprisingly dainty feet. I am often taken aback by the small-ness of many Greek men's feet: no matter the height of the man of a certain age, their often tiny feet seem out of proportion to the rest of their body as though proclaiming some form of arrested development. Athena tells me it is something to do with a shortage of vitamins during the war and the subsequent years of civil turmoil, pointing out later generations have enormous feet in comparison.

"Violet," Vasos bellowed, managing to sound out her name in four elongated syllables. Rubbing his paint stained hands on a grubby rag, he hurtled himself forward and threw his arms around my mother's bulbous frame. Considering that the top of Vasos' head was practically on a level with Violet Burke's ample bosom, he demonstrated an unexpected strength by sweeping her off her feet and spinning her round. Admittedly he did look a tad winded by the time he set her down on solid ground. Violet Burke promptly clouted Vasos on the ear, the blow doing nothing to suppress the enormous grin on his face.

"*I varka sou?*" I said, indicating the boat with my head and asking Vasos if it was his.

"*Nai, psarevo apo afto,*" he replied, pride suffusing his voice as he confirmed his ownership and told me that he used it for fishing. Barely pausing for breath, he added that I must go out with him one morning for a spot of fishing.

"Prepei na vgeis mazi mou gia psarema ena proi."

"What's he saying?" my mother demanded.

"He says I must go out with him in the fishing boat one morning."

"You must want your head examining if you set out to sea in that leaky death trap. You'd need to take a sturdy bucket along to bail you out," Vi scoffed.

"Ti leei?" Vasos asked what my mother was saying.

"Chreizetai ena kathistiko kai ena oraio flitzan tsai," I improvised, telling Vasos that Vi had said she needed a sit down and a nice cup of tea. I didn't consider it would serve any purpose to translate the disparaging insult she had directed towards his boat.

"Tsai. Tha agoraso Violet ena kokteil." Scoffing at the mention of tea, Vasos said he would buy Violet a cocktail. I hoped he didn't intend to get my mother tipsy. With not a whit of consideration for my upholstery, Vasos hurled himself into the back of the Punto and directed me towards the car park. As I parked up, Vasos proposed we go for a cocktail, *"Ela, pame gia kokteil."*

Linking his arm in Violet's, Vasos bounded towards the restaurant. I followed hesitantly in their wake, a tad worried that Vasos may be denied entrance in his scruffy state. Violet Burke didn't exactly look like a fashion plate in her flat lace-ups and her drab travelling clothes. The establishment appeared a bit on the smart side, no doubt more used to welcoming affluent yacht owners rather than grungy proles and bolshie harridans. Still, at least I was suitably clad in long trousers and my tie was from Marks and Spencer. In light of my misgivings, I admit to being rather taken aback when the elegantly attired owner sprang forward, enthusiastically embracing Vasos in welcome.

As the owner, Marinos, ushered us inside to a charming table overlooking the water, Vasos introduced us as his English friends, the beautiful Violet, and her son, Victor, "*Aftoi einai oi Anglikou mou filoi, i omorfi Violet, kai o gios tis, Victor.*" I struggled to keep my face straight at the thought that the chap who owned a restaurant at the marina just happened to be so conveniently named Marinos: perchance he was really another Georgios or Giannis, assuming a posher name to fit in with his business image.

Marinos didn't blink an eye when Vasos ordered sex on the beach cocktails for Violet Burke and himself. Declining the offer of alcohol, I accepted a black coffee, Vasos proclaiming he would keep me company with an *ouzo* to wash down his mid-afternoon cocktail. I supposed he was clueless if the cocktail that he had ordered was to his taste: I rather imagine he had opted for sex on the beach just to show off his acquisition of yet another English word, sex, to his limited vocabulary. I cringed at the thought that it might join his repertoire of English words that he liked to randomly drop on day trippers. If sex became one of his standard tourist greetings, I would be forced to explain the meaning of sex pest to him. I made a mental note to start practising a suitable phrase in his language.

Marinos returned with our drinks and a small plate of complementary *mezedes*. Violet Burke immediately found fault with the selection: the marinated anchovies, the *tzatziki* and the small elongated red peppers stuffed with spicy *tirokafteri*, all a bit too Greek for her taste.

"I'd rather have had a plate of chips or a nice bag of pork scratchings, Vasos," she complained as if the *Kapetainos* was capable of understanding her griping.

"*Ti leei?*" Vasos demanded, looking indulgently at my mother.

"*Leei oti einai ola ta agapimeni tis,*" I falsely translated, telling him that she said they were all her favourites.

Turning to my mother, I told her that she must start addressing Vasos as Vaso when speaking to him directly, explaining that it was customary for the final S of a Greek male name to be omitted when addressing someone. "It's high time you got the hang of it."

"What's the point of him having an S at the end of his name if you expect me to drop it? I'll have you know that I speak proper, you don't hear me going around dropping my aitches," she sneered dismissively.

"It's the Greek way, Mother."

"Well I can't be doing with all these daft foreign customs. Vasos is Vasos and that's the end of it. Tell him that I can't be eating any of this foreign muck; it will likely play havoc with my digestion. Now, I managed to smuggle some mushy peas over in one of my cases," she said, taking a large swig of her cocktail. "Pop out to the car and get them, Son."

Having no intention of rummaging through Violet Burke's belongings in search of a tub of mushy peas or of embarrassing myself by asking Marinos to heat them up in the microwave, I ignored my mother's demand, instead encouraging her to try an anchovy. It wouldn't do to have her think that I was prepared to run round at her beck and call.

"They don't look like they've been cooked properly," Vi said, eyeing the anchovies suspiciously. "They look a bit fishy?"

"*Gavros* aren't meant to be cooked, Mother. Raw anchovies are cured in salt and then marinated in olive oil with garlic and herbs," I explained.

"Have you lost your mind expecting me to eat raw fish? And to think you call yourself a retired public health inspector," Vi scoffed.

"There's no need to scoff. I had a long and illustrious career in the field," I retorted.

"Then you'd think you'd have heard about the dangers of catching vibrating volcano figs from eating uncooked fish. That plate is likely swimming in marine bacteria."

Presuming that mother had boobed, confusing the potentially deadly vibrio vulnificus with the mangled malapropism she uttered, I was nevertheless secretly impressed that she was up on the type of lethal infections that one could contract from eating raw fish. Perhaps such information had become required reading for chip shop employees since I left England: the Foods Standard Agency was forever introducing new regulations.

"The curing process will have removed the bacteria," I assured her.

"I'm not eating raw fish, it's disgusting. I like my fish properly fried with mushy peas," Vi declared, determined to have the last word.

"Mushy peas," Vasos repeated, slowly sounding out the novel words. *"Ti einai mushy peas?"*

As Vasos asked what mushy peas were, I experienced a hideous flashback, recalling the time I had made a laughing stock of myself in the taverna by offering up the words *evaisthitos arakas* as the Greek translation of mushy peas, only to discover I had mistakenly referred to them as sensitive rather than mushy. Before I could attempt to offer an explanation, Vasos simply repeated "Mushy peas" again, an enormous grin on his face. It struck me that it really didn't matter to him what the words meant: now that he had mastered them, he would no doubt randomly drop them with frequent regularity along with the other English words he had memorised, with no consideration of context. At least mushy peas were preferable to sex.

Nudging me sharply in the ribs, Violet Burke winked at me. Dangling a paper napkin in front of Vasos' nose, she slowly sounded out the words, "Spotted dick."

"Spotted dick," Vasos repeated in heavily accented English. After trying out the new words for size several times, he turned to me, saying, *"Spotted dick einai mia chartopetseta, nai?"*

"Nai," I agreed, confirming that spotted dick was indeed a small paper towel. It was much easier to play along with Mother's wind-up rather than attempt to come up with the necessary Greek vocabulary to explain that spotted dick is actually a suet pudding filled with dried fruit: off the top of my head I couldn't conjure up the translations of either suet or dried. I hoped that after downing a couple of *ouzos* on top of his cocktail, Vasos would forget any of the ridiculous words which Violet Burke seemed intent on feeding him.

"Kai poia einai i lexi gia charti ygeias?" Vasos asked what the English word for toilet paper was.

"What's he saying?" my mother demanded.

"He wants to know the word for toilet paper."

Quick as a flash, my mother supplied the words, "Mucky fat."

"Mucky fat," Vasos repeated, clueless he

was being played for a fool and that mucky fat was a northern term for dripping. "Mucky fat."

Yanking a filthy tissue from the depths of his pocket, Vasos waved it in front of my mother. "Bubble and squeak," Violet Burke declared, smiling encouragement as the gullible boat captain repeated her words until he had perfected the English pronunciation.

"You are awful, Mother," I chided as Vasos excused himself to go to the toilet.

"It's all harmless fun; he never has a clue what he's saying in English anyway."

"Well, let us hope that Vasos doesn't turn the tables and teach you a lot of nonsensical Greek," I said.

"He can if he wants. I've no intention of bothering to learn a foreign language at my age. There's no sense to know what anyone is saying, most of it is likely nothing more than hot air and blather. It's the conversation that counts, it doesn't matter what someone's saying."

"If that's how you feel, perhaps you could spare me your endless demands that I translate. There's no point in my bothering if you couldn't care less what the Greeks are saying," I said.

"I only ask out of common politeness. It makes no difference to me what they're blathering on about."

I supposed there was a smidgen of logic in my mother's argument that the subject of a conversation was irrelevant: it had not escaped my notice that women frequently seemed to talk at and over one another, barely bothering to listen to what the other person was saying. Still it amused me to see Violet Burke nearly jump out of her skin when Vasos crept up behind her. Using a strip of toilet paper as a makeshift blindfold, he covered her eyes, shouting "Mucky fat."

His words were impeccably timed to cause maximum embarrassment, drawing the attention of two women who had just walked in and taken a seat at a nearby table.

"One doesn't usually find such common types in here," one of the women sneered, firing a look in our direction so withering that it made one of Marigold's trademark withering looks seem like a visual caress in comparison.

"Shh, they might hear you," her companion shushed, clearly mortified by the other woman's smug superiority. It was the smugness that made the penny drop, prompting me to recall that I had made their acquaintance on a previous occasion.

Chapter 9

Common Types

I recognised the two English women who had just entered the restaurant as members of the expat book club down on the coast. Whilst my mother amused herself by boisterously continuing to encourage Vasos to sound out totally inappropriate English words, my mind flashed back to a summer evening when Smug Bessie had disparaged Milton's 'Delicious Desire' as an unsuitable choice for the Book of the Month. I recalled taking an instant, visceral dislike to the unattractive woman of stumpy stature, her out of proportion protruding bust threatening to tip her over. Exuding an inflated sense of her own self-importance, she rode roughshod over the opinions of her fellow book club members whilst somehow holding them in thrall, presumably by intimidation.

When Violet Burke shouted the words suet dumpling at Vasos, Bessie reacted like a jumped up snob, making no effort to lower her voice when she opined to her friend, "I just cannot abide the sort of common English person who moves to Greece and insists on eating the same unimaginative food they ate back in England."

"Oh, I don't know. There's something very comforting about a suet dumpling at this time of year," Bessie's friend dared to argue. I belatedly recalled her name was Iris. Although we had only met briefly, I remembered that she had suggested to me that Marigold might like to join the book club since they shared a mutual enjoyment in reading books about people up-sticking to foreign parts. Bessie had made it clear that she looked down her nose at such reading matter: she considered such tripe must be penned by literary amateurs and wasn't high-brow enough for the book club. Considering I am penning an up-sticks book of my own, I regard her opinion as total twaddle.

Iris shuffled uncomfortably in her seat as Smug Bessie launched into an attack on suet dumplings, opining it was a filthy practice to eat balls of rendered animal fat. Since Iris was not unattractive, it was inevitable that she caught Vasos' eye. Noticing her shift uncomfortably, he barged over. Clutching a cushion, he offered it to Iris, saying, "*Thelis o* suet dumpling?"

I snorted in laughter at the realisation that Violet Burke had taught Vasos that the English translation of a cushion was suet dumpling.

"I suppose you think you are funny," Bessie spluttered at Vasos.

"*Ti?*" Vasos responded, completely unfazed by Bessie's condescending tone.

"Well, we'll see what the management have to say. I'm sure there are rules barring the likes of you from respectable establishments such as this," Bessie posited.

Her scathing glance lumped me in along with my mother and Vasos as disreputable riff-raff. Before I had chance to retort, Bessie stomped off in search of the management, no doubt intending to have us thrown out. I should add that whilst flounced is my preferred word to describe someone taking off in a tizzy, flounced could never be used to describe the ungracious movements of someone as decidedly frumpy as Bessie.

"Beautiful towel," Vasos said to Iris, clueless that her companion had judged him to be beyond the pale.

"Don't mind Vasos, he's got a heart of gold," I said to Iris. "He can get a tad loud as he's used to competing to be heard over the boat's engine."

"Vasos," Violet Burke shouted, blatantly ignoring my advice to drop the S from the end of his name. "Time for another sex on the beach."

Vasos' eyes lit up with a twinkle as he repeated the only word of mother's sentence that he had understood, "Sex." As he bounded back to Violet Burke, a flush crept over Iris' cheeks. I attributed her blushes to mortification over her friend's judgemental outburst rather than Vasos voicing his new favourite word.

"I'm so sorry about that, I don't know what gets into Bessie sometimes," Iris gulped. "She seems to delight in going out of her way to make people feel uncomfortable."

"I noticed that when I ran into your book club meeting down on the coast back in the summer," I replied. "Why do the other ladies in the book club allow themselves to be pushed around by her?"

Sighing heavily and nervously checking over her shoulder to make sure that Bessie was out of hearing range, Iris hissed her reply. "Bessie founded the book club and expects us all to follow her rules. It doesn't do to get on her bad side. She has banished members that had the nerve to stand up to her and expects the rest of us to ostracise them from our social circle. No one wants to be on the outs, having everyone turn against them. It would be social suicide to find oneself excluded from the expat get-togethers."

"Well, I can't imagine why any of you would allow such a ghastly woman to wield all the power," I observed, just as Bessie returned, dragging along a reluctant Marinos.

Considering her superiority, Bessie's grasp of Greek was a laughing matter. With her vocabulary and tenses all over the place, she did an excellent job of butchering the Greek language. It would be beyond pathetic to pen a transliterated account of the botched attempt at Greek that she spat, but it amused me greatly to hear her proclaim in mangled Greek, "This people is the talked mint. What are you none of them?"

Even though the words that Bessie uttered made no sense when strung together, she spoke them with a certain confidence, no doubt attempting to impress us. Since I had blundered my way through many an incorrect Greek sentence, I could decipher the intent behind Bessie's words, realising she had tried to say we were too noisy and demanding to know what Marinos intended to do about it. However, her incoherent babble left Marinos floundering beyond confused, clueless she had mixed up the word for loud with mint. He stared at her blankly, daring to interrupt with the word "*Ti*?"

"Do you speak English?" Bessie demanded.

"*Eipe oti milas Anglika*?" I helpfully translated.

Bessie shot daggers at me, her sense of indignation deflating as she realised my mastery of Greek put hers to shame. Waving a hand in our direction, she said in English, "These people are noisy and uncouth."

"*Ti*?" Saying what, Marinos winked at me. I gathered he understood Bessie's English but chose not to let on. In the typical manner of entitled Brits abroad, Bessie repeated her words, enunciating each syllable slowly and loudly.

Turning to Vasos, Marinos addressed him

in their native tongue, telling him that the horrible woman was insisting that our small party be slung out for uncouth behaviour. Marinos assured Vasos that the woman was stupid and that Vasos was his good friend and a valued customer. Demonstrating his adeptness at handling an awkward situation, Marinos told Vasos that he would move Bessie to another table: *"Tha tin valo se allo trapezi."*

Confident that Bessie was not well versed enough in Greek to be able to translate my words, I told Marinos that I was sorry that he had to put up with such an ignorant English woman, assuring him that not all English are like that: *"Sygnomi pou prepei na anechteite mia tetoia adia Anglika gynaika. Den einai ola ta Anglika etsi."*

Bessie gawped in fury, her mouth hanging ajar, clearly incensed that my Greek was better than hers and that she was unable to comprehend my meaning. As Marinos led her and Iris to another table at the opposite side of the room, I fired off a parting shot.

"The *Kapetainos* here is a regular and esteemed customer. His boat is bigger than any of the yachts outside."

Following meekly behind Marinos and

Bessie, Iris shrugged apologetically, mouthing to me that I'd be welcome to join them at the book club any time. Perhaps she hoped that I would stand up to Smug Bessie and take her down a peg or two.

"I can't be doing with such snooty types," Violet Burke huffed. "All them fake airs and graces. Her sort give the English abroad a bad name."

Marinos returned with a complimentary *ouzo* for Vasos. As the two men chatted amongst themselves, Violet Burke fixed her attention on the luxury yachts outside. "'Appen I should find myself a rich fellow with a yacht and bag him as my fifth husband."

"I thought that you had sworn off men, Mother," I chortled, wondering what kind of doddery old fool she expected to snare.

"It's something to bear in the mind for the future. A fifth husband might come in useful for sparing me from impoverishment when I get old."

I have to admit that my mother's practical take on life amused me greatly. Here she was on the cusp of her eightieth year, yet talking as though she was still a spring chicken in her prime.

"'Appen it won't come to that. With a bit of luck I can still earn my crust by getting some cleaning work in your village or better yet a job in a chippy."

"Have you seen many chippies in Greece, Mother?"

"Perhaps we should open one then, what with both of us having experience with a chip pan," Vi suggested.

"I think we'd find such a venture would be a bureaucratic nightmare. We would be strangled in red tape. I doubt we would ever manage to get it off the ground," I said. Whilst I had no intention of frying chips for a living, I had to admire my mother's entrepreneurial spirit in suggesting a new business venture at her advanced age.

"I hope you aren't going to tell me the same about cleaning," Vi huffed.

"I'm more than happy to pay you to clean our place," I suggested. "Marigold is forever banging on about us having a woman in to clean and I'd much rather have someone in that I trust. It's either you or a Roomba and I can't imagine the cats taking to a robotic cleaner."

"Why does it not surprise me that Marigold would rather shell out your cash on a char than get her own hands dirty? That lazy wife of yours has you doing most of the cooking, after all."

"I enjoy it, so much so in fact that I am about to commence cookery lessons from my kitchen," I said.

When Marinos disappeared to shake another cocktail for mother, Vasos plonked himself down next to Violet Burke again. Grabbing a paper napkin to wipe the sweat from his brow, Vasos boomed, "Spotted dick."

"Once I get settled in Victor's basement, you'll have to come round for a visit," mother said to Vasos.

"*Ti leei?*" Vasos shouted.

Ignoring his interruption, I corrected my mother. "It isn't a basement; it's an *apothiki*. I spent a small fortune converting it into a comfortable abode."

Ignoring me, she continued, "Tell Vasos if he comes round for a visit, I'll cook him a nice spotted dick and custard."

"*Ti leei?*" Vasos repeated.

"*I mitera leei oti tha sou mageirepsei mia spotted dick kai custard an tin episkeftheis,*" I said, translating Vi's words.

Staring at my mother as though she had lost her marbles, Vasos responded, "*Akousa oti to*

Angliko fagito itan fritiko, alla den ixera oi Vretanoi oti efagan mageiremenes chartopetsetes."

"What's he saying," Mother demanded.

"He said that he'd heard English food was horrible but he'd no idea the British ate cooked paper napkins."

"What's the daft apeth on about? Oh... I get it," she said, the penny dropping. "'Appen I won't tell him that the word custard means bleach. He might think that I have plans to poison him."

Chapter 10

A Sitting Tenant

Our little side trip to the marina had mellowed Violet Burke quite considerably, though whether that was down to Vasos' company or a couple of cocktails was hard to determine. Chattering away on the drive home, I told her that Marigold was very keen to show off the *apothiki* conversion, smiling to myself when my words were met with nothing but rhythmic snoring. It had been a long journey for mother and no doubt a couple of sex on the beach cocktails had contributed to her drowsiness. Ordinarily I would have considered it a shame for Violet Burke to be missing out on the spectacular views from the mountain, but on this occasion the clouds had descended, obscuring the magnificent vista. The rain bounced off the Punto, the windscreen wipers swiping in overdrive. I slowed down: the roads tended to be incredibly slippery after such a long dry spell.

Pulling into Meli, I felt a satisfactory sense of accomplishment. I had successfully persuaded Violet Burke to move to a foreign country for part of the year, something she would never have contemplated in her wildest dreams was it not for our rediscovering each other and forging a mother and son relationship. I felt confident that whilst Greek life may not come naturally to Violet Burke, it would be a vast improvement to seeing out her days on a rundown council estate.

"Mother, we're home," I announced, nudging her in the ribs.

"Look at this miserable weather, it's like I never left Warrington," she griped.

Rushing round to open the passenger door, I offered, "Take my arm, I don't want you tripping over in the dark."

"There's no point rushing my swollen feet…"

"Is that you, Victor? You've been an absolute age," Marigold called down from the balcony.

"We stopped off for a drink in town with Captain Vasos," I explained, relieved beyond measure that my mother appeared to have sobered up. It really wouldn't do if I'd been forced to explain to my wife that I had allowed Violet Burke to get squiffy.

As my mother hauled her considerable bulk out of the car, Marigold called out, "Do you want to come up for a cuppa, Violet, or would you rather see what we've done to the *apothiki* first?"

"I might as well see the place right off since it's going to be my home for the foreseeable," Vi decided.

"We'll be right down then. Barry's with me, he's dying to see your reaction: after all, he did all the work," Marigold called down.

"Bring the cases, Victor," my mother ordered. "I'll be needing my slippers as soon as my poor swollen feet have had a good soak."

Grabbing the cases, I replicated the almost 'giving myself a hernia' moment of earlier. By the weight of her bags, I imagined that Violet Burke must have packed enough tins of Fray Bentos to see out the decade.

"Do you think Victor should carry you over the threshold?" Barry suggested, greeting Violet Burke.

"You daft apeth, he'd give himself a hernia," my mother chortled.

"I believe I've already got one from manhandling your suitcases," I quipped.

The front door opened directly into the sitting room. Violet Burke stepped inside, giving the room the silent once over, Marigold on tenterhooks hoping it met with approval.

"You've done a grand job, Victor, it's hard to believe it's that same filthy storage room that was full of old junk," Vi pronounced.

"It's Barry who really deserves the credit, he did the conversion," I said.

"You've done a grand job, lad, it's not bad for a dingy basement," Vi grudgingly said to Barry.

"It wasn't just me. Vangelis put in plenty of hours," Barry said.

"And of course, I had a great input in the design, they incorporated many of my ideas," Marigold butted in. "I came up with the colour scheme."

"The colour's a bit drab and no mistake. It hardly takes a lot of imagination to slap some dingy beige paint on the walls," Violet Burke pointed out.

"It's not beige, it's orchid white," Marigold protested, wilfully overlooking the fact that the walls were indisputably beige no matter what it said on the tin.

"Victor wanted to stick with the white that is typically found in most Greek houses," Barry explained. "But Marigold argued if we did it white it would turn brown in no time at all from all the chips you'll be frying."

"So you did it in beige."

"Orchid white," Marigold repeated.

"So if Barry and Vangelis did all the labouring and Marigold chose this dreary colour scheme, what did you do, Victor?"

"I paid for it," I stated, wincing at the thought of the gaping hole in my bank account. Even with the family discount Barry had offered, it had cost me an arm and a leg.

Barely pausing to draw breath, Violet Burke marched through from the living room to the bedroom, pronouncing, "You've made it quite cosy and no mistake, even if you did get a bit carried away with the beige. I didn't think you'd be able to make a silk purse out of the sow's ear that was down here, but you've done a good job."

Catching my eye, Barry high-fived me. In truth, neither of us had expected to receive such high praise from my mother.

"I'm surprised that you bothered splashing out on a double bed for me. Are you expecting me to be having gentleman callers?" Violet Burke sniggered. Marigold reddened: never one to tire of matchmaking, I knew that she harboured high hopes that Panos may turn into an overnight guest.

Violet Burke threw her considerable bulk on the bed to test it out, putting enormous strain on the widgets holding the flat pack bed together.

"I put a lovely new electric blanket under the sheets, Vi. It can get quite chilly up here in the mountains at night," Marigold said.

"I can't be doing with one of them deadly contraptions," mother retorted. "What if I spill my cuppa in bed? I'd end up electrocuting myself. It will have to go. It's a good job I brought a couple of hot water bottles over from England. Dig them out of my suitcases, Victor."

Rummaging through one of the two cases in

search of hot water bottles, I mouthed, "I told you so," at my wife, receiving a withering look in return. I actually felt quite smug: in just two years of acquainting myself with the woman that had abandoned me in a bucket, I had come to know her well enough to successfully predict that she would view an electric blanket as a hazardous device and instead hanker after a nice hot water bottle.

"There's a serviceable candlewick bedspread in there too," mother continued. "Dig it out while you're at it, Victor. It will cover up this horrible bedding. I suppose that's down to you, Marigold. You do have shocking taste."

Marigold bit her lip, silently seething. After going to so much trouble to choose lovely things for Violet Burke, it was a kick in the teeth to have her efforts unappreciated.

"I suppose I'd better give the kitchen the once over," Violet Burke decided, moving between rooms. "Ooh, it's a bit nippy in here. What idiot left the window open?"

"I left it ajar to dispel the lingering smell of paint," Marigold admitted, hurrying to close it.

"I suppose this sickly yellow is down to you, too," Violet Burke accused.

"It's daffodil," Marigold corrected.

"Well, it looks like yellow to me," Violet Burke pointed out, ever pragmatic.

Marigold's eyes narrowed in annoyance. Intercepting the pleading look I sent in her direction, she squared her shoulders and slapped a long-suffering smile on her face.

"Look, Vi, I bought you a lovely deep fat fryer. It's the latest model." The enthusiasm in Marigold's voice sounded a tad forced, no doubt she expected her thoughtfulness to be met with carping criticism.

"Ooh, I can't be doing with that, chips need cooking proper in a chip pan. It's a good job I brought one over in my suitcase, dig it out for me will you, Victor."

"You brought a chip pan over in your suitcase?" Marigold asked incredulously.

"Of course I did, it's not as though I'm only going to be here for five minutes. You can't expect me to manage without my chip pan."

"Well, I hope you cleaned it out properly before packing it," Marigold said.

"As if," I muttered under my breath, shaking out a grotesque mustard coloured candlewick bedspread that stank of chips. I decided not to mention that the weight of the chip pan had made a squashed mess of the Warrington eggs stashed beneath it, making them barely recognisable. Mother might be inconsolable at the loss of her favourite snack.

"I brought my toasted sandwich maker over too, dig it out, will you, Victor," mother ordered. "It will come in handy if I get peckish in the night and fancy a Spam toastie."

I hoped that Violet Burke had packed plenty of Gaviscon to wash down her revolting midnight snack. The very thought of it gave me phantom pangs of indigestion.

"They do sell toasted sandwich makers in Greece, Vi. It's not a total backwater," Marigold pointed out, shuddering at the mention of mother's appalling eating habits.

"That's as maybe, but I've got this one nicely worn in. It's absorbed just enough mucky fat to add a bit of flavour to the outside of the bread..."

"You put dripping in the sandwich maker..." My horrified incredulity mirrored Marigold's, the very thought of runny lard smeared on the outside of a toastie enough to turn my stomach.

"Ooh, would you look at that, the plug won't fit in these foreign sockets. You'll have to change it, Victor," mother barked.

"It would be safer if Barry took care of it," Marigold said. "Victor's a bit incompetent when it comes to electrics."

Marigold's words hit home. To celebrate our fifth wedding anniversary, I vividly recalled attempting to purchase a food liquidiser as a gift for my wife. Fighting my way through the crowds in Rumbelows sale, I snagged a liquidiser on special offer. Inspecting the electrical appliance before parting with my hard earned cash, I noticed that it needed a plug attaching. Since my last attempt to attach a plug to something electrical had resulted in a veritable explosion in our fuse box, I duly requested that the salesman fit one. I was quite willing to pay the extra for this service, presuming it would cost a mere pittance in comparison to the emergency callout fees I had shelled out to have the fuse box fixed. I was appalled by the salesman's reluctance to put down his egg mayonnaise sandwich and service my needs. Questioning my competence, he sneered through a mouthful of bread, "You don't know how to fit a plug?"

"Whether I know or not is neither here nor there. I rather doubt that you have the skill set to spot that the egg in your sandwich has turned and is likely to give you a nasty dose of salmonella," I retorted, flouncing out of the shop and marching directly across the road to the rival Currys store. Clearly schooled in the ethos that the customer is always right, the young salesgirl at Currys adeptly fitted a plug at no extra charge. Since I have brought up the subject, I may as well mention that Marigold was less than impressed with my thoughtful gift. She retaliated by buying me a set of screw-drivers that Christmas.

Violet Burke marched towards the bath-room, the three of us trailing in her wake. I sin-cerely doubted she would be able to find fault with the pristine new white bathroom suite which Marigold had chosen. My wife had even gone as far as insisting that the toilet must be equipped with a genuine wooden seat rather than a dodgy plastic one that may groan and crack under mother's weight.

Vangelis had done a masterful job of tiling the room in aqua, even adding a mosaic display as a splash back behind the basin. Although I had winced at this additional unnecessary ex-pense, I had reluctantly handed over my credit card, thinking the fancy mosaic may appeal to any tourists in need of accommodation when mother was back in Warrington. Naturally I hadn't mentioned this to Marigold: she remained adamantly opposed to any suggestion that we should ever welcome paying guests. However, I had by no means given up on the hope of persuading her. Since mother would be living rent free in the *apothiki*, a few tourists with a bit of spare cash to flash could provide a welcome injection to the bank account whenever she flitted back to Warrington.

Violet Burke's nose twitched in satisfaction as the familiar smell of Vim hit her nostrils. Despite the newness of the bath, I had given it a thorough scrubbing before leaving for work that morning. Considering mother's exacting standards when it came to bathroom cleanliness, I hadn't wanted to risk leaving anything to chance.

"You might have made an effort to clean up before I arrived. Look at the state of this place," Violet Burke complained. Taken aback by my mother's scathing words, I exchanged a confused glance with Marigold. Since Violet Burke's considerable bulk was frozen in the bathroom doorway, I had to elbow her aside in order to take up her invitation to look at the state of the place.

"Good grief, what on earth has happened?"

I exclaimed, unable to comprehend how the bathroom had come to be in such a state. The brand new fluffy bath towels which Marigold had draped over the heated towel rail had been flung on the floor in a bedraggled muddy heap. Reams of mutilated toilet paper stretched from the toilet roll holder over the side of the bath, resembling a pathetic display of tattered bunting. The intrusive sight of Cynthia's vile cat, Kouneli, holding court in the middle of the bath filled me with dismay. The mutant feline sprawled out asleep on a nest of ripped up loo roll was evidently responsible for the mess.

"You never mentioned the place had a sitting tenant. I've no intention of putting up with a scabby cat. Can't you control your blasted pets, Marigold?" Vi huffed in annoyance. "I've always said you're soft in the head when it comes to those spoilt cats of yours."

"The horrible creature is nothing to do with me," Marigold defended, her voice barely above a whisper as she choked back tears of outrage. "It's Cynthia's vile cat, it's the scourge of the village. It must have sneaked in through the kitchen window."

"Well, it can go out the same way then," Vi decreed, grabbing the odious mutant by the scruff of its neck and stomping back to the kitchen. Rudely awoken from its catnap, Kouneli hissed and spat at the strange woman manhandling it, growling in outrage as she hurled it through the kitchen window with gay abandon.

"That's a bit extreme," Barry muttered under his breath.

"We're on the ground floor," I reminded him.

"I'm sorry, Violet. Cynthia will be mortified when I tell her that her cat created havoc in your new bathroom," Barry said rather insincerely. Since Anastasia adored Kouneli, Barry tended to be quite indulgent of the Tom's nasty habits.

"It's high time she had the blasted creature put down..." I declared.

"Steady on, Victor, that's going a bit far," Barry feebly protested.

"You wouldn't say that if you were one of the tabbies it ravishes on a regular basis," I argued. "That thing has the morals of an alley cat rather than a tamed domestic."

"I'm so sorry, Violet. I wanted everything to be perfect for your arrival, to make you feel at home. I know what a huge step it must have been for you to move to a foreign country for the winter," Marigold said in a wobbly voice, her eyes tearing up. "I really went to a lot of effort to make everything feel homely and now that horrid cat has ruined everything."

"I know you did, lass, it's not your fault." Violet Burke's carping tone mellowed, a touch of genuine affection inflecting her words as she slipped a comforting arm around Marigold's shoulder. "Come on, love, stick the kettle on and we'll laugh about it over a cuppa. We'll leave Victor and Barry to clean up the mess in the bathroom."

"We're on it," Barry confirmed.

"And make sure you use plenty of Vim. If I pick up a single cat flea from that tub, there'll be hell to pay…"

"Don't worry, Vi. Cynthia had the cat deflead last week."

Scooping up wads of shredded toilet paper, I smiled to myself when I heard Violet Burke reassure Marigold that the bathroom would do nicely, pronouncing the newly installed tub a vast improvement on the washing up bowl we had upstairs.

Chapter 11

Like Riding a Bike

Marigold used the promise of a roast chicken dinner with all the trimmings to lure Violet Burke upstairs to dine with us. I was delighted my mother caved in: it wouldn't be much of an occasion if she celebrated her first night in Greece by tucking into a Fray Bentos in the bath. Whilst I considered my wife's choice of chicken a tad insensitive so soon after burying Mavrodafni, I appreciated the lengths she had gone to in bunging a Lidl bird in the oven to welcome my mother.

Barry had accepted our invitation to join us. About to decline and rush home to his wife and baby, Cynthia had telephoned to tell him she was about to dish up sausage curry. The thought of stomaching briny sausages out of a jar mixed into a watery mess of rice flavoured with a spoonful of curry powder, was enough to change his mind. My brother-in-law, full of high expectations that I could work miracles on his wife's uninspired repertoire of evening meals, had been quick off the mark in signing Cynthia up to attend my cooking classes. Naturally I offered him a family discount.

As Marigold piled roast potatoes and oven roasted caramelised onions onto our plates, Violet Burke remarked, "I hear that you're going back to England tomorrow and leaving poor Victor here to fend for himself."

"He's not exactly helpless," Marigold retorted. "And at least he'll have you here to keep him company."

I fired a withering look at my wife. There was no need for her to go putting daft ideas in Violet Burke's head. I wanted my mother to enjoy her independence without relying on me for company.

"Victor won't be wanting me getting under his feet. Anyway, I've things to be getting on with..."

The three of us waited with bated breath for Violet Burke to elaborate but she was otherwise occupied, shovelling roast potatoes into her mouth.

"Did Victor mention that we'd be delighted if you'd clean the house for us? We'd pay you, of course." Marigold broached the delicate subject tentatively, worried the offer may sound a tad insulting.

"Aye, Victor mentioned your standards are a bit lax. Not that he needed to bother, I can see for myself," Vi replied. With all her attention focused on her chicken breast, she failed to notice Marigold visibly bristling. "I'll have to see if I can fit you in. I'm after a proper job."

"Yes, mother said she'd quite like to get a job cleaning at the taverna," I hastily added, neglecting to mention her lofty ambition of opening a chippy.

"That Dina could do with someone to give the kitchen a proper scrubbing, it's amazing you haven't come down with a bout of something nasty from eating there. And the lav is a disgrace. I'll have it that clean that you could eat your dinner off it," Vi asserted.

"I shouldn't imagine there'd be much demand for that," Barry chortled.

"Now, I'll be needing some way of getting about the village. I can't be walking everywhere on these swollen feet without them exploding," Vi said.

"I didn't know that you could drive, Vi," Marigold said in surprise.

"I can't. It was pointless learning how to since I never had the money to run a car. I could always hop on a bus back in Warrington but I know such things are in short supply over here," Vi complained. "No, I was thinking something more along the lines of a bicycle."

I exhaled in relief. The last thing I wanted was my mother behind the wheel of the Punto.

"Cynthia has an old push-bike that she never uses. I'm sure that she'll be happy to let you use it," Barry suggested.

"That would be grand, lad. I'm sure I'll get the hang of riding one in no time at all."

"They didn't invent the term 'it's like riding a bike' for nothing. It's a skill that you never forget," I pointed out.

"Well, I can't exactly forget something that I never learnt in the first place," Vi admitted.

"But I'm sure there's nothing to it, plenty of wet behind the ear kiddies seem to manage it."

"Do you mean to say that you've never ridden a bicycle before and you intend to take it up at your age?" Barry laughed

"Aye, lad, that I do. I'm sure that Victor can get me started, show me what's what once I get settled in the saddle."

"A bicycle isn't a horse," Marigold interjected.

"Well, it's probably best if you let me give you a few pointers to get you started, rather than Victor," Barry volunteered. "He was clueless when it came to teaching Benjamin how to keep his balance. He did nothing but bang on about the necessity of the poor child wearing a helmet and it wasn't even the law back then."

"One can never take health and safety for granted," I retorted.

"Vangelis has some old stabilisers in his *apothiki* that he used when his boys were little and first learning to ride a bike. I'll fetch them over with Cynthia's bike tomorrow," Barry promised.

"Mother will need a safety helmet, too," I reminded him.

"I'm sure that Spiros could spare the one

that you gifted him for his name day. He never wears it," Marigold pointed out.

"Spiros has a very lackadaisical approach to health and safety. You'd think he would take greater caution considering the amount of people that he ends up burying due to needless accidents."

"Well, I've no objection to sticking a helmet on my head," Violet Burke conceded. "You know that I'm partial to a hat and it will save me wearing a rain-mate if the weather's bad."

"That takes me back, Vi," Marigold laughed. "I haven't heard of rain mates for years. Barry, do you remember how Aunty Beryl always used to keep a plastic rain mate at the ready in her handbag?"

"Along with that pepper shaker in case she ever got mugged," he said, smiling fondly at his sister.

"Bring the bicycle over tomorrow afternoon, Barry," I urged, the prospect of watching Violet Burke learning to ride a bicycle too tempting to resist. "I'm showing the Stranges round Leo's old place at noon."

"Ooh, I hope they like it. I quite took to that Moira. It would be nice to have some pleasant neighbours after putting up with that foul mouthed Edna Billings back home," Vi said. "Marigold, did Victor tell you? Moira Strange has the strangest job."

"Her husband mentioned that she was a model at least a hundred times," Marigold replied, a distinctive twang of jealousy creeping into her tone.

"You should see the look on your face, Marigold. You've gone as green as that soft cow that Barry married," Vi snickered. "'Appen Moira's husband forgot to mention that she's an ear model, did you ever hear the like? Anyway, I'll be around to make sure that Victor doesn't go making eyes at any other women while you're gadding about in Manchester with that gormless friend of yours that can't nab herself a decent husband."

I imagine the look on Marigold's face would be priceless if she hadn't tuned out of the conversation to retrieve the crumble from the oven. Although secure in the knowledge that I would never make eyes at another woman, she had been caught out red-handed harbouring thoughts of petty jealousy about an attractive model moving into the village.

"Well these feet of mine are screaming out for a good soaking so I'm off downstairs for a bath," Violet Burke announced.

"But I've done your favourite pudding, apple crumble and custard," Marigold said.

"Shove it in a bowl for me, lass. I'll eat it in the bath."

"I'll walk you down," Barry offered.

As the two of them took their leave, Marigold hissed, "Do you think I ought to have mentioned that we've got no water pressure again?"

"I'm sure we'll hear all about it in the morning," I sighed.

Chapter 12

A Fawning Farewell

The dark clouds had drifted away, the dismal weather replaced with the promise of radiant sunshine to mark Marigold's departure from Greece. As I carted her suitcases through from the bedroom, they struck me as suspiciously light. No doubt she intended to stuff them with new purchases in England: I had a feeling she would flash far more cash on new frocks in Marks and Sparks than she would in Tesco on silver skin pickles. Still, at least she hadn't laden her cases with essential household belongings, depriving me of our toasted sandwich maker and other assorted kitchen utensils for the week.

"Now you will remember to feed the cats. I'm going to miss them so much," Marigold called out from the bedroom. Considering that I was the one to put the disgusting slop in their bowls every morning, I considered her reminder a tad redundant.

"Catastrophe could afford to miss a few meals, she's bordering on the obese," I retorted. Neither of Marigold's pampered imported domestics took a lick of outdoor exercise, preferring to sprawl out on the furniture shedding hairs. Kyria Maria's namesake tortoise next door exhibited more energy than either of Marigold's overindulged imported moggies.

Marigold emerged from the bedroom, yawning widely. It had been a shock to her system to get out of bed so early two days on the trot. Frank had insisted they make an early start. He wanted to allow plenty of time to get to the airport, apparently calculating the travelling time as though he was pedalling his bicycle there rather than driving a car. Dressed in a neat skirt suit and heels, with not a hair out of place, Marigold looked very chic. Abhorring the latest trend of flying in shell suits and other such comfortable garb, she preferred to mimic the glamorous style popularised by traveller's jet-setting the globe during the golden years of aviation.

Marigold had pulled out all the stops in the hope that if she stood out as suitably smart she may land an upgrade to business class. My wife appeared to have overlooked the fact that she was travelling with Frank and Julie: Frank's unwavering loyalty to Lycra would surely relegate the threesome to seats squashed in next to the toilet with any other badly dressed rabble.

"Now, you're sure that you'll manage okay without me, dear?" Marigold cooed. Like her reminder about feeding the cats, her question struck me as rather redundant: I doubted she had any intention of cancelling her plans if I belatedly claimed that I could not live without her for the week. "You've always got your mother downstairs for company if you start to miss me too much."

Whilst we have never been joined at the hip, Marigold's absence for a full week would be the longest that we had been apart since our wedding day. Although my illustrious career as a public health inspector had taken me away on occasion, I had always returned home to my wife at the weekends. Marigold's odd spa week-end away with Geraldine had never clashed with the weekends I returned home from my in-spection trips.

My visit back to England to assist Violet Burke's move had been a flying one. I rather im-agined that this seven day trip would prove the old adage correct about absence making the heart grow fonder. Marigold had certainly ex-ploited the notion, insisting that we spin out our reunion at Athens Airport the following week into a romantic luxury mini-break in the Greek capital. She had even made a point of warning me that under no circumstance was I to invite Violet Burke to tag along.

"Give Benjamin a hug from me," I said. Our son had promised to drive up to Manchester over the weekend to see Marigold.

"Benjamin said that he would whisk Ger-aldine and me off for dinner at the Bhilai Bhaji tomorrow evening…"

"Well, it wouldn't be fair on Benjamin to let Ashley tag along. I can't see our son suffering such an insufferable bore, not to mention if Ash-ley starts chuntering on about venereal diseases whilst you're tucking into aloo gobi it will ruin your enjoyment of the food," I warned. I doubted that I would ever be able to look a cauliflower dish in the floret again without associating it with the disgusting samples Ashley examined under his microscope.

"Geraldine hopes that Ashley will keep his distance whilst I'm staying with her. She's worried he may spring a proposal on her at any minute. There's no time to lose in making her unattractive to him…"

The sound of a car horn honking below interrupted our conversation. Rushing to the balcony, Marigold called out, "It's Frank and Julie. They're terribly early, they weren't due for another half-hour. Now, let me check that I have everything, ticket and passport, yes."

"But you haven't had any breakfast," I pointed out.

"Hopefully Frank will stop somewhere so I can buy a takeaway *bougatsa*," Marigold said, chivvying me to drag her cases downstairs.

To my surprise, Julie was behind the wheel of the hire car. The expat couple from Nektar leapt out to greet us, Frank obligingly relieving me of Marigold's suitcases.

"It's a good job that we travel light," he said, nodding towards a couple of Lycra backpacks taking up hardly any room in the boot. Marigold visibly winced at the sight of Frank's outfit, an all-in-one skin tight cycling number in bottle green, hugging his bulge a tad too closely. Averting my eyes from the vulgar display, I couldn't help but notice that his legs were completely hairless. Although I had read about the new metrosexual trend of men removing all their body hair, it was the first time I had encountered any solid evidence of it.

The local Greeks seemed more inclined to encourage their bodily hair growth as a symbol of their masculinity, unless their tendency to flaunt a hirsute appearance was down to sheer laziness when it came to shaving. If it wasn't bursting through the buttonholes of their too-tight shirts, it was sprouting out of their noses and ears with gay abandon, or embellishing their lower foreheads in the form of bushy eyebrows. Moustaches remained surprisingly popular too, though beards were sparse until the olive picking season when they were cultivated for warmth. Naturally Papas Andreas maintained his scraggly beard year-round but that was a compulsory requirement of the Orthodox Church.

I had briefly toyed with the idea of nurturing some facial hair of my own, thinking it may help me to look more Greek in appearance. I had a theory that if I looked less British it might put an end to Greeks I was unfamiliar with from automatically responding to me in English when I addressed them in their own language. My experiment was short lived, Marigold refusing to subject her delicate skin to my stubble rash. Considering that perhaps I should take advantage of Marigold's absence to have a second attempt at growing a beard and matching tache, I made a conscious decision to avoid scraping the razor over my face the next morning. If the prickly stage was over with by the time she returned, I imagined I might flaunt my new look at the airport and wow my wife. I rather supposed a neat goatee might give me a distinguished air.

My thoughts were interrupted by Marigold elbowing me in the ribs and rolling her eyes at my seeming preoccupation with Frank's hairless legs.

"You're going to feel the draught when you land in Manchester wearing that," I quipped to Frank.

"I never feel the cold. One of the benefits of cycling," he said, my attempt at humour seemingly going over his head.

"That's good to know. My mother is planning to take up cycling, perhaps it will help to keep her heating bill down," I said.

"Don't be ridiculous, Victor. I can't see your mother racing up mountains on Cynthia's old bicycle. She'll be lucky to wobble around the village without doing herself an injury," Marigold said.

"Well, if she needs any cycling gear, direct her to ours when we next come over," Frank offered.

"I rather doubt that Violet Burke would be able to squeeze her substantial bulk into Lycra, even if it is stretchy," I chortled.

"I was thinking more along the lines of puncture repair kits and bicycle pumps," Frank responded blankly, seemingly perplexed by my gaffe.

As we were chatting, I noticed Guzim attempting to slink furtively through my gate. No matter how many times I told him that roadside access through my garden was out of bounds, he continued to defiantly slip through the hole he had made in the fence and troop through my garden. Since he managed to look even more shifty than usual, my attention was drawn to the eggs he was trying to conceal in the cap he was carrying. Just because I had appreciated his thoughtful gesture in digging a hole for my mutilated deceased chicken, it didn't mean that I was prepared to turn a blind eye to him making off with the newly laid produce of my remaining poultry.

Accosting the Albanian shed dweller, I demanded to know what he was doing with my eggs, "*Ti kaneis me ta avga mou?*"

Presuming that he was running some profitable little side-line flogging what was rightly mine, I was rather taken aback when he retorted that he thought Mrs Bucket might like some fresh eggs for her breakfast, "*Nomiza oti i Kyria Kouvas tha ithele freska avga yia proino.*"

"*Ta echeis vrasei?*" Marigold, still half asleep, asked Guzim if he had boiled them. Having been deprived of her breakfast, she appeared quite eager to satisfy her hunger with an impromptu egg until she could get her hands on a *bougatsa*: she has always been quite partial to a cold hardboiled egg as part of a picnic lunch.

"*I Kyria Kouvas borei na ta vrasei moni tis i na ta tiganisei.*" Guzim's response that Mrs Bucket could boil them herself or fry them made not an iota of sense until he turned his back on us to knock on the door of the *apothiki*. As the penny dropped that he was hand delivering fresh eggs to Violet Burke, a generous and thoughtful gesture indeed, I reddened at the realisation that I had been quick to leap to the assumption that he was running some kind of nefarious egg pilfering racket. Knowing how much my mother intimidated Guzim, I supposed he must be attempting to ingratiate himself in her good books before she could unleash any criticism in his direction. Tapping Guzim on the shoulder, I told him that my mother was Mrs Burke, not Mrs Bucket. *"I mitera mou einai Kyria Burke kai ochi Kyria Kouvas."* It might help his cause if he at least got her name right.

Unfamiliar with the Albanian shed dweller, Frank and Julie openly gawped at Guzim, fearfully putting some distance between them as though he was some dissolute type about to make off with their Lycra backpacks: in fairness he did look particularly shifty, apparently attempting to cultivate a bit of facial hair of his own, no doubt in preparation for olive picking. As the British couple scrutinised Guzim, in turn he spluttered in laughter, flashing off his toothless gums. His reaction was understandable: he'd just got an eyeful of Frank's bizarre cycling outfit.

"There's no need to look so worried, he's my gardener," I assured Frank and Julie.

"Is he quite right in the head? It's pretty odd behaviour to laugh so hysterically at nothing," Frank said.

"He's from Albania," Marigold said, unintentionally aping Basil Fawlty's excuse that Manuel was from Barcelona.

"I don't think that Guzim is familiar with Lycra," I explained.

"Really, Victor. There's nothing remotely funny about Lycra," Marigold warned me with a withering glare. Reading between the lines, I knew that was her subtle way of telling me that she found Lycra to be a fashion faux pas beyond humour.

"Well, Guzim's your man if you ever need to dispose of any old clothes. He will turn your cast-offs into a new fashion trend in Albania. He's a much more environmentally friendly solution than cluttering up the village bins with discarded clothing," I said to Frank. I hoped he took my hint. It would be a total hoot to watch Guzim mucking out the chicken coop in the latest cycling fashion.

"Well, we ought to be making tracks," Frank said, ushering Marigold towards the car, seemingly desperate to get away. "We don't want to risk missing the flight."

"I'll see you next week, darling," Marigold trilled.

"Don't forget to phone me when you arrive tonight," I reminded her. Not too keen on public displays of kissing, we had already dispensed with our tender goodbyes over coffee in bed that morning.

As Marigold moved to step into the hire car, Guzim looked totally confused. "*Pou pas*?" he said, asking her where she was going.

"*Stin Anglia*," Marigold responded, telling him she was going to England.

Guzim reacted in a totally unexpected way, prostrating himself on the pavement and throwing his arms around Marigold's shins to prevent her from moving. With an expression of abject misery on his face, he begged, "*Ochi ochi, parakalo min afisete ton antra sas. Doste tou mia alli efkairia, einai kalos anthropos.*"

"Good grief, what on earth is he doing?" Julie shouted, backing away in case the presumably deranged gardener attempted to forcibly restrain her too.

"He seems to have got it into his head that I am leaving Victor. He's begging me not to go,"

Marigold translated. "I didn't catch the rest of it. What did he say, Victor?"

"He is imploring you not to leave me and to give me a second chance. He says that I am a good man," I explained.

"Why on earth has he got it into his head that I'm deserting you?" Marigold said.

"And more to the point, why is he carrying on as though your departure is the end of the world?" I said, puzzled by Guzim's behaviour.

"You know how he's put me on a pedestal ever since I gave his hovel a makeover. I do wish he wouldn't, I find it most unnerving," Marigold said, attempting to shoo Guzim away. Marigold's efforts to untangle her legs from the Albanian's firm grasp were futile, Guzim clinging on ever tighter as he pleaded with her not to go, "*Min pas.*"

Determined to put an end to Guzim's hysteria, I assured him that my wife was simply going on her holidays and would return the next week. "*I gynaika mou paei diakopes, tha episterpsei tin epomeni evdomada.*"

"*Pas sa thiakopes.*" Guzim spat out the words 'you go on holiday' in relief. As he unhanded my wife, I considered that perhaps a public display of our affection in the form of a tender pavement farewell may have disabused him of the ridiculous notion that we were heading to the divorce courts, without the need to explain ourselves. Whilst Marigold was clearly embarrassed by Guzim's fawning overreaction, I was quite touched by his show of devotion towards my wife and his sincere, heartfelt declaration that I am a good man.

As Guzim returned to knocking on the *apothiki* door, it was suddenly flung open, revealing Violet Burke in all her morning glory. Clad in the bedraggled fuchsia candlewick dressing gown that vividly clashed with her garishly dyed rumpled red hair, she growled, "What's all this din about? I thought this was supposed to be a respectable neighbourhood."

Visibly cowering, Guzim backed away, shaking so much he had to do an impromptu juggling act with the eggs. Marigold, hurrying to get out of the firing line and into the car, called out, "Good Morning, Vi, I'm just off."

Fixing her eyes on Frank in his skin-tight cycling outfit, Violet Burke's surly scowl was replaced with an expression of wry amusement. Subjecting Frank to a most disconcerting come-hither grin and a totally inappropriate suggestive wink, she convulsed in laughter, yelling,

"Are you here to get me started on the bike, lad, or are you just happy to see me?"

Ignoring my mother, Frank jumped into the vehicle, his curdled expression intimating he regarded my mother with the same revulsion I reserved for Ashley's infected samples. As Julie floored the hire car, Marigold sent me a cheery goodbye wave. The expat couple appeared quite desperate to get away, clearly having second thoughts about the wisdom of associating with the Buckets, or at least with me. I supposed they had been shielded from the peculiarities of Greek village life by the relative seclusion of their holiday home on the outskirts of Nektar: there again, no Greeks had been involved in the eccentric pavement activities that had just transpired, only a European couple with Greek residency, a bolshie and uncouth British harridan and a shabby Albanian.

Frank's look of startled horror as Violet Burke subjected him to a suggestive wink stuck in my mind as the car roared away. One would really think that a grown man who pranced around in skin-tight Lycra might have a more developed sense of humour.

Shooing Guzim away before he could irritate my mother, I instructed him to give me the eggs, reminding him that Nikos would be angry if he was late, "*Dose mou ta avga. O Nikos tha einai thymomenos an argisete.*"

Scurrying away, the ungrateful wretch grumbled that he hated picking olives, "*Miso na mazevo elies.*" I made a mental reminder to volunteer my services to Dimitris for a couple of hours in the coming days. It really was high time that I discovered what the olive harvest fuss was all about first-hand whilst avoiding working under Nikos' slave driving tutelage.

"How was your first night, Mother?" I asked.

"There's something wrong with the bath, I could barely get more than a puddle of water," she complained. "I had to resort to sticking my swollen feet in the washing up bowl."

"That's nothing to do with the actual bath. I'm afraid the water pressure is a tad low at the moment," I explained, cringing at the thought that her feet had already contaminated the brand new plastic bowl I'd bought her.

"Well, turn the water pressure up then," she demanded.

"I can't just turn up the pressure. It doesn't work like that…"

"Well, ring the water board and get them to

sort it then," she demanded, folding her arms stubbornly.

Across the road, Kyrios Stavropoulos ambled along on his way to the shop for his regular morning coffee. Having the temerity to stare across at the candlewick ensconced bulbous creature propping up the doorway, he received a dagger's drawn look from Violet Burke. Not content with fixing him with an intimidating glare, she shouted across, "Have you had a good look?" It appeared that my mother had been unduly influenced by living next door to the gobby Edna Billings.

Fixing his gaze on the ground, Kyrios Stavropoulos muttered under his breath. I imagined that such an unwarranted confrontation might drive him to adding a *Metaxa* to his early morning coffee.

"The water supply is under the province of the *Dimarcheio*, a bureaucratic body not known for its speed," I told my mother. "You will just have to be patient. I'm afraid an erratic water supply is one of the vagaries you must become accustomed to in Meli."

"'Appen I'd better start leaving the taps running when I go to bed then. With a bit of luck the bath might have filled up by morning."

"More likely you'd just end up flooding the bathroom…" I pointed out, cringing as Papas Andreas stepped out of the neighbouring house. Muttering a subdued "*Kalimera,*" he averted his eyes from the sight of Violet Burke filling the doorway in her nightclothes. Whatever her other faults, one would never find Kyria Maria standing around streetside in anything less decorous than her black widow's weeds.

Embarrassed by the exhibition she was making of herself, I suggested, "Perhaps we should step indoors, Mother."

"I like it out here. I can keep my eye on things, see what's what…"

Her voice trailed off as Vangelis and Barry roared by in the builder's van. Slamming the brakes on, Vangelis reversed, leaving the engine running as Barry rolled down the window, calling out, "Vi, have you seen Kouneli?"

"Kou what?" she responded.

"Cynthia's cat. He's gone on the missing list and poor Cyn is quite distraught. He didn't come home last night."

"I know for a fact that the vile creature often stays out all night so why on earth is Cynthia getting in a tizzy about it now?" I interjected. I recalled the numerous times I had been forced to sweep the feline menace out of my house in the mornings after it had sneaked in through the open balcony doors with all the stealth of a cat burglar.

"Since Anastasia became so attached to Kouneli, he always comes home to see her first thing in the morning. They like to share a bit of brekkie, it's become their morning routine."

Hearing Barry's explanation, I bit my lip to prevent myself from laughing aloud at the thought that flashed through my mind. I wondered if little Ana shared her breakfast with the cat or if she had inherited her Aunt Marigold's habit of taste testing cat food.

"Cynthia knows that Violet was the last person to see Kouneli," Barry continued.

"Why would Cynthia get it into her head that my mother was the last person to see her cat?" I asked.

"Because I happened to mention that Vi chucked it out of her kitchen window and the cat hasn't shown its face since," Barry admitted.

"Shame on you for telling tales out of school, lad. I've only been in the village five minutes and you're already maligning my good name," Violet Burke spluttered.

"To be fair, mother did chuck it out of the

ground floor window," I reminded Barry as Violet Burke stormed inside, slamming the door in our faces. I emitted a grateful sigh, relieved that the rest of the villagers would be spared the sight of my stroppy mother cluttering the doorway in candlewick. Since the eggs were going begging, I headed upstairs with thoughts of scrambling in mind.

Chapter 13

Defacing Lamp Posts

With the morning to kill before I was scheduled to show the Stranges around Leo's house, I decided it would be an opportune time to ensure everything was in perfect readiness for my first cookery class the next afternoon. I must confess to feeling a smidgen of excitement at the prospect of finally launching my practical classes, having every confidence they would be a roaring success under my skilful and erudite tutelage. I was not a complete novice in conducting classes, having once stepped in to deliver a series of lectures on food hygiene at the local technical college when the regular lecturer came down with a suspicious case of listeria. After proving I could be unflappable in front of a rabble of unruly and disinterested teenagers on day-release, I could certainly hold my own in front of a handful of expats.

Although initially Marigold had been less than keen on my opening up our kitchen to a bunch of culinary challenged expats, I had used all my persuasive charm to talk her around, assuring Marigold that I had no expectations of her assuming the role of Major Johnnie to my Fanny Cradock. My convincing selling point had been that after a course of lessons the quality of food produced by the members of the expat dining club would be sure to improve. Even though my wife insisted on dragging us along to every tedious dinner party, she had to admit that the standard of most of the foreign themed inedible slop served up left a lot to be desired.

Cynthia had been the only reluctant sign-up amongst the village expats, initially challenging my credentials. Even though she had scraped her plate clean every time she had dined at my table, she dared to have the temerity to ask if I even had such a thing as an O-level in domestic science. I gave her short shrift, pointing out that I am well versed in creating Greek cuisine due to my experience cheffing in an authentic Greek taverna of excellent repute. When Cynthia had the nerve to snigger, claiming that a bunch of Greek pensioners are hardly the most discerning of judges, I reminded her that she had considered the taverna good enough for her own wedding reception, subtly reminding her that I coughed up the cash for the celebration. With my reminder that I successfully lead the popular Greek gastronomic tour for the travel company, Cynthia was forced to admit that I am indeed an authority on Greek produce with a wealth of experience in the subject under my belt. She had to agree that the customer satisfaction surveys from the tours are nothing less than glowing.

First on the agenda was ensuring that I had all the necessary ingredients to hand for the dish that I would be demonstrating: Greek beef stew with olives, *vodino katsaroles me elies.* Having taken the precaution of pre-ordering the stewing beef from Tina, I checked my list to see if I was missing anything else before I strolled over to the shop to collect the meat.

V.D. BUCKET

As I ran my eye down the list of ingredients it occurred to me that I could offer extra value for money by teaching my pupils the Greek words for the food items they would be handling. Most of the expats I would be tutoring remained perpetually challenged by *i Elliniki glossa;* that is to say the Greek language. Recalling that Cynthia would be in attendance, I dragged out my trusty English to Greek dictionary to ensure my translations were accurate. It wouldn't do to be shown up in my own kitchen by my linguistically superior sister-in-law correcting my pronunciation of bay leaves.

I found it most satisfying to realise that apart from the meat, the olives and the tinned tomatoes, the rest of the ingredients were all to be found growing in my garden: I didn't dare let Norman loose in my kitchen near fresh tomatoes after the microwave horror he'd splattered over his kitchen. It was only my scruples about eating my pet chickens that prevented me from boasting that I was as self-sufficient as Tom and Barbara Good, the suburban couple of 70s sitcom fame who chucked in the rat race to grow their own. Of course it was doubtful that their somewhat lackadaisical approach to hygiene standards would have met the rigorous requirements of the 1990 Food Safety Act, the rulings of which I endeavour to strictly adhere to. Since my Greek neighbours appeared to be welded to their insanitary swill habit: I found it a running battle to convince them of the importance of sticking to what they regarded as pesky and unnecessarily intrusive regulations.

As Marigold had taken over the kitchen the previous day to cook up a chicken dinner with all the trimmings, the place was in desperate need of a good scrubbing. I could only imagine the sly glances and raised eyebrows if I conducted my lessons in anything less than a scrupulously hygienic environment: with my illustrious reputation as a retired public health inspector to uphold, it was beholden on me to set a sanitary example. Since it struck me as a tad unseemly to press my mother into service by making her clean my kitchen on her first morning in Greece, I shoved my hands into a pair of Marigolds and got stuck in with the Vim. After an exhausting hour of elbow grease, the kitchen positively gleamed. Duly divesting myself of the rubber gloves, I headed over to the shop to collect the meat.

No sooner had my feet hit the street, than I collided with Cynthia. My sister-in-law narrowly avoided running the pram over my toes before stopping to attach a poster of her missing feline to the nearest lamp post. Considering the amount of times the vile creature stayed out overnight on a mission to ravish any random ferals, I presumed that Cynthia must keep a job lot of posters on hand. Staring up at the large glossy photograph of the ugly cat with a distinctive black stripe running sideways across its mutant face, I gave serious thought to dobbing Cynthia in to the authorities for defacing lamp posts. Kouneli's glossy image was most decidedly a blot on the village landscape.

"I was just about to knock on your mother's door to see what she has to say for herself. I've a good mind to report her for hurling my cat out of her window," Cynthia grumbled. Considering how overawed Cynthia became whenever she was in my mother's presence, I imagined she was all talk. I very much doubted she had the slightest intention of confronting my harridan of a mother.

"It was the ground floor window," I protested, thinking my sister-in-law was making an awful fuss over nothing. The mutant tomcat had survived being swept to the street from my first floor balcony too many times to recall, not to mention the odd occasion when it had leapt from the roof terrace to avoid my advancing broom. I made a mental note to research if the old English proverb about cats having nine lives applied to Greek felines: perchance they were blessed with more.

In a desperate attempt to steer the subject away from my mother's manhandling of the cat, I went into charm mode, telling Cynthia, "I can see that little Anastasia has inherited your lustrous hair."

"Oh, do you think so?" Cynthia simpered.

"Definitely," I assured her, whilst wondering if Ana's glossy locks were in fact an inherited trait or an unintended consequence of the baby sharing Kouneli's cat food at breakfast.

"Anastasia is so upset that the cat is missing," Cynthia sighed, even though little Ana appeared anything but unduly traumatised by Kouneli being on the missing list. As I peered into the pram, the baby gurgled with excited delight at the sight of her Uncle Victor.

"Anastasia is always welcome at ours to play with Pickles," I suggested before heading on my way, leaving Cynthia to find some more lamp posts to deface.

Making my way to the shop, I paused to

watch with interest as some distant figures laid olive nets in a hilly green grove, the slope of the land making me wonder how they would position their three-legged wooden olive ladders securely. This first stage of the harvest was thankfully peaceful before the machines came into play, but there was a general hum of activity from areas where the more usual sounds were limited to those of nature. Fallen olives dotted the village lane. Blackened from human tread, they were barely discernible from a fresh deposit of goat droppings. Reaching the village square, the fallen leaves carpeting the ground in rich and rustic autumnal colours, rustled under my feet. I pondered if the plane trees dominating the square had their roots in ancient times, *plantania* having a noble history in Ancient Greek lore.

Kyrios Stavropoulos cut a solitary figure sipping coffee outside the shop, one of the usual tables removed to make room for Tina's display of olive picking paraphernalia. By this time of the morning the old chap was usually engaged in a fierce *tavli* battle with one of his fellow old cronies.

"*Monos sou simera, Kyrios,*" I said, observing that he was on his own today.

BUCKET TO GREECE (VOL.9)

"*Oi filoi mou kanoun tis elies. Den boro na voi-thiso kathos i plati mou paizetai,*" he replied, telling me his friends were doing the olives but he couldn't help as his back was playing up.

"*Tha sou steilo ena tsipouro,*" I offered, telling him I would send him a *tsipouro*. The strong spirit might act as a painkiller. I was quite impressed that his usual coffee companions were off doing the harvest since I doubted any of them would ever see eighty again. I hoped that my enthusiastic adoption of the Greek lifestyle would ensure that I would be as fit and active as them in twenty years, though they certainly had the edge on me already in the fitness stakes.

"*Yassou*, Victor," Tina greeted me, coming out from behind the counter to deposit kisses on my cheeks. "I am the happy to see you. Please to watch the shop for the minute. I go the upstairs to check the *mama*. She has to been banging on the floor all the morning."

I nodded in weary agreement, thinking that Tina was definitely taking advantage of my good nature. Apart from my stint running the shop this coming Sunday when Tina was taking the day off to settle Despina back in her own home, my days of manning the shop were thankfully over.

"Really, I will be only the minute," Tina pleaded, having mistakenly interpreted my nod as the typical Greek sign of refusal.

"Go," I assured her. Reluctantly tying the proffered pinny round my waist, I dropped a couple of coins in the till and delivered a small bottle of *tsipouro* to Kyrios Stavropoulos. Despite his Communist sympathies, I had rather come to enjoy the old chap's company, finding him a hive of historical information about the village and the surrounding area. I found that the odd bribe of liquor occasionally lubricated his tongue enough to open up about his fascinating experiences during the war and the subsequent Greek civil war, a subject too sensitive to broach when he was sober. Unfortunately the arrival of customers meant that the verbal grilling would have to be postponed for another day.

As a line formed at the till, I spotted someone shamelessly queue jumping, failing at first to recognise that it was Nikos. His often unkempt stubble was now well hidden beneath a white streaked beard, whilst his tall lean body appeared to have filled out almost overnight. I realised that Nikos' sudden weight gain was merely a visual illusion brought on by the excess padding of his layering a couple of fleece lined, checked flannel shirts so popular at this time of year. The familiar laughter lines on his handsome face stood out in craggy relief when he addressed me with the popular greeting of, *"Pos eisai file mou?"* meaning, 'How are you my friend?'

Having charmed his way to the front of the queue by pointing out that he was only purchasing a single olive rake, Nikos then held everyone else up by settling in for a chat. The queue of villagers behind him resigned themselves to the wait, a tad irritated when Nikos switched to English, thus thwarting their efforts to listen in.

"Victor, you must to help me with the olives. You cannot to call yourself the *Ellinas* until you have the harvest under your waistband," Nikos insisted.

"Belt," I corrected. "You mean under my belt, not under my waistband. Anyway, I don't go round declaring that I am a Greek man. I prefer to describe myself as a European citizen with Greek residency."

"But the olive he is the tradition, Victor. I know how you to love to embrace the Greek custom," Nikos cajoled. "You to throw yourself into the wine and bread making"

"You may have taken me in with your quintessentially Greek spiel when it came to bread and wine, but you're not getting one over on me when it comes to the olives. I've heard you complain often enough that it is backbreaking work," I pointed out.

"You have also to hear me say that the oil from the olives is the nectar of life. Like the blood that pump the heart, the olive oil is the life blood of the Greek," Nikos persisted.

"There's no point in trying to woo me with your romantic vision of olive picking," I said bluntly. Nikos threw his hands up in a gesture of defeat, his eyes twinkling in amusement when he realised I was impervious to his attempts to make me view olive picking through rose-coloured glasses. "I'd quite like to come along to the olive press with you once you've filled all your sacks. I'd rather enjoy seeing the oil making process."

"When all the work he is done," Nikos scoffed.

"You have Guzim to do the hard work this year."

"He already to break the rake," Nikos grumbled, handing the money over for the new one.

"And I expect Kostis is hard at work on the olives too," I said.

"The Kostis is the useless, he go off to try to win back the Eleni..."

"Ah yes, I heard that she had left him," I sympathised.

"I not to blame her. The Eleni is the good girl and the son he is the..." Nikos inserted a string of Greek expletives too offensive for the delicate ears of my readers. I will simply translate his words as 'bad husband.'

"But the Dina she feel it here," Nikos cried, pressing his hand firmly against the right hand breast pocket of the flannel shirt. I got his drift. Dina was feeling the loss of her daughter-in-law and infant granddaughter keenly. "And the Dina she miss the help from the Eleni, she say she should be the retire, not the cook and the clean so many the hour."

"I might be able to help you out there..." I said.

"It is the woman's work, Victor, I tell you before," Nikos interrupted.

"Violet Burke is here and she's after some cleaning work," I clarified. "Unlike Dina, she derives a great deal of satisfaction in scouring the lavatory and slopping a mop around."

"I not concern myself with the woman's work, I have the olive to pick. The Violet must speak to the Dina," Nikos said firmly, wisely absolving himself of all responsibility. Undoubtedly he would never hear the end of it if he took it upon himself to bring another woman into Dina's kitchen.

"Perhaps I should bring her along later to speak to Dina," I suggested. "I'll be able to translate."

"And will you to be there to translate when she to work?" Nikos fired back, pointing out the flaw in my plan. "If the Dina and the Violet cannot to understand one the other, she will be no the use to help. They must to communicate without the word."

"You make a valid point, my friend. They may have to resort to mime."

"What is this mime?"

Since I found the Greek translation of mime rather stumped me, I grabbed the mop from behind the counter and mimed using it, much to the amusement of the ever expanding line of customers. Whilst the bulk of the villagers were generally in no hurry and happy to linger if it kept them up to date with all the local gossip, their patience was being stretched thin by their inability to make head or tail of our conversation.

"*Den echo oli tin imera. Prepei na pao sto farmakeio.*" Shuffling impatiently, an elderly lady shouted that she didn't have all day; she had to go to the pharmacy. Taking the hint, I waved Nikos away and got to work ringing up her purchases.

Another half-hour dragged by. I had just seen off the last of the customers when Tina finally deigned to reappear, apologising for being a tad longer than the promised minute.

"The *mama* make the many demand, I am the sorry, Victor," Tina said.

"Well it's not long now until you can pack her off home on Sunday."

"It cannot to come the soon enough," she sighed wearily as I grabbed a couple of tins of tomatoes and reminded her of my order for meat. Presumably in recompense for the time I had spent covering for her, Tina insisted my purchases were on the house. It was difficult to calculate what my going rate was worth when my wages were paid in stewing beef and tinned tomatoes instead of hard cash, but I suspected I was being seriously undervalued. With an eight hour day in the shop looming on Sunday, I would have to watch out that Tina didn't try to fob me off by paying my wages in close to expiration stock.

Strolling home, I paused to take a hearty breath of the clear autumnal air. Lacking the sapping humidity of summer, I imagined it was a healthy tonic that would bring in a fortune if bottled. Gazing down to the sea in the distance, I spotted a solitary fishing boat on the horizon. The idea of being cast adrift from land in a small fishing boat surrounded by nothing but silence and clear blue water that rippled when I cast a line, held a certain appeal. Perhaps I would take *Kapetainos* Vasos up on his offer to go out with him in his fishing boat. Aware that my presence in his boat would flout the Greek law prohibiting fishing boats from carrying passengers, I made a mental note to check if such a flagrant breach of the regulations would get me in trouble if we were caught or if it would only land Vasos in it. The very notion of deliberately defying the law was so uncharacteristic that it made me feel like a carefree daredevil, putting a noticeable bounce in my step as I continued homeward.

Recalling Nikos saying that Violet Burke would need to speak to Dina directly about cleaning, I stopped to knock at the door of the *apothiki* before heading upstairs. When there was no reply, I pondered that she may have gone back to bed with jet lag or that she may have popped next door to renew her friendship with Kyria Maria. Either way, I didn't linger. It wouldn't do to give the impression that I was never off my mother's doorstep: I may well come across as the sort of poor sap who was at a loss when his wife was away.

Chapter 14

Part of the Fixes and Fits

Do you fancy celebrating together in the taverna this evening if the Stranges put in an offer on the house?" I asked Spiros as we waited in the doorway of Leo's house for the potential house buyers to arrive. Leaning against the stonework, plumes of smoke spiralled around Spiros' head as he frantically puffed away on a cigarette, his foot tapping nervously.

"Tonight I promise to *romantikos* the Sampaguita." Spiros wiggled his bushy eyebrows up and down in a gesture designed to indicate more than romance might be on the cards. "I tell the Sampaguita they will to buy and she have agree to pack and move the in with me today."

"I hope you aren't counting your chickens before..." I began to say before realising I hadn't got the energy to explain the saying to Spiros. Changing tack, I said, "So Sampaguita has overcome her reluctance to live in sin."

"How can the love to be the sin, Victor? I tell that to the Sampaguita many time. It not the easy to persuade the him to live with the me before the marry."

"But she's finally agreed to move in with you. That's excellent news. How did you finally win her over?" I was genuinely curious, aware how sensitive Sampaguita could be about curtain twitchers.

"I to promise him she can to bring the cat to live with the us," Spiros said with a wink. "I had to hope to sell the cat with the house as part of the, how you to say in English, the fixes and fits?"

"A cat wouldn't qualify as part of the fixtures and fittings," I said, astounded that Spiros had even considered it would.

"The Sampaguita, he...

"She," I corrected, wishing Spiros could get a grasp of the English genders. The stress of trying to persuade Sampaguita to live in sin was causing his grammar to lurch into slapdash territory.

"She," Spiros repeated, "She go the berserk when I tell to her I try to sell the cat with the house. I tell to her it is the home of the cat but she not the listen to reason. She to say if I sell the cat, the wedding he is the off."

I knew that the undertaker had no time for cats, considering them a blasted nuisance. However, I hadn't realised he could be so insensitive to Sampaguita's feelings that he would even suggest flogging the cat along with the house. I knew from experience how emotionally attached women could get to their pets. The way that my wife made such an infernal fuss of Catastrophe and Clawsome, one could be forgiven for thinking that Marigold had personally birthed the creatures. Spiros should have twigged that Sampaguita had doted over Tesco from the moment I cunningly rid our home of it by palming it off on Leontiades as an emotional support animal. Sampaguita had inherited Pickles' brother when Leo passed.

Now that Spiros had agreed to Sampaguita

bringing her beloved pet to live with them, I hoped for his sake that Tesco hadn't inherited any filthy habits from its feline father, the infamous Kouneli. We had been most fortunate with Pickles: although it tended to roam at will, spending more time out than in, I had heard no scathing reports that it prowled the village in search of ferals to ravish. Still, if Marigold was to be believed, Clawsome, the imported feline mother of both Tesco and Pickles, was of impeccable pedigree.

"You think they will to buy the house for sure?" Spiros asked.

"I think so. I met Moira at the bus station and she seemed quite keen on the house from what Gordon had told her about it."

"The model wife." Spiros' eyes lit up with excitement at the prospect of meeting a great beauty who made a living from tripping the catwalks. Devoted though he was to his fiancée, his habit of having an eye for the ladies was firmly ingrained.

"She's not an actual model as such," I said.

"Victor, you must to be the mistake. The Gordon say many the time that the wife he is the model."

"She's actually an ear model," I said.

Spiros' crestfallen face was a picture. "She model the ear?" Slipping into Greek, he added in a sceptical tone that he never heard of such a thing, "*Den akouo pote kati tetoio.*"

"*Einai alethia.*" Assuring Spiros it was true, I added that Moira does have beautiful ears, "*I Moira echei omorfa aftia,*" though I did feel a tad guilty for wiping the grin off his face.

Puffing away silently on his cigarette, Spiros pondered the odd notion of women modelling only bits of their bodies before changing the subject.

"I not to like the weekend, Victor…"

"What's wrong the weekend. Have you got a funeral to do?"

"No, the weekend the lawyer not to work. We must to wait to the next week for the signing the paper. I not want them to have the time to change his mind," Spiros explained.

"Ah, I understand. You're worried that if the Stranges put in an offer today, they may still back out as nothing can be formalised until next week. You're not usually this jittery when it comes to a sale," I observed.

"What is this jittery?"

"Antsy…"

"What is the *myrminkia* to do with him?"

"Not ants, antsy. It's an expression; it means to be on edge…"

Spiros stared at me blankly, failing to comprehend my meaning.

"Agitated, anxious…" I continued, determined to drive my point home.

"Ah, I know what you mean, like the cat on the hot ceiling…"

"I believe the common idiom is like a cat on a hot tin roof or a cat on hot bricks…"

"You must to speak the Greek more, Victor. I would to understand you if you just to say you think I am the *anisychos*."

"You've lost me, Spiro," I admitted, struggling to translate the Greek word.

"*Anisychos* is the anxious. If they to say the yes, we go to my house to celebrate the lunch, yes," he invited.

"Yes, that sounds like an excellent plan," I agreed.

Spiros' offer of a celebratory lunch in his home made me more determined than ever to convince the Stranges to buy Leo's house. Whilst the thought of the commission was extremely appealing, I must confess to being intrigued to discover how Spiros actually lived. Although the friendly undertaker had been a visitor in my home on countless occasions, I had yet to cross the threshold of Spiros' house. It wasn't really a Greek thing for single men to entertain in their homes, limiting their socialising to cafes and tavernas. I was of course familiar with the abodes of his three deceased uncles, having been a party to each of their sales. I couldn't help but wonder if Spiros' home emulated the rather confused chaotic state that his Uncle Pedros had lived in before plummeting from the roof, or if Spiros leant more towards the ordered and well maintained style of his late Uncle Leo. With a bit of luck, all would be revealed at lunch.

At the sound of a car approaching, I said, "This could be the Stranges now."

"No, it is the Ioanna car, she to drive the Sampaguita back," Spiros exclaimed. Standing to attention, he spat on his finger, using it to tease his bushy eyebrows into some semblance of tidiness. "The Sampaguita look after the Ioanna *pateras* in Nektar this the morning."

"How is the old fellow?" I asked, recalling that Sampaguita worked several mornings a week as a carer for the grandfather of Giannis, the handsome bee man. Giannis' mother, Ioanna, found it too much to cope with her apparently demanding and querulous father alone. Despite his inability to get around much, the old man refused to move in with his daughter and grandson in Meli. Ioanna, having found Sampaguita's help as a part-time carer a lifeline, never failed to proclaim that Sampaguita was an absolute angel whenever I ran into her around the village. For some strange reason, Ioanna had got it into her head that I was somehow related to the delightful Filipina: perhaps it was because Sampaguita was often to be seen out and about with my niece when she looked after little Anastasia.

Ioanna's battered old car drew up alongside us. As Sampaguita alighted, Ioanna wound her window down. Midnight black curls teased her face, highly defined cheekbones emphasising her ageless grace. It was easy to see where Giannis got his remarkable good looks from. Dispensing with the usual greetings, Ioanna proclaimed, "*I Sampaguita einai enas apolytos angelos*," reiterating her usual sentiment that Sampaguita is an absolute angel.

"*I Sampaguita einai ena aromatiko louloudi*," Spiros replied, attesting that Sampaguita is a fragrant flower.

Beaming with delight, Sampaguita told

Spiros to stop, saying that he made her blush: *"Stamata ta Spiro, me kaneis rouz."*

About to drive away, Ioanna remembered that she had a message for me from Giannis. Drumming a finger against her forehead as she tried to recall the message, the light bulb went on.

"O gios mou leei oti echei ligo xylo gia ti fotia sou," she said, telling me that her son had said he had some wood for me for the fire.

"Pou?" I said, asking where.

"To xylo einai sto chorafi me ta koutia melisson," she replied, telling me the wood was in the field with the bee boxes.

Waving Ioanna away, I coughed discreetly, not wishing to intrude as Spiros hugged Sampaguita, slathering soppy kisses on the face and neck of his fiancée.

"Hello, Mr Bucket," Sampaguita said, her pronounced accent making her words almost lyrical.

"Victor, please," I reminded her for the umpteenth time.

"I hope I am not late. I want to make sure everything is perfect for the English people that are viewing the house," Sampaguita said.

"The Sampaguita keep the place like the

palace," Spiros boasted, lighting another cigarette.

"Oh no, I remember the work surface needs a wipe and I still have some clothes on the washing line. It will make it look untidy. What will they think?" Sampaguita said, turning to rush indoors.

"Put the dress into the suitcase," Spiros urged.

"Spiros has talked me into moving in him with today," Sampaguita confided with another blush.

"I hope you'll be very happy together," I said heartily as she dashed inside to tidy up.

Hearing another car approaching up the narrow lane, I predicted, "This must be them now."

"I cannot to wait to see the ears," Spiros said, grinding his cigarette out with his heel and springing forward ready to greet the Stranges.

Chapter 15

Attached to the Cat

Welcome, welcome," Spiros enthused, leaning over to gallantly
kiss Moira's hand as introductions
were made, his contorted efforts to get an eyeful
of her ears anything but discreet. Moira was
charm personified, pretending not to notice the
Greek's unnatural interest in her lobes.

"Hear how the quiet it is. Away from the
maddening crowd of tourists you will breathe
pure mountain air in the peace and tranquillity." Spiros' gushing words sounded overly

familiar to my ears. If I wasn't mistaken, he had used the exact same ones to sell the honeyed dream of Meli to the Buckets. It struck me that since his spiel was more grammatically correct than his usual efforts in English, he had no doubt memorised the words, having probably stolen from some cheesy greetings card. I hoped that the Stranges were as easily suckered into the honeyed dream as we had been.

"I do hope we've not kept you waiting. I wanted to walk round the village first to get a feel for the place," Moira said.

"What did you think?" I asked.

"Meli is absolutely charming. The buildings have such character and the whole place is so picturesque. It fulfilled all my expectations of a quintessentially Greek village," she said.

"I knew that you'd fall in love with the place," Gordon said. "It's the perfect spot for us."

"Oh, what a delightful house," Moira trilled as her gaze settled on the home that could soon be theirs. The house certainly looked appealing. Thanks to Sampaguita's efforts, every last pane of glass glistened in the November sunshine, the windows artfully framed with deep blue wooden shutters carrying the distinctive whiff of furniture polish.

"Oh, and the smell of herbs. Can you smell them, Gordon? I'm sure there's a hint of lemon rosemary."

"The Sampaguita cultivate the special herb garden," Spiros told them, ushering the couple indoors.

"Oh, look at the tiles, Gordon. The design is just wonderful," Moira cooed as they tripped through the entrance hall into the living room. "And I just love the high wooden ceiling and the fireplace. Even without a fire burning in the grate it feels lovely and warm in here. I know it's warm outside but our hotel room had a definite nip about it. This feels really cosy."

"The warm is the air conditioner. The uncle he put in the every room," Spiros explained.

Since the Stranges appeared a tad flummoxed by the notion that the air conditioning emitted hot air, I jumped in to clarify, "The air conditioning units double up as room heaters. That way, you can regulate the temperature to suit you, no matter the time of year."

Spiros sent me an appreciative glance. He was well aware of my personal reservations about unhygienic air conditioners and the filthy way they recirculated contaminated air with no regard for the spreading of insanitary germs.

Crossing his fingers behind his back, Spiros led the way through to the kitchen. I had cautioned him that although Gordon had been adamant that his wife was happy to go along with his decision about the house, he should take such rash words with a pinch of salt. In my experience it was invariably the woman that made the decision, most usually based on whether or not she could live with the kitchen.

Having fallen in love with the roof terrace at our place, Marigold had been sold on the house before we even stepped inside. Whilst the kitchen had been something of a jumbled nightmare complete with a bed squashed in next to the fridge, she had seen past the clutter by simply decreeing that we would install a new kitchen. Even though her dream Shaker kitchen had failed to materialise, she was happy enough with our IKEA one for the time being.

The refreshing scent of lemon and vinegar permeated the kitchen; Sampaguita was giving the surfaces a quick wipe. Pausing as we entered the kitchen, she smiled shyly at the house hunters.

"Oh, everything is so lovely and fresh," Moira gushed before putting her foot in it by saying to Spiros, "I do appreciate the effort you went to in getting a cleaner in to make the place sparkle."

"A cleaner?" Spiros queried, his brow furrowing in a frown.

"The foreign lady," Moira hissed none too discreetly. Fortunately discretion wasn't necessary as Sampaguita had stepped outside to remove her washing from the line. "Do you think there's any chance that we could keep her on? Good cleaners are so hard to come by."

"They are certainly hard to find in Salisbury," Gordon agreed. "It's a constant worry that the neighbours will lure our char away with the offer of an extra 50p an hour. We'd be quite lost without our woman that comes in and does."

"The Sampaguita is not the cleaner, she is the fiancée," Spiros bristled, staring Moira down with a flinty expression.

"The fiancée," Moira parroted in confusion.

"Sampaguita lived here as the carer for Spiros' old Uncle Leontiades when he began to go senile. Spiros inherited the house when his uncle passed earlier this year and Sampaguita stayed on," I explained.

"Ah, I understand. So this Samp..." Moira

paused, unable to master the unusual pronunciation of the Filipino name. "This foreign carer received a marriage proposal from the elderly gent and became his fiancée."

"The Uncle Leo was likely the homosexual..." Spiros began to say.

"So this foreign woman took advantage of his senility even though he was gay. And she's still living here?" Moira interrupted. Without waiting for a reply, she tactlessly blundered on, "I do hope it isn't going to complicate the sale of the house if she refuses to move out. As your deceased uncle's fiancée, does she have any legal claim on the property?"

"You to have the wrong end of the twig," Spiros said, visibly attempting to temper his annoyance, realising an outburst of anger might throw a spanner at the potential sale. "The Sampaguita is the engage to me, not to the dead uncle."

Moira's hand flew up to cover her gaping mouth as it belatedly dawned on her that she had put her foot in it. "I'm so sorry, I just assumed she was the cleaner...I didn't mean to cause offence."

If there was any offence to be taken it was in Moira's half-spoken implication that Sampaguita was a gold-digger taking advantage of a senile homosexual, rather than in the assumption that she was engaged as a cleaner.

"There's nothing to take offence at. Cleaning is a noble occupation," I insisted, refusing to lose sight of the main prize: the sale of the house. "There's no shame in working as a cleaner, it's good honest work. In fact my own mother is hoping to secure some cleaning work in the village."

"Violet...surely she's getting on a bit to be thinking of working," Moira said.

"Don't let her hear you say that," I warned. "She's not ready to hang up her scrubbing brush quite yet. She's determined to keep busy rather than vegetate. There's nothing she enjoys more than a spot of scrubbing and scouring."

"I could tell that she had high standards when we chatted on the bus," Moira said.

"Between you and me..." I lowered my voice to a confidential whisper before continuing. "The truth is my mother is a tad obsessed with hygiene."

"What better obsession could one wish for in a cleaner? Gordon, we simply must snap up Violet to clean this place for us. She'd be an absolute treasure," Moira cried, before turning to me and asking, "Do you think you could put in a good word with your mother for us? It would make life so much easier to know that we have an English speaking cleaner. I imagine they aren't easy to come by out here. And it would put our minds at rest knowing she could keep an eye on the place when we're back in England."

"Don't you think we should sort out buying the place before you think about employing a cleaner?" Gordon pointed out.

"We must buy the house, it's perfect," Moira said with determination.

"You not to need to look at the bedrooms?" Spiros said, barely able to contain his excitement at such enthusiasm.

"Well, I'll take a look of course but Gordon was right. I love the house, we'll take it. Just promise that you won't show it to anyone else. I couldn't bear it if it was snapped up from under our noses," Moira said, oblivious that the house had been on the house for eight long months with nary a nibble.

"We can to visit the lawyer to draw the paper after the weekend," Spiros suggested.

"That would be perfect, wouldn't it Gordon. We're happy to give you a cash deposit now to secure it," Moira said, apparently eager to splash the cash.

"The after the weekend will to do. Today we will to celebrate with the lunch at my house," Spiros beamed, elated that he had finally snared a buyer.

"And you will speak to your mother about cleaning for us?" Moira reminded me.

As the Stranges wandered off to look at the bedrooms, Spiros winked at me, delighted everything was going so smoothly. Moira returned to the kitchen, looking round the room appreciatively, her smile only fading when she spotted Tesco sprawled out in the kitchen sink licking its privates. It must have leapt in when our backs were turned.

"I didn't realise that you kept cats in the house," Moira said, more than a hint of revulsion in her tone. The way her lip curled in disdain anyone would think that she'd discovered a skeleton in the basement rather than a cat in the sink.

"Just the one," I assured her. "Tesco is the offspring of my wife's pedigree and my sister-in-law's tom."

"This could complicate things. I can't imagine that Waffles would take to living in a house with a cat," she sighed.

"Waffles can't stand cats, they unnerve him," Gordon said in a tone that suggested the dog's personal preferences may factor into their decision.

"The cat doesn't come with the house," I assured them, jokingly adding, "Spiros would have to put the price up if it did."

"The cat will be to move into my house," Spiros said.

"We'll get my mother in once the cat has moved out," I declared. "By the time she's finished giving it her special treatment, Waffles will never detect that a cat has ever been near the place."

"I think that should make it okay, Gordon. Waffles need never know that a cat was ever in his territory if every last trace is scrubbed away," Moira said. Turning to me, she apologetically added, "It's not that either of us has anything against cats. It's just that Waffles is very particular."

"Just the sniff of a cat sends him into a frenzy, he's terrified of the things," Gordon revealed as the two of them stepped outside to take a look at the yard.

"The poodle dog is the afraid of the cat,"

Spiros chortled once we were alone.

"Let's hope that the pair of them don't notice that they're moving into a village that is knee deep in ferals," I replied.

"I think it the best if I not to move the cat to my house till after the lunch," Spiros mused pragmatically. "I think it is the Moira, not the poodle, that is afraid of the cat."

Chapter 16

A Celebratory Lunch

Prior to our convoy of cars setting off to Spiros' house in the village square, Spiros and Sampaguita busied themselves filling the back of the hearse with Tupperware boxes of food. Sampaguita had prepared a celebratory lunch the evening before in anticipation of the Stranges making an offer on Leo's house. Spiros' earlier invitation had not been a casual one and he had planned to invite the English couple if they were poised to buy.

Although it struck me that it would have

been easier to simply dine at Leo's house, I was eager to see how Spiros lived, not to mention it seemed a wise move to put some distance between the Stranges and Tesco, Moira appeared irrationally unnerved by the cat's presence. I couldn't help but wonder if she suffered from ailurophobia, a fear of cats. Perchance, or should that be purrchance, she simply dragged up her dog, Waffles, as a convenient excuse to hide her embarrassing phobia.

Entering Spiros' home, I was struck by an overwhelming sense of déjà vu, flooded with memories of how our village house had looked before we engaged Vangelis to transform it. Spiros clearly favoured the style of his late Uncle Pedros, not to mention his love of old icons. Completely gob smacked by the amount of random clutter crowding the place, it struck me that Sampaguita's apparent reluctance to move in with her beloved was perhaps due to the disordered state of the place rather than her self-professed out-dated reservations about living in sin.

Considering that Spiros' hearse was never anything less than immaculate, I admit to being rather taken aback to discover that his living room could easily be mistaken for the sort of

flea-pit more usually associated with the bedroom of a teenage boy. It didn't help that the distinctive stench of sweaty socks was noticeable in
the room. Naturally I attempted to conceal my
shock that Spiros was content to live in such
messy squalor, but Moira and Gordon's dumb-
founded faces said it all, their mouths falling
open when they had to sidle around a couple of
coffins to get into the living room.

The eclectic mix of furniture piled high with
random junk was a bizarre combination of tacky
looking plastic, drearily dated MDF and the odd
promising looking antique. Reams of paper-
work were messily heaped on top of a formal
dining table surrounded by eight uncomfortably stiff chairs: Spiros obviously used the table
as a makeshift office for his undertaking business. Sweeping the papers together, Spiros said,
"I move him so we can to eat at the table."

Peering around in search of a suitable spot
to dump the papers, Spiros plumped for filing
them in an open coffin, before inviting Gordon
and Moira to take a seat. As we gathered round
the table, Spiros grabbed a random dirty sock
draped over the back of a chair and stuffed it
into the breast pocket of his suit jacket, a look of
embarrassment creeping over his face as he

belatedly realised the place was a veritable pig-sty.

"Spiros has been living the bachelor life-style," I explained to his guests. "It's a good thing that Sampaguita is going to be moving in to give the place a much needed woman's touch."

"We understand," Moira said with a long drawn out sigh. "Our son went through an ex-tended teenage boy stage too."

"Until he was about thirty," Gordon added.

"We hoped that Matt would mend his ways when he got a flat of his own. It was only when he met a girl that he wanted to move in with that it finally dawned on him that dirty clothes don't walk to the laundry hamper on their own," Moira shared.

"He went through quite a long phase of con-fusing the area under his bed with the kitchen sink," Gordon added. "Moira had to put her foot down when there were more plates grow-ing mould under his bed than in the kitchen cupboards."

"He seemed to think that the washing up fairy would miraculously appear," Moira con-tinued, rolling her eyes.

"Suzy was the making of him. She refused

to live with Matt unless he promised to transform his slobbish ways," Gordon said. "And goodness knows what state our home would be in if we didn't have Mrs Thing who comes in and does."

"Mrs Thing does have a name you know," Moira snapped, sending a withering glance in her husband's direction. "It's Mrs Lubenov. She's from Bulgaria; her English isn't up too much. It will be quite the coup if Violet can be persuaded to char for us here. No pesky language misunderstandings."

"But I thought you'd picked up a bit of Bulgarian from Mrs Thing," Gordon said.

"Well. I managed to get my tongue round the Bulgarian for polish but it did help that it only has one syllable." We all looked at Moira expectantly, hoping she would enlighten us with the Bulgarian word for polish. "It's lak."

"You'd better not ask for *lak* in the village shop or you'll end up polishing your furniture with hair spray," I chortled.

"*Lak* is the Greek word for hairspray? I do believe you have taught me my first Greek word, Victor. And it's one that is so easy to not only pronounce but to remember," Moira exclaimed delightedly. "It will be so handy to know when I need a good spraying after a cut and blow. I suppose I will need to drive up to town to get my hair done. I need to have it done regularly. It's crucial for my job that my hair doesn't grow over my ears. I must keep them hair free at all times in case a modelling job comes up at short notice."

"If you to have the hair to grow inside the ear, the Apostolos in the village is good to re-move," Spiros volunteered.

Brushing over his rather insulting implica-tion that Moira might suffer from an inner ear growth of fuzz, I hastened to say, "There's no need to go up to town to have your hair done, Moira. Meli boasts a wonderful ladies' hair-dresser, Athena. Marigold goes to her regularly and her Titian tresses always look lovely."

"I didn't notice a salon when we walked through the village earlier," Moira said.

"The Athena to cut the hair in the kitchen," Spiros blurted.

Moira recoiled at his statement. Clearly she considered such a set up on a par with having one's tonsils removed by a veterinarian.

An awkward silence descended, only bro-ken when Spiros waved his arms around to point out the mess, saying, "I to apologise for the not clean up…" Rather like the Stranges' son Matt, it seemed that Spiros had only belatedly realised the place was in no fit state to welcome visitors. "I have no the time… the funeral…the harvest."

Meanwhile Sampaguita busied herself in the open plan kitchen which filled one side of the room, unpacking the food she had prepared. Fortunately there wasn't a bed cluttering up the basic kitchen, its tidiness indicating that Sampaguita had claimed that area as her domain even before she had formally moved in.

Sampaguita signalled to Spiros to give her space to give the dusty dining table a good scrubbing before she served lunch. Taking the hint, Spiros invited, "*Ela*, look the beautiful view from the *balkoni*." The four of us duly stepped outside, ducking under a washing line displaying Spiros' dripping boxers and narrowly avoiding tripping over a parched looking plant in dire need of a good watering. Grabbing a broom, Spiros hastily swept away a pile of withered leaves that had fallen onto the neglected balcony from a nearby plane tree. I imagined in summer the stately tree must provide welcome shade from the sun.

The view from Spiros' balcony was magnificent, more than compensating for the disorder inside. Overlooking the village square, the balcony offered a bird's eye view of all his neighbours comings and goings. I gave a friendly wave to Dimitris, perched on a chair just outside his front door. His nose buried in a book, the professor didn't notice my presence above him. In deference to his hatred of loud noises, I refrained from yelling down to him.

The landscape to one side of the square was dominated by the Byzantium church with its impressive red tiled dome. As one gazed over the village square, the sea was visible in the distance, its deep blue colour blending seamlessly into the paler blue of the sky as the two dovetailed together on the far horizon.

Spiros' house was, in estate agent parlance, situated in a prime location. Personally I preferred the relative peace our own house offered, being a tad removed from the centre of the village. The close proximity to the church would have driven Marigold mad since she would find it impossible to indulge in her daily lie-ins with the intrusive sound of the church bells pealing. My wife has the habit or rather irreverently referring to the sound of the church bells as a god-awful din, though she would never dream of being so crass as to drop such a clanger in front of Papas Andreas.

Leaving Spiros to chat with the Stranges, I stepped back inside, offering to give Sampaguita a hand with the food.

"Thank you, Victor. You could carry the dips to the table and I will make the salads and cut the *syglino.*"

"Spiros' house must make you feel as though you're slumming it after living in the relative luxury of Leo's house," I remarked.

"There is much slum housing in my own country. The people that live in the real poverty would consider Spiros' home a palace," Sampaguita confided, making me wish I could take back my tactless remark. "I like this house very much but there is much work to make it tidy…"

"You'll have to keep after Spiros, make him pull his weight. Try nagging him a bit…"

"I don't like to nag him but I think I might have to. Spiros has lived alone for too long and fallen into lazy habits. The place is too messy. At least I have put the kitchen in good order but the comfort room…ugh," Sampaguita shuddered.

"The comfort room?" I queried.

"That is my Filipino English, I mean the bathroom. It is the opposite of comfortable."

"You should get Barry and Vangelis in to fit a new one," I suggested.

"I don't like to take liberties in Spiros' home."

"You're going to be married and this will be your home too," I reminded her.

"Anyway, I am glad to move out of Leo's house. It saddened me to be surrounded by memories of him. I was very fond of him." Sampaguita's words reminded me how much she had cared for the old fellow. "I think it would have made him happy that I am to marry his nephew."

"I'm sure it would, Leo was very fond of you. He would have been delighted to welcome you as a family member. So, do you think you'll adapt quite easily to living here after the relative luxury of Leo's house?" I asked.

"I would happily live in a cardboard box with Spiros," Sampaguita responded with genuine sincerity.

"At least he couldn't make such a mess in a box," I quipped before remembering that the undertaker had even managed to make a coffin look slovenly by using it is as a receptacle for his junk.

Placing the last of the dishes on the table,

BUCKET TO GREECE (VOL.9)

Sampaguita called out to Spiros to come inside, telling him the food was on the table, *"Ela Spiro, to fagito einai sto trapezi."* As always I was impressed by the seemingly effortless way in which Sampaguita switched between English and Greek.

The sight of the table laden with appetising dishes appeared to distract the Stranges from the general clutter. As we sat down to eat, Spiros worked his charm: in no time at all the couple were putty in his hands, oblivious to the mess.

"The Sampaguita make the wonderful cooking," Spiros proclaimed, inviting the Stranges to tuck in. "She make very good the Philippine food but for me she learn the Greek favourite like the *yiayia* to cook."

"Like his grandmother cooked," I duly translated.

"It all looks most tempting," Moira said. "You'll have to tell us what everything is."

The generous spread which Sampaguita had prepared the evening before included a tempting array of dips to be eaten with bread. In addition she served *feta* cheese and Kalamata olives, and a platter of *syglino,* cold smoked pork preserved with herbs, a speciality of the Mani. Whilst we had been chatting in the kitchen she had whipped up a selection of fresh salads: *lahanosalata*, a winter salad of shredded cabbage dressed with lemon juice and olive oil, and a *tonosalata*, chunks of tuna mixed in with diced vegetables and capers.

"Would you like to try some *pasta*?" Sampaguita asked shyly, offering a small dish of thick green paste to Moira.

"Pasta?" Moira queried, her brow scrunched in confusion.

"The name may be a tad confusing if you were expecting to see a bowl of spaghetti or fusilli. *Pasta elies* is the Greek word for a delicious olive paste," I explained. "Greek *pasta* is rather like a tapenade. The flavour can be quite overpowering. Just try a little, it's an acquired taste."

"Oh, I adore anything with olives," Moira effused. Sampling the *pasta* she practically swooned in pleasure, having discovered a taste of olive heaven.

"The *psomi*, the bread, he come from the outside oven of the Dina at the taverna," Spiros said, pointing towards the basket of bread. Since it was Friday, the day when Dina baked a huge batch of bread to keep the villagers supplied for the week, it was fresh from the oven and still warm to the touch. Pointing at the crispy breadsticks, Spiros added, "He is the *kritsinia*."

"Tina sells them in the village shop," I volunteered.

"Oh, we poked our head round the door earlier, it looked wonderful," Moira said. "So many unusual Greek foods, we didn't have a clue what half of them were."

"Discovering the delight of traditional Greek foods will be an adventure for you," I assured her. Although I was tempted to sign them up for my Greek cookery classes, I resisted, thinking there would be time enough once they had moved into the house. "The local food is fabulous and everything is so remarkably fresh."

"Victor made a superb Greek onion soup followed by a sun-dried tomato quiche the other evening. He turned simple ingredients into the sort of feast you'd expect in a five star restaurant," Gordon gushed. Whilst I appreciated his praise, I disavowed his opinion that there was anything simple about knocking out a batch of perfect, lump-free pastry.

"Are there any good restaurants locally?" Moira asked.

"The village taverna has a simple menu but it is the best food you'll ever taste," I said.

"Nikos grows and rears everything on the menu…"

"Not the water. The water he is nothing to do with the Nikos," Spiros said, making a spoiler of Nikos' famous punch line. No doubt it would still make the Stranges smile when they heard Nikos deliver it for the first time in his own unique way. Filling our glasses with wine, Spiros added, "This is the *krasi* from Nikos, it is the *spitiko*…"

"Homemade wine," I translated.

"And the Dina, he cook the best *tiganites patates*…" Spiros continued.

"Chips. Dina will have a challenge on her hands to maintain her reputation for making the best chips for miles now that Violet Burke has moved to the village," I interrupted. Rather bizarrely, an image of the two women facing off with chip pans at dawn invaded my mind. I could picture myself and Nikos, turned out in our best suits, standing as seconds with refills of oil.

"Violet promised to show me how to cook perfect chips," Sampaguita told us, a smile gracing her lips as she spoke. For some inexplicable reason, she was inordinately fond of my mother.

"She's certainly an expert after all the years

she put in at the chippy," I said.

"What are these dips called?" Gordon asked.

"He is the *tirokafteri*," Spiros said, pointing towards a pale red creamy dip.

"Feta cheese spiced up with roasted red peppers," I duly translated.

"He the *skordalia*," Spiros added, indicating a creamy coloured dip garnished with fresh parsley.

"A garlicky potato dip," I explained.

"Very good strong," Spiros added. "The Sampaguita not to shrimp on the garlic."

"I think you mean scrimp," I corrected.

"Is not the same thing, the shrimp and the scrimp?" Spiros queried.

"No, a shrimp is a *garida*," I said.

"Ah, there is no the *garida* in the *skordalia*, only the not scrimp *skordo*." I was impressed how quickly Spiros turned his shrimp gaffe into a witty joke.

"It's very garlicky," Gordon confirmed, hastily glugging some wine to cleanse his over-loaded palate.

"*Skordalia* is a wonderful accompaniment to *bakaliaros* which is crispy fried salt cod. Dina sometimes adds it to the winter menu in the taverna," I added. "You can buy dried cod from the village shop; you'll find it in big wooden barrels packed with salt."

"And he is the *tzatziki*...." Spiros continued.

"Ah, we know that one. It's cucumber and yoghurt," Gordon said, sparing me the need to translate.

"With garlic and mint," I added.

"And this?" Gordon questioned, pointing towards the *syglino.*

"That is *syglino,* salted and smoked pork, a regional speciality of the Mani. After it has been cured it is boiled with wine and oranges. It really captures the intense flavours."

"I didn't make it. A local farmer, Panos, prepared it," Sampaguita admitted. I was surprised to hear that the welly wearing farmer had a hand in preparing the pork. I made a mental note to warn Violet Burke that she should expect a personal delivery of smoked pork from her admirer. I do of course use the term admirer loosely; simply repeating what my wife has convinced herself is the case.

"It can be enjoyed as part of a *meze* or it can be added to beans and sauces for extra flavour," I elaborated.

"I'm very tempted to try it," Gordon said.

"Try it, yes. The *syglino* will to make you to forget all this *chortofagos skoupidia* and make you into the *kreatofagos*," Spiros urged.

Gordon and Moira stared at Spiros with vacant expressions until I jumped in with a helpful translation. "Spiros says if you taste the *syglino* it will make you forget all this vegetarian rubbish and turn you into a meat eater."

"You're not still on that vegetarian kick, Gordon. I was hoping you'd have dropped it by now. It's such a nuisance to check that there's no trace of any meat in Marks and Sparks ready meals," Moira grumbled. I considered her gripe about Gordon's vegetarianism a touch ironic considering that the wonderful spread in front of us was entirely meat free apart from the *syglino*.

"I think this is the moment when I turn my back on vegetarianism," Gordon said, reaching for a piece of *syglino*." One taste of the aromatic pork and it was clear by his expression that he was a meat convert. "The flavours are just divine, so intense."

The wine and the conversation flowed as we enjoyed the delicious lunch, Moira and Gordon eager to learn more about the village and the area. During a lull in the conversation, I asked Spiros why he had elected to stay in this house when he'd been spoilt for choice, having inherited three other local houses from his now sadly deceased uncles. Whilst the run down house in Nektar and the one I had bought had both been in urgent need of modernising, his Uncle Leo's house was in excellent nick and fitted out with all mod cons.

"This the house I grew the up in, it is the best situate in the village. Only two the minute to the shop and only one to the church. Always I am the surround with the good neighbour," Spiros said.

"That's certainly a convincing argument for staying put," I agreed, impressed with his reasoning.

"The moving the house mean more the tax to pay," Spiros spat. Turning to Gordon, he edged in close, hissing, "You to pay the objective value of the Leo's house and the rest under the table, yes?"

"We don't want to flout any laws," Gordon said worriedly.

"The lawyer he fix it. It is, how you say in English, the unwritten law."

"It goes on all the time," I confirmed.

When Gordon reminded me that I had

promised to show him the cave in Nektar, I ran over my busy schedule in my mind, suggesting I could slot him in the next morning. With the cave date duly arranged, I patted my stomach to indicate I had eaten my fill when Sampaguita offered more salad. Glancing at my watch, I realised I must hurry if I didn't want to be tardy for Violet Burke's first cycling lesson.

"I really must be off," I said. "I don't want to miss being on hand when my mother takes to the bicycle saddle for the very first time."

The others appeared intrigued at the thought of a near octogenarian taking up cycling. "We can to watch from the *balkoni*," Spiros promised since there was no sign of the lunch party breaking up.

"That reminds me, I need to borrow that cycling helmet I gave you, Spiro. You never wear it," I said.

"It make me look stupid," Spiros responded.

"Never mind your vanity. It would spare you any more scars. The one you picked up when you cycled into that pothole is still visible," I pointed out.

"I not to mind it. The scar he make me to look the rapey..."

"Raffish," I hastily corrected.

"I think the Violet make better the use of the helmet," Spiros said. "*Ela*, it is in the hearse."

"Why on earth is it the hearse?" I asked.

"Last week I have the very tall corpse. I stuff the head in the helmet to stop it to banging on the coffin on the bend. It not to look good if the family to see the dead with the new bruises. They might to think I the corpse beater."

Following Spiros down to the hearse to re-trieve the cycling helmet, I couldn't control my laughter, Spiros' bizarre reasoning truly making my mind boggle.

Chapter 17

Riding Along on the Pushbike,
Honey

The tinny clang of a bell clacking repetitively down on the street announced Barry's arrival on Cynthia's old bicycle.

"Give it a rest, Barry," I called down from the balcony. "Some of the neighbours may be taking a siesta."

Gingerly grabbing Spiros' cycling helmet which I had prudently taken the precaution of spraying with disinfectant to eradicate any lingering traces of the recent corpse, I joined my brother-in-law in the street. Casting a critical eye over Violet Burke's borrowed transportation, I deduced from the dated style of the contraption that Cynthia's purchase must have been second-hand at the very least. I was relieved to note that Barry had clearly put in a bit of effort to ensure it was in good enough nick to bear the weight of my mother. I would hazard a guess that the ancient looking machine was older than Barry's wife: it may even have more years on its metaphorical clock than my mother.

"It's a vintage model and no mistake," Barry remarked. "I put some air in the tyres, oiled the chain and checked the brakes before I rode over, it made for a smooth ride. Can you believe I provided a bit of free entertainment for those old codgers drinking coffee outside the shop? They had plenty to say about a fellow riding a ladies' bicycle but if I'd turned up on a boy's bike then your mother would never have been able to get her leg over," Barry chortled.

"I just hope the pedals are wide enough to take the strain of her swollen feet," I said, ignoring Barry's lewd jibe.

"Never mind her feet," Barry said with a worried expression. "I'm more concerned how she's going to fit that broad backside of hers on the saddle."

There was no ignoring the fact that my brother-in-law had a valid point. Clacking the bell again, Barry urged me to rouse Violet Burke. "Tell her to get a move on, I haven't got all day."

"I'll give her a knock. Hadn't you better attach the stabilisers?" I reminded him, spotting the set of child's training wheels poking out of the wicker basket on the front of the cycle.

"I'll get right on it. I'd have been even more of a laughing stock if I'd put them on before I rode over," Barry guffawed.

"She's not answering the door," I said in exasperation when Violet Burke failed to respond to my knocks.

"Perhaps you should let yourself in and make sure that she's okay," Barry suggested.

"I'm not sure that's a precedent that I want to set. If I just let myself in, she may get the impression she can start doing the same upstairs," I mused. "I think it's important that we establish some kind of boundaries."

"Well, you'll have to give her a key if she's going to be doing your cleaning," Barry pointed out.

Although the key to the *apothiki* was burning

a hole in my pocket, I was reluctant to barge in unannounced. I wanted my mother to feel that I respected her privacy and to be afforded the same respect in return. As I dithered, Barry said, "Hang on, she's not in there. That's her coming down the street now."

Shielding my eyes against the sunshine, I spotted Violet Burke trundling wearily towards us, swinging a red plastic bucket as though it was the latest fashion accessory.

"Get a move on, Vi. Have you forgotten I'm here to get you started on the bike?" Barry called out.

"Hold your horses, lad. If I go any faster my swollen feet will likely explode," Violet Burke retorted.

As my mother drew level with us, Barry tried to peer in the bucket, bluntly demanding, "What's with the bucket?"

"It's not full of gutted cat if that's what you're thinking," my mother snapped, clearly still smarting from the accusation that she had done something unsavoury to the missing cat. "If you must know, I took my bucket and Vim along to that mucky taverna to show them what a bit of honest elbow grease can do. That Dina hasn't got a clue about hygiene. I refused to shift until I landed myself a cleaning job."

"Bravo, Vi, that was certainly enterprising of you," Barry applauded.

"Well, I didn't want Victor here thinking I'd be nowt but a burden on him."

"You certainly didn't waste any time..." Barry continued.

"I'm not one to let the grass grow, lad," she interrupted.

"How did you manage to communicate with Dina?" I asked, genuinely curious since neither of them knew a word of the other's language.

"I demonstrated my worth by giving the place a good bottoming, there's no arguing with the results," Vi revealed. "We bartered my hours and rate of pay by scrawling some figures on a paper tablecloth. I'll be going in regular at five every day to clean up the place and peel the spuds for the chips. Can you credit the place doesn't even have a decent potato peeler? It's a good job I brought a couple over in my luggage."

"Good grief, five o'clock is early, even for me," I exclaimed in surprise. Even though mother is an early riser like me, it usually takes a couple of strong Tetley brews to get her moving.

"Five in the afternoon, you lemon. I need to find out how the land lies for some other cleaning work during the day," Vi clarified. "Do you suppose some of those wealthy expats in the village will be needing my services?"

"Sherry certainly has money to burn," Barry suggested. "Mind you, you'd have to stomach all her jolly-hockey-sticks prattling. It fair near drove Vangelis and me insane."

"Vangelis? Doesn't his wife cut hair in her kitchen? 'Appen she'd appreciate having someone in to give the place a good sweeping. There's nowt more disgusting than getting a mouthful of hair in your dinner," Vi shuddered.

"I think that's why Vangelis never brings a packed lunch. I'll have a word with him for you, Vi," Barry offered. Opening his big mouth even wider, he put his foot in it. "Victor is having most of the local expats over tomorrow afternoon for his cookery class. You should pop upstairs and corner them, see if any of them have any cleaning going."

"Aye, 'appen I'll do that, lad," Vi said, impervious to the withering look I was firing at Barry. The last thing I needed was Violet Burke gate-crashing my very first cookery class and undermining me by whipping out her chip pan.

"So are you ready to get started on the bicycle?" Barry asked.

"Don't be daft. I'll be done for flashing if I start pedalling around the village in this skirt. Give me two ticks. I've got some trousers inside; I picked them up at the charity shop for nearly nowt." Dumping her bucket on the pavement, Violet Burke dashed inside the *apothiki*.

"Thank goodness she brought some trousers out with her," I sighed in relief. "I'd never live it down if my mother got a reputation for flashing."

"As if that tweed number she was wearing would ride up enough to have her flashing her drawers," Barry laughed. "I doubt it had enough give to get her in the saddle."

"Her clothes do appear to be a tad on the tight side. It seems she has recklessly disregarded her doctor's advice to lose some weight," I said worriedly.

"Carting her chip pan across the continent doesn't really say that she's sticking to a diet," Barry pointed out. "Perhaps she'll shift some weight when she starts cycling. It's good healthy exercise."

"Let's see if she's capable of mastering the

pedals while keeping her balance first," I said.

The pair of us struggled to keep our faces straight when Violet Burke emerged from the *apothiki* clad in a pair of denim bell-bottom jeans. Noticing our bemused stares, she announced, "I don't normally resort to cast-off clothes, I bought these special with a bike in mind. Still, they're as good as new after I gave them a good boil wash."

"Barry had a pair just like them back in the 70s," I chortled.

"Don't remind me," Barry cringed

"During his mullet phase," I added, rubbing it in. "Between the tache and the mullet, he looked a right plonker."

Blatantly ignoring my reference to the disastrous style he had favoured back in the 70s, Barry said, "I'm not sure that denim is ideal, Vi. It could get heavy if you get caught in the rain when you're cycling and it can chafe something awful."

"Phhh, don't be such a sissy, lad. I lived through the war. I can put up with a bit of chafing," Vi pronounced.

"Well, at least roll up the legs or they'll get caught in the chains," Barry advised.

"No need for that, I've got some laccy bands

here," Vi retorted, leaning her considerable bulk on Barry's shoulder whilst she bent down to secure her bell-bottomed trouser legs with rubber bands.

"Don't forget the safety helmet," I reminded her, passing over Spiros' helmet and fervently hoping I had removed every trace of its last wearer. I'd never hear the end of it Violet Burke discovered the helmet had effectively been plucked from the head of a dead man.

"That thing will play havoc with my hairdo," Vi complained as she popped it on her head. Whilst I had gone out of my way to ensure she would be safely helmeted up, I had failed to take into account the size of her enormous bulbous head. The helmet ended up perched ridiculously on the top of her hair, the chin strap stubbornly dangling on a level with her ears. No matter how much she yanked the straps, they refused to stretch enough to wrap round her double chin. I suppressed a snort as she made a ridiculous attempt to secure it beneath her nose.

"I've got a balaclava that I brought over in case it gets really cold. It will have to do instead," Vi said.

"You really need a helmet, Mother," I insisted. "I won't be party to you flouting any health and safety laws."

"Do you ever give your health and safety obsession a rest?" Barry griped. "You didn't see me cycling over here in a helmet."

"Considering the number of potholes riddling the road, it was pure luck that your head remains intact then," I snapped.

"Hand me the helmet, Vi. The straps probably just need adjusting," Barry said. Muttering "potholes" under his breath as though it was an exotic expletive, Barry fiddled around with the helmet's straps. "There, try it now, Vi."

Forcing the helmet into place and buckling it under her chins, she decreed, "That's better. Now, let me see if the basket is roomy enough for my bucket. Aye, that'll do nicely but I doubt it will hold my mop. I'll have to find somewhere else to stick it."

I sent Barry a warning look. I could do without any of his crude suggestions as to where Violet Burke could stick her mop.

"Victor, give me a hand up onto this contraption," mother ordered.

It took the pair of us to hoist Violet Burke onto the saddle which instantly disappeared from sight beneath the sizeable bulk of her denim clad bottom. I took it to be a good sign that the bicycle didn't immediately collapse under her weight and that her hands instinctively reached for the handlebars.

"Now you just need to lift your feet onto the pedals, Vi," Barry encouraged. "Don't worry, it won't tip over. The stand is down and the stabilisers will keep it balanced."

"Are they properly fettled?"

"I fixed them myself," he assured her. "There, how does that feel?"

"A bit peculiar, lad, if I'm honest. It's a good long while since I had anything rubbing up against my crotch area."

I hastily glanced around to ensure that no random pedestrians had been subjected to an earful of my mother's unique brand of vulgarity. Realistically, I knew that I ought to prepare myself for my mother becoming a somewhat permanent embarrassment.

"Stand up a sec while I adjust the saddle. There, is that better? You'll soon get the feel for it," Barry encouraged. "Now, these are the brakes, give them a firm squeeze. You don't need to worry about getting to grips with the gears as this bike is so old it doesn't have any. Luckily, you'll be mainly on the flat if you stick to Meli. If you venture further afield, you'll have to get off and push it up the hills."

"That would rather defeat the object of sparing her swollen feet," I piped up. "Best if you stick to Meli, Mother, and watch out for any stray cats leaping out in front of the wheels."

"And random goats," Barry said.

"Not to mention erratic Greek drivers," I added, determined to have the last word.

"Right, Vi. I'm going to kick the stand out of the way so you'll need to move your knees and start pedalling," Barry instructed, demonstrating remarkable patience. I supposed it would be good practice for the day when little Anastasia got her first bicycle.

"It feels good to take the weight off my feet," Vi commented, her swollen feet engaging with the pedals.

"Don't worry, I'll keep one hand on the handlebars and run along beside you until you get the feel for it," Barry told her.

I watched with a mixture of anxiety and amusement as Barry guided my mother along on the bicycle, his support coupled with the stabilisers ensuring she didn't wobble over. I have to confess the sight of Violet Burke on a bicycle was one I had never expected to behold. If she could get the hang of it, it would certainly help her to be independent and save me the bother of being at her beck, obliged to ferry her around in the Punto.

"Do you remember that song from the 70s, Victor? 'Riding Along on the Pushbike, Honey,'" Barry called out.

The lyrics of the song instantly sprang to mind and I found myself swaying as I hummed the catchy tune.

"Do you remember how everyone said that the girl on the bike in the video had a look of Marigold about her?" Barry reminded me.

"But because the video was shot in black and white, we never knew if she had red hair like Marigold," I replied, remembering how chuffed Marigold had been when everyone pointed out her likeness to the attractive young woman in the video.

"The Mixtures, that was the group that sang it," Barry reminded me.

Barry's words were a tad breathless. Struggling to keep pace with Violet Burke on the bicycle was taking the wind out of him

"I think I'm getting the hang of this," Vi shouted.

"Do you think you'll be all right if I let go?" Barry's question was superfluous. The bicycle hit a slight decline in the road and he lost his grip on the handlebar, Violet Burke soaring off into the distance with nary a wobble. "Don't forget to squeeze the brakes, Vi," Barry yelled after her. Bending over, he planted his hands on his knees, panting heavily.

Gasping for breath, Barry instructed me, "Trot after her, Victor, and point her back in this direction. She needs a bit more practice before I let her loose on her lonesome."

"I'm not sure I'm quite cut out for trotting," I retorted, obediently striding speedily down the lane to catch up with my mother, all the while doing my best to ignore the bemused villagers who were gathering in their doorways to watch the free entertainment. I couldn't imagine the likes of Kyria Maria or Kyria Kompogiannnopoulou venturing onto a push-bike at their advanced years, though Dina was often to be seen riding side-saddle on the back of Nikos' decrepit moped. As promised, Spiros and the Stranges were hanging over his balcony watching the rather absurd spectacle with interest. There was no doubt that Violet Burke had plenty of pluck for a pensioner: perhaps that was where I had inherited my recently discovered daredevil nature from, even though it was still in the early development phase.

"This is a bit of all right, lad," Vi shouted out, her voice suffused with pleasure as she threw her head back and laughed when I finally caught up with the bicycle. A couple of loose red tendrils escaped from the helmet and her cheeks flushed from exertion. It was the first time I had ever seen a look of genuine, carefree happiness on Violet Burke's customary grim countenance: I must confess to a warm and fuzzy feeling in my insides, crediting the transformation to her move to Greece. "I'll be able to get around a darn sight faster on this thing than I would on my poor puffed up feet. I felt like I was fair flying except for not being all squashed up like I am on a plane."

Having mastered the brakes, she had come to a halt. Taking a breather, she cautiously lifted her swollen feet off the pedals as I kicked the stand into place to offer additional support. I was relieved to see that my mother's height meant that her feet could easily touch the road rather than dangling precariously above ground while she was stuck in the saddle. At least if the brakes failed, she would be able to slow the contraption down with her feet.

"I've just got to work out how to turn it

round and then I'll bike back to Barry," Vi announced once she'd recovered her breath. Kicking the stand out of the way, I beamed with pleasure as she successfully repeated the return trip in one piece.

By the time I'd trotted back to the *apothiki* doorway, my mother was urging Barry to remove the stabilisers, complaining that they slowed her down.

"I'd feel happier if you kept them on for a day or two until you've really got the hang of keeping your balance," Barry said.

"'Appen you would but you aren't the one having all them people sniggering at the sight of a grown woman using training wheels. Take them off, Barry, there's a good lad," she insisted. "Once I'm rid of them, I'll be able to go faster. I've a fancy for feeling the wind in my hair."

"On your head be it," Barry grumbled, reluctantly removing the stabilisers.

"My head's protected with this helmet, so stop your griping," Vi retorted.

Chapter 18

An Undignified Landing

I really don't think that removing the stabilisers so soon was a sensible move," I opined, watching as Violet Burke flew down the street on the borrowed bicycle, fingers clamped tightly around the handlebars, her back ramrod straight. "She hasn't even got any L-plates on to warn any unsuspecting road users that she's likely to be a menace."

"I suppose if you had your way, you'd make L-plates compulsory on bicycles," Barry snorted, demonstrating his contempt for what he considered my overzealous adherence to health and safety regulations. "Anyway, you heard what Vi said. She wants to feel the wind in her hair."

"It may have escaped your notice but there's not even the whiff of a breeze today. Even if it was windy, it would never blow enough to muss her hair up under that helmet she's wearing," I pointed out, craning my neck as the bulbous figure of Violet Burke swerved round a bend in the road before disappearing from view. "I hope she's got the hang of turning it round."

"If she keeps on past the village square, she'll end up going down that sharp incline that leads to Nektar," Barry posited, a note of worry creeping into his tone.

"Lots of hairpins on that stretch of road…"

"Perhaps we ought to go after her…" Barry suggested, breaking into a hasty stride.

"Perhaps we should," I agreed, hurrying to keep pace with him. It had seemingly dawned on us at the exact same moment that we had been more than a tad reckless allowing Violet Burke free rein on the road without more intensive tutelage. Admittedly it was difficult to argue with Vi: she had a tendency to be bolshie when her mind is made up about something. I should have put my foot down and forbidden Barry from removing the stabilisers. Such a precipitous move on his part could well result in my mother coming a cropper.

"She's got lots of padding to protect her if she falls off," Barry wheezed as we speeded up.

"There's not much of a cushion in denim," I argued.

"I meant natural padding. Your mother isn't exactly sylphlike."

"That's an understatement," I gasped.

"Course, she'll be all right if she lands on her fat arse…"

"This is not the moment for vulgarity, Barry," I carped.

Approaching the village square, we collided with a rather shell-shocked looking Dimitris. Grabbing my arm, the retired professor pointed down the road, shouting, "*Victor, ela grigora. I mitera sou espese apo to podiliato tis.*"

My heart sank as Dimitris' words sank in. He was urging me to hurry, telling me that my mother had fallen off her bicycle.

"*Petaxe akrivos diple mou, schedon me chtypise apo tin karekla mou,*" Dimitris cried, meaning, 'She flew right by me, nearly knocking me off my chair.'

Breaking into a sprint, Barry and I left Dimitris flapping around like a spare part on his doorstep, no practical use in a crisis. Even though we were running, there was no sign of Violet Burke in the direction that Dimitris had indicated.

"Victor, *stamata*," Spiros yelled down from his balcony, telling me to stop. "You have to runned right past the Violet."

Spinning round, I could see no sign of my mother. Peering every which way in desperation, Barry appeared equally flummoxed. Realisation only dawned that she must have toppled off the bicycle and landed in the prickly hedgerow skirting the front of Milton's house when I spotted a denim clad leg flailing around in the greenery and heard a peevish voice accusing, "What's your game, Violet Burke? Trying to throw yourself at my husband's feet, I suppose. You'll try any cheap trick to get my Milton to notice you."

I barely recognised the toxic voice as that of Edna Hancock. The impoverished and genteel pensioner, who always acted as though butter wouldn't melt, sounded anything but genteel. Standing outside her house with her arms firmly folded like a fishwife, Edna talked down to my mother, sprawled at her feet in an ungainly heap.

"Can't you keep your bloody cats under control?" my mother retorted.

"Are you hurt, Vi?" Barry was the first to hurl himself on the ground next to the prostrate form of my mother.

"Don't try to move, Mother," I advised, pushing a random cat out of the way before it could sink its claws into her bell-bottoms. "You might have broken something."

"Only my dignity," Vi snapped, picking some prickly burrs from her denim clad knees before extending her hands so that we could haul her up. It hadn't escaped my notice that Edna miraculously changed her tune the moment she clocked our arrival to assist my mother. She might well slap a fake look of concern on her face but her blatant hypocrisy didn't fool me for a moment. Not only had I overheard Edna's disparaging comment that Violet Burke had deliberately engineered her fall to attract Milton's attention, I had spotted her gloating with smug satisfaction at my mother's unfortunate tumble before she twigged that she had an audience. Edna instantly went way down in my estimation. I knew that she harboured a jealous dislike of my mother because Milton had fessed up that he'd carried a torch for Violet Burke ever since the war, but to derive any form of pleasure from seeing an elderly woman fall off a bicycle struck me as callous and unfeeling.

"Perhaps you could bring her inside and I'll fetch her a cup of sweet tea," Edna reluctantly suggested, feigning concern. "Sweet tea is good for shock."

"I take it that pathetic husband of yours isn't at home then or you wouldn't be giving me house room." Edna's blush indicated that Violet Burke had hit the nail on the head.

"No, Milton isn't at home," Edna confirmed. "Norman gave him a lift to the supermarket on the coast to stock up on cat food."

"'Appen if you had proper control of your verminous pets in the first place, the buggers wouldn't be catting it round in the road tripping up innocent bicyclists. It's a disgrace. No doubt you'd have plenty to say if I'd squashed one of your precious cats under my wheels," Vi complained as we yanked her upright.

Edna may have felt superior standing over Violet Burke when the latter's toppled position left her at a disadvantage, but once she was firmly back on two feet, my mother towered over the shorter and much slighter woman. Edna scuttled backwards, putting some distance between them as though expecting my mother to hurl a cat at her. After inadvertently exposing her petty malicious streak, Edna's attempt to hang onto what little dignity she had left was lost when she tripped over one of her own mangy cats. Were it not for Barry's razor-sharp reflexes, Edna would have taken a nasty tumble of her own, most likely ending up with a dodgy hip to match that of her husband.

"You're lucky Barry caught hold of you," Violet Burke taunted. "Being nowt but skin and bones you'd 'appen have broke something if you'd had a fall."

"I wish I'd reached you in time to catch you and break your fall, Vi," Barry said guiltily. "I should never have let you ride off without stabilisers."

"Don't be so wet, lad. I was having the time of my life till Edna's scabby cat sprang out of nowhere. You could see for yourself, I'm a natural on a bike." Groaning aloud, Violet Burke pressed her hands into her lower back. "Bloody hell, I reckon I've gone and knackered my coccyx.."

"Blimey, that sounds painful," Barry sympathised.

"Perhaps Edna has a bag of frozen peas..." I suggested.

"I'll see what I can rustle up," Edna said peevishly, turning towards the house.

"Never mind frozen peas, what I need is a large medicinal brandy. That Edna will be hearing from my solicitor if my bike is damaged," Vi vented.

"No damage done beyond a bit of a wonky wheel, Vi," Barry pronounced, taking a quick look at the overturned bicycle as the two of us assisted my mother inside. "If Edna's got a hammer lying around, I can knock it back into shape in two shakes of a cat's tail."

"It's a lamb's tail," I corrected. Lowering my voice to a hiss, I warned Barry, "Since it appears that avoiding mangling a cat with the bicycle is what got her into this mess, the less said about cat's tails in front of my mother, the better."

"Fair point," Barry acknowledged.

Chapter 19

Weak Tea and Frozen Chips

You'll have to get the bike fixed for to-morrow, Barry. I'll be needing it to get to my job at the taverna. It's a good job I peeled the spuds already for this evening. I can't be traipsing backwards and forwards on my puffed up feet without them exploding, not to mention the state my poor bruised coccyx is in," Vi bellyached. My arms ached from the strain of supporting Violet Burke's substantial bulk as we led her through to Edna's living room. "I can feel it turning black and blue already."

"I'll sort the wheel now if Edna's got a hammer handy," Barry promised, following Edna into the kitchen in search of a toolbox.

"Never mind the bicycle, Mother. It's you that I'm concerned about," I said, shooing a dozen cats off the sofa to make room for my mother.

As I eased her down gently, she scrunched her nose in disgust, complaining, "They keep a mucky house and no mistake."

Presuming that my mother's reference to a mucky house meant that I must have outed Milton as penning porn under a pseudonym, I tried to recall if I had ever told her about his erotica hobby or what he got up to as Scarlett Bottom on one of Vi's previous visits to Meli.

"I didn't spot a red light outside," I quipped.

"What are you on about now?" My witty jest implying that the Hancocks ran a house of ill-repute was lost on Violet Burke.

"Look at the state of this sofa, it's knee deep in filthy cat hairs," Vi grumbled, elbowing a particular persistent adopted stray out of her way. I gathered from her words that rather than alluding to Milton's erotic leanings, Vi had actually been referencing Edna's noticeably lax housekeeping skills when she'd declared that the house was mucky. It struck me as a pity that the Hancocks were too impoverished to engage Violet Burke as a cleaner.

"Here, Victor, take some of my weight while I adjust myself enough to stick this cushion under my coccyx," Vi instructed, groaning in pain.

"That isn't a cushion, Mother. It's a cat," I said, relieving her of the docile feline and shoving an actual cushion in the vicinity of her tailbone. "Perhaps I should nip back and get the Punto to run you down to the clinic. A contused coccyx is no laughing matter."

"Who's laughing? It was no joke landing on my backside…"

"At least it's well padded," Barry said, emerging from the kitchen with a brandy snifter and a bottle.

"Just because you're vaguely related, lad, it doesn't give you the right to go getting overly familiar," Vi snapped.

"Better that you landed on your bottom rather than going over the handlebars and landing on your head," Barry continued.

"My head's protected if you hadn't noticed.

Or did you think I was wearing this lump of ugly plastic because I mistook it for the height of fashion?"

"Get some of this down your neck, Vi," Barry said, pouring a cloudy liquid into the glass. "Apparently the Hancocks' finances don't run to medicinal brandy, but I found this bottle of homemade potato wine that Milton brewed."

"Here Victor, give me a hand to loosen this helmet strap, it's fair digging in my chin," Vi demanded, gulping the potato wine down in one. I noted mother was certainly made of strong stuff, not even wincing as the potato brew went down.

"Never mind that, Mother. I really think I should get you to the doctor."

"I'm in no mood to be prodded and poked by some foreign quack…"

"I doubt that the doctor will be foreign. I think most of the local medical personnel are Greek…"

"Well, Greek is foreign, you muppet."

"Not in Greece it isn't. You're the foreigner here," Barry pointed out, his remark leaving my mother for once at a complete loss for words.

Violet Burke fired a contemptuous look at Edna as she returned to the living room with a cup of tea.

"I've put two sugars in it for the shock and I've wrapped a packet of frozen chips in a tea towel," Edna said grudgingly.

"Phhh, I might have known you were the sort of lazy cow that can't be arsed to peel and fry your own chips," Vi spat with open contempt. "I'm not putting that tea towel anywhere near my bruising unless it's had a good boil wash. Likely it's riddled with cat hairs like the rest of this dirty place. I suppose you think you're too grand to give it a good bottoming."

"I went round with a feather duster earlier…"

"Feathers are a poncy substitute for a good scouring with Vim," Vi sneered.

"The tea towel is clean," Edna feebly protested as Violet Burke inspected the tea cup for stains.

"Yuck, this brew tastes like cat's piss. Have you never heard of giving the tea bag a good mashing?"

Going by previous form, I suspected the tea bag was likely on its third or fourth dunking.

Refusing to rise to the bait, Edna's nostrils flared in disdain as she made no attempt to conceal her dislike of my mother. Consulting her watch, Edna didn't bother to be discreet, the expression on her face making it clear that she was desperate to rid the house of unwanted intruders before Milton arrived home. It struck me that Edna's obvious contempt for Violet Burke was irrational to say the least. I would happily affirm in a courtroom that my mother had done nothing to encourage Milton: in fact she barely afforded him the time of day. She would happily swerve his company altogether was it not for the pesky inconvenience of the Bucket household being on friendly terms with the neighbourhood purveyor of porn. There really was no avoiding one's neighbours in a village as small and close-knit as Meli.

Barry didn't help matters by dragging Milton's name up, asking Edna how her husband was keeping.

"He's fine…"

"Your husband is that lanky piece of string that's always banging on about meeting me in the Dirty Bird back in 43?" Vi said, her statement sounding more like a question.

Edna nodded curtly before prising her tight lips apart enough to respond, "You know he is."

"I can't see why you're getting your knickers in a twist about whatever went on down the pub more than six decades ago," Vi said, shaking her head in disbelief. "I'm telling you straight, I've no recollection of ever running into your husband during the war."

"You did more than just run into him. You kissed him," Edna accused.

"So, I kissed plenty of fella's during the war, it meant nowt. A girl had to kiss a lot of frogs back then to keep her legs in nylons."

"Edna, were you even married to Milton, back then?" Barry asked, belatedly picking up on the tension between the two women triggered by Edna's jealousy.

"I didn't meet Milton until after the war," Edna admitted.

"So why is your face stuck like a sour lemon? It's not as if I was mushing on with a fella that was already spoken for," Vi spat.

"You know as well as I do that Milton has carried a torch for you ever since first setting eyes on you..." Edna whined.

"I'm sure this is the first I've ever heard of it..." Vi stubbornly retorted. As she pinched the top of her nose above her spectacles, I recognised this as a familiar habit she adopted whenever she was giving something a great deal of thought. I could practically visualise the cogs in her brain turning as she cast her mind back, trying to recall any impassioned declarations of love that may have slipped her memory. "I've hardly been short of admirers. This Milton bloke wouldn't be the first sap to carry on like a lovesick fool over me. I was quite the looker back in the day on account of my shapely legs and my full bosom."

"And of course your red hair didn't come out of a bottle back then," I reminded her.

"Aye, my hair was my crowning glory."

Although my mother flatly denied being aware of Milton's long-held infatuation, I distinctly remembered telling her about his obsession with her in order to avoid any embarrassment if she chanced to run into the Hancocks at Barry's wedding. However, I didn't for one moment believe that my mother was being deliberately obtuse. She genuinely couldn't recall our conversation because Milton had failed to make any impression on her, neither sixty years ago or in the present. I doubted she would even recognise him were he to walk through the front door at that very moment. To put it bluntly, Milton was a complete nonentity in mother's mind, his infatuation a matter of complete indifference to her.

Considering how Vi had reeled off a list of likely candidates as possible contenders for my paternity, she had not only been a bit free with her kisses during the war but with her more intimate favours. It was hardly surprising that a casual pucker didn't stand out against a sea of more memorable fumblings.

"Ever since Milton confessed his feelings for you, I've been terrified of losing him to you." Dumping her own insecurities on Vi's shoulders, Edna's tone was reproachful.

"How many more times? I wouldn't look twice at that weedy wimp you call a husband, even if I hadn't sworn off men," Vi insisted, drumming her knuckles against her forehead as she spoke. I instinctively interpreted her gesture as being symbolic of banging her head against a brick wall.

"Have you any idea how it makes me feel to know that Milton is consumed with thoughts of you? And all the while you claim to have never even spared him a second thought," Edna cried, her voice quivering with emotion.

"Make your mind up. Are you seriously complaining that I didn't reciprocate his daft feelings?"

"Cold hearted trollops like you…"

"Who are you calling a trollop, you cheeky mare?" Vi interrupted.

"You can never imagine how it feels to know that your husband has eyes for another woman?" Edna said, retrieving a handkerchief from her sleeve and blowing her nose loudly.

"Course I can. Lionel Blumenkrantz did more than make eyes at that trollop in the Odeon; he went and got her pregnant with triplets..."

"Lionel Blumenkrantz?" Edna repeated.

"My third husband. I'm not too proud to admit the cheating scrote not only deserted me for his bit on the side, but the divorce left me well and truly skint," Vi said bluntly.

"I'd no idea. I know what it is to fall on hard times after all that sorry business with the fake Liberian orphans..." Edna said.

"You reckon to know all about hard times, do you? You know nowt, lass. Look at you, living the dream in this lovely house in Greece with enough farthings to rub together to feed the entire stray cat population..."

Catching Barry's eye, I suppressed a snort. It was amazing how quickly Edna's home had gone from a filthy cat ridden flea-pit to a lovely house.

"And then there was Arthur Burke. I'll never live down his philandering swindling. He didn't just go round making eyes at other women, he went and bigamously married lord knows how many of them before emptying their bank accounts and fleecing them of their bits of jewellery."

"Oh…" Edna's gasp was barely a whisper.

"Oh, indeed. Grow a backbone, you snivelling creature. The trouble with women like you is you have too much time on your hands to let your imagination run away with your common sense," Vi pronounced.

"It's Milton's imagination running away with thoughts of you that plays havoc with my peace of mind," Edna cried.

"Oh, give it a rest. So your husband has the odd fancy for other women, so what? I'll bet you it's only his eyes that stray. You can't fix nature and men are programmed to look. At least your husband stuck by you for all these years, and let's face it, it couldn't have been easy for any fella to be faithful to a cold stuck-up fish like you."

Edna squirmed uncomfortably, the truth hitting home.

"I can see how your husband having the

odd mental flirtation makes you feel hard done by...not," Violet Burke scoffed. "If only my Lionel and Arthur had stuck to dreaming about someone else instead of dipping their wicks in, then I wouldn't have been left slaving away in a chippy long past my rightful retirement age."

"But it's not just the odd thought about another woman," Edna persisted. "In Milton's mind, you are his ideal woman. It makes me feel that I'm not good enough. How can I possibly compete with the dream woman that you are in his mind?"

"Are you saying you never had the hots for some handsome bloke that caught your eye, or for a movie star?" Vi clucked her tongue at Edna's blank look. Tempted though I was to interrupt and point out that clucking her tongue was very Greek, I held my tongue. Glancing over at Barry, I could tell that he was as curious as me to see where this was going.

"I don't mind admitting that I wouldn't have kicked that hunky Rock Hudson out of my bed. It didn't put me off him neither when it came out that he was one of them closet homosexuals."

As my mother fired off her own dose of pragmatic realism, Edna stopped snivelling enough to let the sage words sink in.

"That's the thing about people we fantasise about, it's all in the head," Vi continued. "We get a fancy for someone and start to idolise them. But these ideal images only exist in our minds because they're nowt to do with real life. I'm sure I'd have turned the cold shoulder on Rock pretty sharpish if he'd given me any lip about putting the bins out. And I'd have pulled a headache pretty sharpish on Rock if he'd rolled in drunk on a Friday night, too plastered to remember to pick up my battered cod and some mushy peas from the chippy on his way home from the pub. It sounds to me that whatever your husband has done to wrong you has been all in in your head."

"So you're saying that if Milton perhaps got to know you a bit better in real life, the idealistic image of you that he carries around might be shattered," Edna mused aloud. "It might dawn on him that you have a mouth like a sewer and feet of clay."

"I don't know about clay but it's no picnic putting up with these swollen feet. Your Milton might have carried an idealised memory of my shapely legs around in his head for years, but the reality of my flabby thighs is enough to put a grown man off his dinner."

"Milton always told me that I was the inspiration for his book but after he confessed the feelings you stirred in him when he met you during the war, I couldn't get it out of my head that you were his true muse." Voicing her fear that Violet Burke had supplanted her as Milton's muse, seemed to finally put things into perspective for Edna. "I can't really see Milton being inspired by flabby thighs…"

"You daft cow, you are his muse. Cynthia told me that Milton described you to a tee when he wrote that blonde character, Brandy, in that mucky book of his." Noticing our gaping mouths, Vi added, "You needn't look like that. Cynthia devoured 'Delicious Desire' right before her wedding. She said that she'd give me a lend of the book but I told her straight that it didn't grab my fancy. I like to get stuck into a good serial killer; porn's not my cup of tea."

"Erotica," I corrected for the first time ever. I hated the thought of my mother being associated with porn, even if it was only in Edna's fevered imagination.

"So I really am Milton's muse… and you're not interested in him at all?" Edna exclaimed, the penny finally dropping.

"For the love of God," Vi screeched, her cry of frustration so loud that a dozen cats practically trampled each other in their dash to find an exit. For some reason Vi's explosive reaction triggered a fit of the giggles in the two women.

"I must confess that I used to have a secret crush on Rock Hudson too. He was such a heart-throb in 'Pillow Talk,'" Edna chortled.

"It was 'Magnificent Obsession,' that did it for me," Vi said, absentmindedly stroking the solitary cat that remained, too lazy to have shifted. "Rock did a sight more than put the bins out in my fantasies, I can tell you. Now if I was 'appen ten years younger, I wouldn't kick that Captain Vasos out of my bed. He's not got the movie star looks but he's a real charmer, plus he's got a big yacht. Still, a youngster like him wouldn't look twice at me now I'm past my prime…"

Unable to contain himself any longer at Vi's description of the inebriated boat captain as a charmer with a yacht, Barry let loose with a snort. My mother sent him a withering look before scaling back her expectations and demonstrating a more practical bent.

"Course, if I was to ever give courting another go, 'appen I'd have to make do with the likes of that farmer with the mucky wellies. I think he's quite keen. Last time I was over he was forever popping round, trying to woo me with bags of spuds and pans of tripe soup."

"Potatoes are far more practical than a bunch of wilted carnations when you get to our age. Shall I make you another cuppa, Violet? I'll use a fresh teabag and slip in a drop of Milton's homemade potato brew," Edna offered, extending an olive branch.

With a tentative truce established between the two women, Violet Burke rolled her eyes as Edna went through to the kitchen.

"How's your coccyx holding up, Mother," I asked.

"I can't say I nary gave it a thought, Victor. 'Appen all Edna's daft mithering took my mind off it," Vi winked.

Chapter 20

In the Mood for Fray Bentos

After parking my mother downstairs in the *apothiki* with a hot water bottle to relieve the swelling of her contused coccyx, I escaped upstairs to the peace and quiet of my own domain. I was on a determined mission to pen some more words in my book. It was hard to write without any distractions when Marigold was around, constantly disturbing me. I planned to take full advantage of her absence to knock out another couple of chapters. Throwing myself on the sofa with a notepad and pen, I defied Marigold's house rules by planting my stockinged feet on the coffee table.

Although it seemed an age since I had added any additional material to the sequel of my still unpublished moving abroad adventures, I slipped back into writing with relative ease. It struck me as ironic that with my mother finally installed downstairs in the *apothiki*, I had reached the point in my penned saga where it was time to relive the moment when Violet Burke first turned up on our doorstep in Greece and barged into our dinner party.

Even though I have admittedly grown quite fond of my mother, I could still vividly recall my initial impression of her as a vulgar and overdone bulbous harridan. As the words flowed onto the page, I smiled to myself, remembering Barry's horror when Violet Burke threw her arms around him in a suffocating embrace. Pressing Barry's head into her ample bosom, Violet Burke had dramatically cried, "My son, I have found you at last." Barry had been none too pleased to be mistaken for me.

Scribbling away with gay abandon, I reached the last page in my notebook, a tad irritated that I would need to break off to find a new one. Fortunately I noticed a spare notebook half concealed behind a cushion on the sofa. Opening the notebook expecting to encounter a virgin leaf, I was surprised to recognise Marigold's handwriting defacing the page. Presuming she had left me a note, hopefully of the billet-doux variety rather than a Dear John, I glanced down at the exclamation littered prose.

It may not be every girl's dream to be swept off her feet over a galvanised metal bucket in B&Q but I wouldn't change a thing!!!

My wife's words brought a smile to my lips and I wondered if she was perhaps composing something special to write in our anniversary card. I suppose I could overlook the odd exclamation mark if they were used to commemorate our first meeting.

The words below the ones I had read were obscured, indecipherable due to the unsightly lines drawn through them with a red marker pen. Perchance Marigold was struggling to put her feelings about our first encounter into words: she does strive to be a perfectionist.

Turning the page, I must confess to feeling perplexed as I read on, at first confusing the words with a shopping list.

I managed to send Victor off on a fool's errand!! I told him I had a craving for gluten, salt and sugar free organic Ready Brek!!! A quick search on the internet revealed it is impossible to find in Greece so the wild goose chase should keep him from getting under my feet for hours!!!

From the dark recesses of my mind, I dredged up a memory of Marigold dispatching me on a fruitless errand for Ready Brek, though as best as I could recall it was at least a year ago. I had worried that I would be letting my wife down when I eventually returned home bearing an uninspiring packet of cheap porridge oats from Lidl. Marigold had tossed them to one side without even bothering to scan the packet to see if the oats met all her essential free demands. I recall being a tad puzzled why she was suddenly demanding sugar free items when she never missed the opportunity to guzzle a custard laden *bougatsa* doused in icing sugar. When Marigold belatedly remembered that she hadn't been able to face a bowl of porridge ever since I'd compared Norman to a bowl of the lumpy and congealed breakfast choice, I ended up throwing the oats in a batch of homemade flapjacks.

Flicking through the pages, I read a little more.

Earlier this morning I was flashed by that

horrible little Albanian that lives in the shed!!! It put me right off my breakfast! I must tell Victor to have words with him. At least it will keep Victor from getting under my feet!! He will probably spend the morning locked in his office memorising the Greek for don't flash your private bits at my wife – bit being the operative word!!!

I laughed aloud at Marigold's description alluding to Guzim falling rather short in the privates department. Still, it was a timely reminder to ensure that Guzim understands that he must in future always shower under the outside hose-pipe with his underpants on. It wouldn't do for Violet Burke to get another glimpse of Guzim's privates or she may mock him relentlessly. Rather than coming down with a fit of the vapours the first time Guzim had flashed her, Violet Burke had been rather disparaging.

My eyes moved down the page, this passage catching my eye.

I have to say I was quite taken with the charming young man we ran into at the vets. He's a bit of a dish!! I do like a man in manly leathers! The leather may be a foil!!! Any man who keeps a beribboned poodle must be gay!!

Shoving the notebook back behind the cushion, I realised that I had unwittingly invaded my wife's privacy by reading what, it was now apparent to me, was her personal diary. Filled with self-loathing for my accidental snooping, I retrieved a fresh notebook from my office and continued my writing.

I felt a tad choked with emotion as I wrote about the incredible, unconditional support my brother-in-law had offered when I was thrown for a loop by Violet Burke's impromptu arrival in Meli. Even though my relative count has increased with the number of newly discovered half-brothers that had crawled out of the woodwork recently, I could never ask for a better brother than Barry. I decided to give him a call later and see if he fancied spending the evening together. I could perhaps knock up something for us to eat, sparing him Cynthia's uninspired cooking. I made a mental note to pay extra attention to Cynthia's efforts once my cooking classes were underway. I owed it to Barry to turn his wife into a competent cook.

My concentration was broken by a knock at the door. Presuming my mother had popped upstairs, I slapped a smile on my face and prepared to give her a warmer welcome than I had two years ago when she had first burst so unceremoniously into my life.

"I say, hope I'm not disturbing you, old chap," Milton said as I reluctantly invited him. On reflection I wasn't too surprised that it wasn't Violet Burke on the doorstep: she would most likely have bulldozed her way in rather than knocking. Pondering that thought, I realised the necessity of establishing some boundaries, sooner rather than later, for when my mother took it into her head to just casually pop upstairs. I would need to approach the subject tactfully or my mother may get it into her head that I didn't really want her in Greece. With my mind thus occupied, I missed whatever it was that Milton was chuntering on about.

"Sorry, Milton, I was miles away. Could you repeat whatever it was you were saying?"

"I was just filling you in on Scarlett Bottom's latest batch of fan mail, bit racy, what. Still, you probably don't want to hear all about that..." Milton's words tailed off as he clocked my look of impatience. "I'm here on a mission of mercy: Edna sent me round. She heard that Marigold is away and insisted I bring you home to eat with us. Can't have you stuck on your lonesome and all that, old chap. I know I'd be lost without Edna, struggle to boil an egg and all that..."

"Really, there's no need..."

"It won't be anything fancy, just beans on toast. Can't run to Heinz, I'm afraid, shocking price to import. Edna has a trick up her sleeve though to make those Greek tins of beans that Tina sells almost edible. She adds a bit of water and a dollop of ketchup, makes them a bit saucier, what. Still, if we play our cards right, Edna may chuck a fried egg on top if we've get enough to go round."

"No really, my mother is staying..." I protested, shamelessly using Violet Burke as a convenient excuse. I deliberately implied that Vi was a guest in the house since it was no business of Milton's that mother had moved in downstairs: she certainly wouldn't appreciate it if her fawning admirer turned up on the doorstep of the *apothiki*. "Didn't Edna mention that my mother is over for a visit?"

"She did. She's just been telling me that she had Violet round for a cuppa earlier. You could have knocked me down with a feather, what. Never thought I'd see the day when Edna could bring herself to be civil to Violet."

The way that Milton's eyes lit up with excitement when he mentioned my mother indicated that he still carried a torch. I had an idea that Edna would make it her mission to extinguish said torch by regaling her husband with examples of Violet Burke's clay feet. No doubt a few grumbles about Vi's loathing of the Hancocks' adopted cats coupled with the odd mention of flabby thighs and a mouth like a sewer would work like a charm in no time at all to knock Violet Burke off Milton's pedestal. It would be a relief all round when the penny finally dropped in Milton's mind that my mother is in reality a bulbous and bolshie harridan rather than the captivating siren he'd fallen for back in 1943.

"I'll tell Edna that you have other plans," Milton said.

"Here, take some eggs home with you, the chickens are laying nicely at the moment," I offered, pressing half-a-dozen onto Milton. It was a small price to pay if Edna was genuine about offering an olive branch to Violet Burke.

"Jolly decent of you, old chap. They'll certainly liven up the beans," Milton said as I pushed him through the door.

"*Tipota.*"

"What?"

"It's nothing," I said, shaking my head in disbelief that after all these years of living in Greece, Milton was still ignorant to the meaning of one of the most common words in the Greek language.

"I'll see you at the cookery class tomorrow," I said.

"'Fraid not, old chap. Edna won the coin toss for first dibs. Don't forget to pass that copy of 'Delicious Desire' onto Violet," Milton reminded me as I slammed the door shut. I didn't bother confessing that I'd left his porn behind at the café in town opposite the bus station, serving as convenient padding to stop the wonky table from wobbling. I couldn't think of a better use for his erotic drivel.

Milton had barely had a chance to make his way down the outside staircase when I was disturbed by another rap on the door. Wondering what my elderly expat neighbour wanted now, I threw the door open in exasperation, surprised to find Doreen rather than Milton on the doorstep.

"Did Marigold get off all right?" Doreen enquired, pushing her way indoors before I had the chance to reply. "Now, I'm just calling round to invite you to eat at ours this evening. Marigold would never forgive me if I left you to fend for yourself. If you're anything like Norman, you'll probably starve."

The outrageous suggestion that I was anything like Norman made my toes curl whilst the thought of attempting to force Doreen's inedible cooking down my gullet turned my stomach. It was only to appease Marigold that I had suffered through two years of the expat dinner parties that Doreen hosted. Admittedly Doreen applied plenty of imagination to the indigestible slop she cooked up, but the woman lacked even the most basic of kitchen skills. I supposed it was quite an art to dish up burnt food that was simultaneously raw inside.

"Rest assured that I am hardly likely to starve. I am more than capable of cooking for myself, Doreen," I pointed out. "It appears to have slipped your mind that you will be relying on my expertise tomorrow when I instruct you in the finer points of Greek cooking."

"There's no need to get on your high horse. I only invited you because I thought that Marigold would expect it of me. Just let her know that I extended an invitation when you speak to her."

"I'll be sure to do that," I promised. Hoping that my rather curt rejection wouldn't deter her from attending my first class the next day, I reminded her that we'd be gathering in my kitchen at 2pm.

"I haven't forgotten. I'm really hoping that your classes will spark some interest in Norman. He's not been himself lately." Sighing deeply, Doreen lowered her voice, confiding, "Norman's lost his got-up-and-go recently."

"Oh," I said non-committedly, amazed to hear that Norman had ever had any get-up-and-go to lose. He had been about as interesting as a bowl of cold porridge for the duration of the two years I had known him.

"If he's not careful, he's going to turn into a couch potato with a drinking problem. He's got no hobbies to keep him occupied…"

"Surely he's got his traffic cones…"

"Yes, but there's only so much one can do with a traffic cone. Once he's got his hands on the latest design, the excitement wears off quite quickly and there's nothing to occupy him beyond running a duster over them once a week," Doreen revealed. Her voice was laden with worry as she continued to speak. "I'd hoped that he'd show an interest in the garden or help with the housework but I can barely get him to budge from the sofa recently."

"Retiring abroad isn't for everyone. Perhaps he's missing England," I suggested.

"He'd be even worse there. At least out here we've got a bit of a social life, and good friends like you and Marigold."

"Well, tomorrow I will endeavour to spark enough interest in Norman to turn him into a cooking convert," I promised, thinking it really was a sad state of affairs if Norman imagined we were good friends. I regarded him as a tedious bore to be avoided at all costs at the ghastly ex-pat dinner parties Marigold insisted we attend.

"Thank you, Victor. And I'd appreciate it if we could keep our little chat between ourselves."

"Mum's the word," I said. The assurance I gave was genuine. Whilst I didn't have much time for Norman, Marigold valued Doreen's friendship and would expect no less of me. I would make a special effort to impart a love of cooking in Norman to add some purpose to his life, whilst ensuring I kept him well away from the cooking sherry.

With another chapter of the book under my belt, my stomach emitted a loud rumble, prompting my thoughts to turn to dinner. It was rather a novelty to have only myself to think of, with no need to consider Marigold's preferences when it came to cooking. Knowing that I would be spending the next afternoon slaving over a hot stove in front of an audience rather dampened my enthusiasm for getting creative in the kitchen now. A defiant thought occurred to me: since my wife would be none the wiser if I simply lobbed a Fray Bentos pie in the oven, I would be spared her scathing judgement.

Unable to recall the last time I had indulged in a processed steak and kidney topped with puff pastry, I threw caution to the wind and raided the cupboard only to discover it was painfully bereft of anything remotely resembling a tinned pie. Marigold must have had a clean out, no doubt stocking up Violet Burke's new daffodil kitchen cupboards with my despised pie collection.

Chapter 21

Meals on Wheels

With the lazy option of slinging a Fray Bentos in the oven no longer on the table, I eyed the contents of the fridge for inspiration, shivering slightly as the chilly blast from within hit me. It was later than I had realised: the evening had crept up on me stealthily and it was already dark outside. Before closing the French windows to prevent the cold night air from rushing in, I stepped onto the balcony, mindful that Marigold had reminded me to check it was clear of cats before locking up for the night.

My wife never ceases to drag up the one occasion when I accidentally locked Clawsome out overnight on the balcony. Although Greek cats can be found littering the pavement of every village in Greece, sprawled out beneath public bins and curled up sleeping in plant pots, the option to roam at will is ruled out for Marigold's imported pampered domestics. My wife claims her cats are of a far too delicate nature to ever rough it in the great Greek outdoors. On the occasion when Marigold couldn't locate Clawsome at bed time, she turned into a nervous wreck, pulling her hair out and ranting and raving, at least metaphorically. Her hysterical cries along with the bucketing rain drowned out the sound of the cat clamouring to be let in from the balcony where it was effectively trapped. Whereas Pickles would have made a daring leap from the balcony down to the street, Clawsome was far too cosseted, not to mention fat, to attempt anything requiring so much energy.

When Clawsome was eventually discovered after a wet night outside, Marigold had been so distraught at the sight of the soaked and bedraggled feline that she had tried to make an appointment to have the thing groomed and blow dried in Athena's kitchen. Whilst Athena appeared to seriously toy with the idea of experimentally preening pets in her kitchen, Vangelis put his foot down, pointing out that she wasn't suitably qualified. Saying it was bad enough to be forever finding human hair in his food, Vangelis drew the line at picking animal hair out of his teeth.

The familiar scent of burning olive wood drifted across the balcony, hinting the villagers were lighting the first fires of the season in their fireplaces and *sombas*. The smell reminded me that Giannis had put some wood on one side for me: I made a mental note to collect it during my walk to the cave in Nektar with Gordon the next morning. A single light moving in slow motion on the horizon caught my eye. Guessing it was a fishing boat, I marvelled at the skill it must take to fish in such complete darkness. I could barely imagine how it must feel to be a lone fisherman cast adrift in the night, the enveloping blackness closing in around the boat from all sides, with who knew what lurking beneath the surface of the forbidding black water.

I briefly considered suggesting to *Kapetainos* Vasos that I join him sometime for an evening's fishing, immediately discounting the idea when it struck me that the noisy Greek would ruin any ambiance. Any peace to found in night-time fishing would be shattered by Vasos' endless spouting of English words that were nothing short of nonsensical when barked out of context. Instead of hankering after new experiences, I decided to appreciate life in the moment and bask in the peace of the evening.

"Mr Bucket, may I come up?" Recognising the lilting voice of Sampaguita calling from the street, I invited her up, reminding her not to stand on formality but to please call me Victor. Scanning the balcony for the final time to ensure I hadn't overlooked any cats, I closed the French windows and went through to welcome Sampaguita.

"I didn't expect to see you this evening," I said. "I thought Spiros had grand plans to romance you."

"I told him that I would find it very romantic if he tidied up," Sampaguita laughed. "I just popped over to bring you this dish of pork adobo. I cooked too much for just me and Spiros. If you are anything like Spiros, you won't be looking after yourself properly while Marigold is away. Spiros has the terrible habit of living on pies if I don't cook for him."

"Fray Bentos," I quipped.

"I don't understand…"

"I'd show you but it appears that Marigold has smuggled my own supply of tinned Fray Bentos pies downstairs."

From the expression on Sampaguita's face, it was clear that she thought I was barking mad. Perchance tinned pies weren't an actual thing in the Philippines.

"Spiros likes best the *loukanikopita* and *spanakopitas*," she said, referencing Spiros' preference for sausage rolls and spinach pies. "I think the pork adobo is tastier than pies. I hope you enjoy it."

"I'm sure I will. It was most thoughtful of you to bring it round," I assured her as she rushed back down the outside stairs, keen to get away from the barking Brit and back to her untidy Greek. Carrying the dish through to the kitchen, I inhaled the aromatic scent of the meat and recalled enjoying the same delicious Filipino dish once before: Sampaguita had cooked it for me when I babysat for Leo back when Spiros had first been courting her. I was touched by Sampaguita's kind gesture in bringing the same dish over this evening, particularly as I suspected she had deliberately prepared extra so there would be enough for me. The meal looked so delicious that I decided to tuck in straight away. Alas, I was forced to turn my back on the food before taking a bite, disturbed by the sound of another caller at my door.

I was surprised to find Dina on the doorstep clutching a large casserole dish.

"*Kalispera, Victor. Pos eisai, agori mou.*" Dina wished me good evening before asking how I was. The way she referred to me as 'her boy' made me feel like a positive youngster. Not waiting to be invited in, Dina pushed past me, making her way through to the kitchen where she put the large casserole dish down next to Sampaguita's pork adobo. With her hands finally free, I picked Dina up and twirled her around, always delighted to see the motherly Greek lady. Once she was firmly back on her feet, Dina lifted the lid from the casserole dish, saying that she had brought me some stuffed vine leaves in an egg and lemon sauce because she had heard that my wife was away. "*Sas efera merika dolmadkia avgolemono giati akouo oti i gynaika sou einai makria.*"

Knowing that the tasty dish took a lot of fiddly preparation and didn't feature on the taverna menu, I was touched by Dina's thoughtfulness. Still, I was surprised that she felt the need to cook for me since Dina knew better than anyone else in the village that I was more than capable of cooking for myself. We had after all rubbed shoulders together in the taverna kitchen for long enough to have formed a special bond.

"*Pragmatika den ypirche ananki, xerete oti boro na mageirovo,*" I said, telling her really there was no need, she knew I could cook.

"*O Nikos eipe oti den einai sosta na kaneis ta douleia tis gynaikas.*" Dina threw her head back in laughter as she told me that Nikos had said it was not right for me to do the woman's work. I knew full well that Nikos would rather see me slaving over his olive harvest than knocking up something edible in the kitchen.

"*Itan evgeniko na doseis sti matera mou douleia katharismou,*" I said, telling Dina it was kind of her to give my mother a cleaning job.

"*Den to ekana gia na eimai evgenikos,*" Dina replied, telling me she didn't do it to be kind. Explaining her motives, Dina told me that she hated cleaning and it was too much work on top of cooking for the taverna: "*To ekana epeidi miso ton katharismo, einai para poly douleia pano apo to mageirema gia tin taverna.*"

Taking the weight off, Dina sank into a chair and began to lament the loss of her daughter-in-law, Eleni, and her beloved granddaughter, Nikoleta. She told me that when Kostis married, she had been grateful to hang up her mop and retire her scrubbing brush, passing the burden of responsibility down to the next generation in keeping with Greek tradition. Whilst the taverna kitchen remained her personal domain, she hoped in time to pass on enough of her culinary secrets to hand all the cooking over to Eleni. Emotion filtered into Dina's words and the tears started flowing. I must confess to feeling a tad out of my depth, fervently wishing that Marigold was by my side. My wife is an excellent person to have around in an emotional crisis, being much better suited to mopping up tears and dishing out comfort than I am.

Dabbing her eyes with a tea towel, Dina berated her son for being such a useless husband that he had driven Eleni away. To be frank, I was shocked to hear Dina not only criticise her precious offspring but to use some extremely choice language to do so, too choice to repeat in translation without causing possible offence to my readers. Kostis, for all his many faults, has always been the apple of Dina's eye, epitomising the spoilt and pampered Greek son who can do no wrong in the eyes of his doting mother. Dina had until now always treated her son as nothing less than a Greek god, but now it appeared that the scales had well and truly fallen from Dina's eyes. Content to turn a blind eye to his habits of hunting, carousing and chasing women, she drew the line at his ripping her obedient daughter-in-law and her darling granddaughter from her bosom.

I was grateful beyond measure to hear yet another caller at the door, hoping that the prospect of an audience might encourage Dina to get a grip and pull herself together. Leaving Dina to flood the kitchen with her tears, I opened the front door to the lovely Litsa, inviting the black clad widow in. Although I was somewhat surprised that the elderly woman had ventured out to call on me in the dark, I could guess the reason for her visit. I was beginning to cotton on that the village ladies regarded me as a helpless male in need of home cooked food during my wife's absence. As Litsa shoved a large pan under my nose, I realised my home was turning into a depository for the Greek equivalent of Meals on Wheels.

"*Perase mesa,*" I said, inviting her in.

"*Ochi. Oi anthropoi tha milisoun an eimai monos to vrady sto spiti me enan xeno,*" Litsa protested, saying people would talk if she was alone at night in the house with a foreigner. Litsa went on to tell me that she just wanted to give me a pan of *hortasoupa,* vegetable soup. Having heard that my wife was in England, she didn't want me to go hungry.

"*Parakalo elate, i Dina einai stin kouzina,*" I said, asking her to please come in and telling her that Dina was in the kitchen.

"*Entaxei,*" she agreed, apparently reassured by the mention of Dina's presence that she wouldn't be the target of scandalous gossip by being alone with a man in the Bucket household.

I relieved Litsa of the heavy pan and she followed me through to the kitchen, telling me that the soup was full of carrots, leeks and potatoes, "*I soupa einai gemati karota, prasa kai patates.*"

"*Myrizei yperocha,*" I said, telling her 'it smells delicious.'

"*Eftiaxa arketa gia ton Barry,*" she said with a blush, telling me she had made enough for Barry too. Litsa has always had a soft spot for my brother-in-law.

Catching sight of Dina's tear strewn face, Litsa nearly tripped over her walking stick in her haste to rush over and comfort her friend.

"*Ekei, min klais.*" Comforting Dina, Litsa said, 'There, there, don't cry.' Waving her walking stick around in a threatening manner, she added that she could swing for Kostis. "*Tha borousa na talentevo ton Kosti.*"

Standing around in my own kitchen, I felt like a spare part, superfluous to requirements. The two elderly women gabbled away in such rapid-fire Greek that I could barely make head or tail of their conversation. Kostis' name was bandied about between them, usually preceded with the sort of expletive one wouldn't expect to hear ejaculated from the lips of such a pair of lovely Greek grannies. Even the sound of my rumbling stomach was drowned out by their relentless chatter.

Despite the fact that I was now faced with the delicious choice of homemade vegetable soup, stuffed vine leaves and pork adobo, I considered it would be impolite to eat in front of my visitors unless I could persuade them to join me. Interrupting their conversation, I asked them if they would like something to eat, "*Tha itheles kati na fas?*"

"*Ochi, ochi, einai akoma to apogevma,*" Dina refused, saying it was still afternoon despite the fact that it was getting on for nearly seven o'clock.

"*Oi xenoi trone se perierges ores,*" Litsa hissed to Dina. It took me a moment to mentally translate that she had just said that foreigners eat at odd hours. I must confess to feeling rather deflated by her comment, having convinced myself that I was no longer considered a foreigner by the local Greeks.

Ruffling my hair, Dina told Litsa that I am in the habit of getting up very early in the morning so it was no wonder that I was hungry by the afternoon. I had to fight back a tear of my own when Dina proclaimed that I wasn't foreign to her and that she thought of me like a second son, "*O Victor den einai xenos gia mena. Skeftomai ton Victor san deftero gio.*"

"*Skeftomai ton Barry san ton antra pou efyge,*" Litsa replied, sending both women into convulsions of laughter. Mentally translating her words, I understood that Litsa had said that she thought of Barry as the husband that got away, I joined in their laughter. It would make Barry's day when I told him, though it would probably be best if I didn't repeat it in front of Cynthia. She could be a tad jealous when it came to elderly Greek widows flirting with my brother-in-law.

Chapter 22

An Available Object of Fancy

No sooner had Dina and Litsa departed together than I was interrupted by yet another uninvited caller. The Bucket household was beginning to resemble Piccadilly Circus at rush hour. Wishing I'd had the foresight to dim the lights to give the impression that no one was home, I found it impossible to ignore the relentless knocking at the door. I determined to briskly see off whoever it was, turn off the lights and settle down to tuck into Dina's delicious *dolmadkia avgolemono* by candlelight.

Throwing the door open, I was rather taken aback when Sherry practically fell through the door, struggling to maintain her balance in a pair of ridiculously teetering heels and nearly suffocating me with the overpowering scent of Poison. I should point out that I am only familiar with the noxious perfume because Marigold had once splurged on a bottle of the finest Dior only to discover it brought her out in an unsightly rash. Since my olfactory senses confused the perfume with the toxic scent of fly killer, I was relieved when Marigold binned it, blaming her allergy. Fortunately the Poison hives were not contagious: it would have given a terrible impression if a blotchy health inspector had turned up in a commercial kitchen, particularly as I had such an illustrious reputation to maintain.

Reaching a hand out to steady Sherry, I recoiled pretty sharpish when she attempted to clumsily embrace me. Knowing full well that I would need to endure her jolly-hockey-sticks cheerleading the next afternoon as she had been the first enthusiastic sign up for my cookery classes, I could do without an extra dose of her ruining my evening.

Swinging a carrier bag recklessly, Sherry

narrowly avoided lamping Clawsome, the cat having followed me faithfully to the door. Fearing that Sherry had somehow got wind of the apparent Greek custom of delivering home-made meals to men when their wives were absent, I dreaded to think what sorry excuse for a meal she was schlepping around in the carrier bag. Wasting no time, Sherry delved in the bag, producing a bottle of wine. Whilst grateful that the bag didn't contain anything she had the presumption to consider edible, the bottle of wine rather alarmed me. Sherry hadn't scrimped by picking up a bottle of the cheap plastic stuff from the local shop but had splashed the cash on a bottle of the good stuff from Lidl. Although the wine alone may not have unnerved me, coupled with the predatory look in her eyes and the nasty reek of too much Poison, it sent terror coursing through my veins. It was clear to me that Sherry had turned up with a specific mission in mind.

Before I had the chance to gather my wits and expel her, Sherry bulldozed her way through to the grand salon with her bottle. Throwing herself on the sofa in a pathetic semblance of a come-hither posture, she adjusted her blouse to expose a lumpy looking cleavage.

Flashing her horsey dentures, she declared, "You know it's like falling off a horse, Victor. The best thing you can do now is drown your sorrows and then throw yourself straight back into the saddle."

Not having the slightest clue what she was talking about, I assured her, "I have no sorrows to drown."

"Ah, you must have been expecting it then, rather than it coming out of the blue?" The predatory gleam was back in her eyes as she brayed, "We'll need a cork screw, Victor. If you don't need to drown your sorrows perhaps we should raise a glass to the next chapter in your life. Think of it as an opportunity to embrace new beginnings."

"It appears that you've had rather enough to drink already," I said, assuming she must be half-cut. "Perhaps you should go home and sleep it off."

"I've not had a drop, silly. We can drink this together," she said waving the bottle so violently than it sent the recumbent Catastrophe scuttling off behind the sofa. "I called round to cheer you up now that you're all on your lonesome. You will let me cheer you up, won't you Victor? We singles must stick together."

"Singles?" I repeated, a glimmer of an inkling beginning to form in my mind.

"It may be hard for you to come to terms with the idea that you're back on the market again, but I find it best not to deny reality…"

"I am neither single nor back on the market as you so crudely put it," I stated. "I am a happily married man."

"But Marigold has left you…"

"What on earth put such a ridiculous notion in your head?"

Sherry has a reputation for being relentlessly enthusiastic and it appeared that I was now experiencing first hand her enthusiasm for the notion of my being a deserted husband. I was determined to disavow her of the absurd idea before she got any ideas about propositioning me.

"Marigold has not left me, nor has she any intention of doing so," I stated with every confidence in my assertion. One thing I have never doubted is Marigold's unwavering loyalty and love. "My wife has simply flown back to England to spend the week with her friend Geraldine and to catch up with our son Benjamin."

"But… but I heard she had walked out on you…you mean to say that you aren't getting a divorce?" Sherry's crestfallen face reddened, her mouth gaping so wide that it was impossible for me to miss the piece of greenery stuck in her dentures. I decided it was probably prudent not to point it out in case the deluded woman mistook such a personal observation as a come-on.

"On the contrary, we are a devoted couple. In fact our marriage is such a happy one that I have been thinking about surprising Marigold with a special ceremony to renew our vows. Nothing would make Marigold happier than celebrating our love in front of all our friends and family," I blurted, desperate to disillusion Sherry that I was up for grabs. Having never given the slightest consideration to renewing our vows, I had no idea what prompted me to say such a thing beyond the necessity of convincing Sherry that we were both committed to our marriage. Since Marigold and I have always honoured the vows we exchanged at our wedding, it struck me as a wasteful extravagance to go through the whole rigmarole again.

"Oh, that's so romantic," Sherry gushed. "It's one of the most romantic things I've ever heard. What made you think of it?"

"Some of our friends and family missed out

on our wedding," I improvised, feeling obliged to maintain the pretence that such a ceremony was on the cards. The idea was quite ridiculous: we didn't have enough beds to put up all the people that had missed out on our wedding if they all flew to Greece for a repeat celebration. Of course, Violet Burke wouldn't need a bed in the house now that she was bedded down in the *apothiki*, and technically Benjamin had been at the wedding since Marigold had been pregnant. Still, there was my newly discovered half-brother Douglas and his family to consider, along with Benjamin's life partner Adam and Marigold's best pal Geraldine. It didn't seem right not to include them all in a shindig.

"Marigold is a lucky woman to have such a thoughtful husband." As Sherry's words brought me back to the present, I realised I had been mentally compiling a guest list for an event that I had not the slightest intention of organising since it was never going to happen. There was no vow renewal ceremony: it was simply a convenient ruse I had fabricated to convince Sherry there was no chink in my marriage.

"I am the lucky one," I said truthfully.

"I feel such a fool now," Sherry said. "I heard it on good authority that Marigold had left you and that with divorce on the cards she would never be returning to Greece."

There was no doubt that unfounded gossip tended to be rife in the village but it rather stumped me when I began to wonder where such a nasty rumour could have originated. Shocked to the core to hear the word divorce being bandied around in my home, I demanded to know, "Where did you hear such a preposterous lie?"

"I heard it from a woman who'd heard it while she was in the waiting room at the hospital. Now let me think where she said she'd heard it…oh yes, there was a Greek woman waiting to have the all clear for her new knee…apparently she'd told this other woman all about it."

The penny dropped. It dawned on me that the malicious loose-tongued gossip waiting to have her knee checked was most certainly Despina, the wart-faced old hag who delighted in malevolent meddling and spreading misery. It never failed to amaze me that such a lovely woman as Tina had the misfortune to be saddled with such a sour and embittered old bat of a mother. It wouldn't surprise me to learn that Tina had been abandoned in a bucket and snatched up by an evil imposter.

"You have to believe I would never have thrown myself at your head, Victor, if I'd thought for a moment it was just idle gossip." Sherry looked suitably mortified as she spoke. "It's not even as though you're my type, it's just that I get so lonely on my own. It can be so difficult being a single woman."

I didn't know whether to be insulted or relieved to hear that I wasn't Sherry's type. On balance I decided to go with relieved, realising that she must be desperately lonely if she was prepared to throw herself at a man for no other reason than she fancied he was available, rather than him being an object of fancy. I have no delusions that I am wildly attractive to the opposite sex, but I imagine I could perhaps be considered a catch in the eyes of a woman craving coupledom as an antidote to singlehood. However, the blatantly obvious combination of Sherry's cleavage, the heels and the scent, led me to deduce that she'd had more than just friendly companionship in mind when she landed on my doorstep flaunting her fancy Lidl wine.

I have it on the good authority of my sister-in-law, Cynthia, that single women can feel excluded because expat social gatherings tend to revolve around couples getting together. She assures me that some married women can feel terribly threatened by a single woman joining their social circle. I have always taken Cynthia's argument with a pinch of salt because Marigold has never shown any reservations about including any single women in our social circle, as demonstrated indeed by the way in which she took Sherry under her wing. Secure in our relationship, my wife knows that I would never stray if some unattached woman tried to attach herself to me, or worry that a pair of fluttering eyelashes or an underwired bosom thrust under my nose would turn my head.

I remember Cynthia telling me that back in the days before she met Barry, even Doreen had been reluctant to include her in expat gatherings, worried that Cynthia may make a play for Norman. Delving into the psychology behind her theory, Cynthia had explained that if a single woman successfully snared Norman away from Doreen, then Doreen would be the one relegated to the excluded ranks of single women, the ranks of which not only included spinsters, but widows and divorcees. Apparently any random lesbians would not be an issue since the wives needn't angst about them having designs on their husbands.

Whilst neither Doreen nor Cynthia could in any sane world seriously consider Norman a catch, he was by default of being a man more likely to be included rather than excluded, along with whatever woman he had on his available arm. Cynthia had told me that the local Greeks had always been happy to welcome her, but she did have the advantage of being able to communicate, whilst Sherry was still out in the cold language wise with the Greeks. Ironically, considering Cynthia's theory, my sister-in-law was not inclined to include Sherry if she could avoid it. However, Cynthia's reluctance to befriend Sherry stemmed from Sherry snubbing Barry when she first moved here, dismissing him as the help, rather than any jealous worries that Sherry was likely to pounce on her man. Cynthia was well aware that Barry found Sherry insufferable.

Whilst still not convinced by Cynthia's theory, I had to admit that it was unlikely that Marigold would have been the recipient of a constant delivery of Meals on Wheels if she been the one to be alone in the village whilst I gadded off to England. The food had been cooked up by women concerned that I wouldn't be able to cope alone as a helpless man. I pondered that if the fancy took me, I could pop over to the taverna and catch up with friends. On the other hand, Marigold would not dream of dropping into the taverna alone in case she gave the wrong impression to the local male clientele. Admittedly, most of them were on the wrong side of eighty, but that wouldn't deter them from raising false hopes if an attractive woman fancied a night out on her own in the only night-spot in Meli.

"Really, Victor, I mean it, you're not my type." Sherry's words dragged me out of my reverie. "I'm genuinely happy that Marigold isn't divorcing you. Marigold is so lovely, she always invites me to everything."

"Marigold goes out of her way to match-make for her single friends. She is a great believer that everyone deserves to find the same happiness that we have found together," I said, thinking how my wife racks her brains to drum up eligible bachelors to dangle in front of her friends. I recalled how Marigold had not only arranged a dinner party but scraped the barrel in order to parade Spiros, Dimitris and Panos in front of Geraldine. Admittedly Marigold's

meddling hadn't borne fruit: our celibate cleri-
cal neighbour, Papas Andreas, being the one to
catch Geraldine's eye rather than any of Marigold's carefully selected line-up of bachelors. By
the time Sherry turned up in Meli, Spiros was
already spoken for and Marigold had ear-
marked Panos for Violet Burke. Still, Marigold
had insisted on dragging Sherry along to Apostolos' name day party in the hope that she could
find a single male with a pulse to fix up with her
new friend. It struck me that while my wife had
been keen to introduce Sherry to eligible bachelors, she hadn't planned on Sherry mistaking me
for one of them.

"What is Marigold ever going to think of me
now?" Sherry stammered, her horsey confidence momentarily deserting her. The prospect
of Sherry giving in to tears of remorse was too
much for me to cope with on top of Dina's earlier weeping. Although I found Sherry's usual
jolly-hockey-sticks manner quite excruciating, it
was certainly preferable to uncontrolled water-
works.

"I expect that Marigold will find it hilarious
that I am still able to attract a woman," I said,
trying to jolly Sherry up. "She likes to jest that
no one else would put up with my hygiene

obsession."

"But I don't find you attractive, Victor, not at all," Sherry protested, yanking her blouse up to thankfully conceal her wobbly cleavage.

"It didn't stop you from coming round here with seduction in mind," I retorted.

"Well, you can't blame me for trying in the circumstances," the ever thick-skinned Sherry attempted to excuse herself. "If it had been true that Marigold had left you, you might have appreciated me trying to cheer you up with a nice bottle of wine. It wouldn't have been neighbourly for me to have left you alone to wallow in self-pity."

"So you were just trying to cheer me up," I said in the hope that we could perhaps bluff our way out of the embarrassing situation by pretending it was just a case of crossed wires.

"Exactly. And now that Marigold hasn't left you, we don't need to say anything more about it."

Before I could respond, our attention was diverted by the sound of someone knocking at the door. Running a list of the local Greek ladies through my mind, I tried to guess which one of them might be ministering to my rumbling stomach now. At least I hoped it was yet another delivery of Meals on Wheels rather than another amorous woman who had heard the same rumours as Sherry and got it into her head that I was available.

I was quite touched to find Athena on my doorstep bearing food. Between helping Tina out at the shop and cutting hair in her kitchen, it was amazing that she had enough free time to think of cooking for me.

"*Kalispera, Victor. Prepei na leipesis to Marigold,*" Athena greeted me, saying I must be missing Marigold.

"*Apeiche mono apo simera to proi,*" I replied, pointing out that she'd only been away since the morning.

"*To xero, alla O Vangelis tha chathei choris emena,*" she said, telling me she knew but that Vangelis would be lost without her.

"*Mou leipei i Marigold,*" I said, admitting I did miss Marigold. Certainly if Marigold hadn't gone gadding off to England, I would not have been forced to suffer Sherry throwing herself at me. I thought it best not to mention the embarrassing matter to Athena or tongues would undoubtedly start wagging.

"*Sas efera ligo chtapodi me macaronia.*" I attempted to feign delight when Athena told me that she'd brought me some octopus and macaroni. Although a nice bit of octopus is one of my favourite Greek culinary treats, I didn't trust Athena to handle frozen marine life in a safe and hygienic manner. I recalled from our very first meeting that she has a very blasé attitude when it comes to refreezing bulk purchases of frozen *chtapodia* that had been left out to defrost and turn in the heat. I would hazard a guess that the eight-limbed mollusc she had cooked up this evening may have been hanging around in her chest freezer for a couple of years, the frigid temperature preserving the growth of bacteria that latched onto the octopus back when it had been sunning itself in the back of Vangelis' pick-up.

Whilst not spurning Athena's offering of octopus outright, I decided it would be prudent to feed a sample of it to the cats first to see if it had a deleterious effect on their stomachs. If they came down with a nasty case of food poisoning, I would definitely give it a miss. It struck me that Marigold's pampered imported felines had their uses after all, if only as convenient food testers.

Athena barged through to the kitchen, raising her eyebrows when she spotted Sherry lounging around in the grand salon. Taking in the heels and coughing as she was near asphyxiated with Poison, Athena clearly did not like what she saw. Wasting no time, she got straight to the point, demanding to know what Sherry was doing there when Marigold was away. I deduced that Athena must have a nose for sniffing out predatory females up to no good.

"*Ti kanei edo otan i Marigold einai makria?*" Frowning at the guilty looking interloper, Athena astutely commented that she was trying to get her feet under my table, "*Prospathntas na valei ta podia tis kato apo to trapezi sas.*"

"*Den proskalesa i Sherry,*" I said, telling Athena that I hadn't invited Sherry to call. Thinking on my feet, I asked Athena if she would take Sherry away with her when she left, "*Boreite na tin parete mazi sas otan fygete.*"

"*Ela, ora na fygo. Oi anthropoi tha milisoun ean eiste mazi me ton Victor otan i gynaika tou einai makria,*" Athena addressed Sherry directly in a commanding tone.

"I don't understand what she's saying," Sherry said, shuffling uncomfortably under Athena's unwavering gaze.

"She says it's time for you to leave. She says that people will talk if you are alone with me while my wife is away."

"*Tha prepei na vrei enan diko tis andras,*" Athena decreed.

"*I Marigold prospathei na tin vrei,*" I responded.

"What are you saying?" Sherry questioned, her eyes swivelling between us.

"Nothing, just talking about the weather," I lied. It may hurt Sherry's feelings if I told her that Athena had said she must find a man of her own. In Sherry's defence, I had told Athena that Marigold was trying to find her one. In truth, I was actually quite touched that Athena cared enough about Marigold to worry when she found an unattached woman brazenly hanging around making eyes at her friend's husband.

"*Ela, pame,*" Athena barked at Sherry, meaning, 'Come, we'll go.' Not prepared to argue the matter, she firmly planted her arm under Sherry's and frog-marched her towards the door.

"I'll see you tomorrow at the cookery classes," Sherry cried out as the other woman steered her towards the exit. "Do say hello to Marigold if you speak to her."

"*Efcharisto, Athena.*" Thanking the Greek woman, I sent her a look of gratitude for the no-

nonsense way in which she was taking control of the insufferable Sherry.

Opening the front door to facilitate their exit, I was surprised to discover Kyria Kompogiannopoulou lurking on the doorstep clutching a giant pan. As I invited her to step indoors, it amused me to note that Athena raised no objection to my inviting the elderly woman in: presumably a visit from the Greek grandmother would not have a negative impact on my reputation. The two of us had become quite friendly over the last several weeks as she had done the odd shift alongside me in the village shop. Unfortunately, Kyria Kompogiannopoulou had proved about as useful as a chocolate teapot, spending most of her time dashing to the toilet with her dodgy bladder. No doubt I would hear all about her bladder in glorious Technicolor detail on Sunday when she was rostered to give me a hand in the shop.

"*Se ekana merika patsas,*" Kyria Kompogiannopoulou said, telling me she had made me tripe soup. As she lifted the lid off the soup pan to reveal the contents, I recoiled in disgust at the stench of offal and innards. I have never developed a taste for the stuff.

"*Fainetai nostimo,*" I lied, telling her it looked

delicious before inviting her in for a cup of tea.

"*Den boro na meino, prepei na epistreso stin toualeta.*" Declining the offer of a cuppa, Kyria Kompogiannopoulou said that she couldn't stop, she had to get back to the toilet.

Hauling the giant pan of disgusting soup through to the kitchen, I decided that instead of chucking it out, I would invite Barry over to join me. There's nothing my brother-in-law loves more than a nice bit of tripe.

"Not tonight, Victor." Barry declined my invitation when I phoned to invite him over to tuck into tripe soup. "We've got a roaring fire going and we're just about to roast some chestnuts and eat them in candlelight."

"Oh, is your electric off over there? There's no problem here?"

"No, we just thought it would make the place romantic."

"It sounds nice and warm. I haven't had a spare minute to see to lighting a fire yet," I said, waiting expectantly for Barry to extend an invitation for me to join them. "You know how much I enjoy roasted chestnuts."

Despite my blatant hint, Barry didn't pick up on it. Since no invitation was forthcoming, I was forced to suggest that I pop over to join them, playing on my brother-in-law's sympathy by reminding him that Marigold had gone to England and left me all on my lonesome. "I could bring the tripe soup with me. You know how you love a nice bowl of *patsas*, Barry"

"Look, Victor, I don't mean to be rude but don't you get it?" Barry sighed. "I've got the scene all set with candles and a log fire. Me and Cynthia are trying to have a romantic evening alone and we really don't need a third wheel playing gooseberry."

"You should be grateful that I didn't take that attitude when you were over at ours all the time playing gooseberry before you met Cynthia," I bristled.

"That was different. You and Marigold weren't newlyweds like me and Cyn," Barry argued. Lowering his voice to a whisper, he said, "Look, I could be on a promise tonight if this romantic scene I've set does the trick."

"But I've got tripe soup," I wheedled.

"Look, Victor. If you're lonely and missing Marigold, why not pop downstairs and spend the evening with your mother."

"I'm not some sad sap that can't enjoy an evening alone in my own company," I retorted, hanging up on my brother-in-law.

Chapter 23

High Time for a bit of Mothering

Although the kitchen table positively groaned under the weight of delectable dishes so kindly delivered by my generous Greek neighbours, the vile smell of the *patsas* had rather killed my appetite. Realising that although I had enough food to throw a party, knowing Marigold wasn't there to share it with me made me feel a tad lonely. Perhaps I should just pop down to the *apothiki* and invite Violet Burke upstairs to join me. I reflected that surely such an invitation would make me appear like a thoughtful and dutiful son with plenty of food going begging, rather than a sad sap missing his wife and turning to his mother for company.

Throughout the course of the evening, I had been aware of the occasional sound of knocking drifting up from the street, indicating that perhaps Violet Burke had also been the recipient of my neighbours' largesse. Of course, since the *apothiki* door was directly on the street it was entirely possible that rather than receiving actual visitors, Violet Burke may have been subjected to random door knockers, perchance the Greek equivalent of Jehovah's Witnesses.

The God squad had never been off our doorstep back in Manchester, along with door to door charity collectors and annoying children wanting me to sponsor them for something distinctly unimpressive such as holding their tongues for thirty minutes. My usual modus operandi had been to send the lot of them packing with a flea in their ear, but being rather impressed with one small boy's determination to break the world record for eating garden worms, I had bunged him a fiver. I even let him keep it when he vomited the worms up all over my neighbour's doorstep when he called round to collect his sponsorship cash. I found the Jehovah's Witnesses particularly persistent on Sunday mornings, or perhaps it was the Mormons. Either way, one ought to have been afforded a bit of peace on the Sabbath since the God botherers should have been off genuflecting in church rather than disturbing Marigold's lie in. Since our own Greek front door was tucked out of sight behind a gate and at the top of a perilous stone staircase, we were blessedly spared such nuisance callers these days, if such things even existed in Greece since Harold had repatriated himself to Old Blighty.

The *apothiki* door was flung open by Kyria Maria from next door. The black clad widow invited me in, indicating with a gesture that my mother was in the bedroom. I was instantly alarmed, thinking that mother's bruised coccyx must have been worse that I'd realised if she had taken to her bed. I should have insisted that she let me take her down to the clinic to be checked out by a doctor. I ought to have realised that with her stoic nature she would have naturally played down her injury.

"*Einai se poly pono*?" I said, asking Maria if my mother was in much pain.

"*Tha zisei,*" Kyria Maria replied, saying

she'd live.

"Who's out there?" Violet Burke yelled from the bedroom.

"It's me, Victor."

"I'll be right out, lad. I'm just getting my slap on before Panos fetches the car round."

Mother's words filled me with guilt. Surely she shouldn't need to depend on the goodwill of the neighbours to drive her to the clinic. She had only been in Greece for five minutes and I had already let her down.

"*Se eftiaxa keftedakia kai macaronia, alla kalesa tin Violet kai tis edosa ant aftou,*" Kyria Maria said, telling me she had made me some meatballs and macaroni but she called in on Violet and my mother had devoured the lot, "*Ola afta.*"

I was very surprised to hear that my mother had eaten the meal Kyria Maria had prepared for me since I was well acquainted with Violet Burke's scathing opinion of foreign food. Still, I was relieved to be spared Maria's *keftedakia kai macaronia.* I could never eat that particular dish without remembering my overindulgence on top of bacon sandwiches and too much sun. The combination had literally floored me, Marigold discovering me collapsed on the bathroom floor at the home of Poppy's parents.

"*Echeis dei tin kokkyyx tis?*" Maria demanded, asking if I had seen Vi's coccyx.

"*Ochi,*" I admitted, thinking it entirely inappropriate for me to go around peering at my mother's tail bone.

"*Einai aschimo.*" Maria confirmed it was nasty before elaborating; telling me it was black and blue, "*Ola mavro kai ble.*"

The bedroom door opened and I braced myself for the sight of the poor suffering invalid. You could have knocked me down with a feather when Violet Burke emerged as bold as brass, dressed up in her finest tweed with a layer of garish makeup plastered all over face, her dyed red hair backcombed to within an inch of its life.

"*Fainesai omorfi,*" Maria exclaimed, telling my mother she looked beautiful.

"Not bad for getting on for eighty, eh Victor," my mother preened. "I think this skirt must have shrunk in the wash. I had to use a safety pin to hold it closed 'cos the button popped off."

It certainly appeared that the overly-tight tweed skirt was straining at the seams but I would hazard a guess that it was down to too many chips rather than the vagaries of the washing machine.

"You seem rather done up, Mother," I observed.

"Well I thought I'd make an effort since a gentleman caller is taking me out."

"A gentleman caller?"

"Aye, that Panos with the mucky wellies. He's persistent, I'll give him that. He popped round earlier with that bunch of flowers and wouldn't take no for an answer."

Following mother's glance, I spied a bunch of trampled and wilting flowers on the mantelpiece. By the looks of them they had never been anywhere near a petrol station forecourt, much less an actual florists, rather resembling something regurgitated by one of Panos' sheep.

"You should put those outside, Mother," I advised. "Otherwise the place will be thick with mites."

"'Appen any mites will eat the fleas that scabby cat of Cynthia's left behind," my mother chortled.

"*Ti leei?*" Maria asked what mother was saying.

"*Tipota,*" I replied, telling her nothing.

"So what brings you downstairs, Victor?" my mother asked.

"I thought you might like some company. I've plenty of food upstairs if you'd like to come up and join me," I invited.

"You don't want me cramping your style, lad. You mustn't worry about me, I've had plenty of company. Maria's here of course, and Panos popped in, oh and that odd fellow who brought me that book." Mother nodded towards the coffee table. "Course, I can't make head or tail of it as it's in some peculiar foreign language. I told him to come back with a nice serial killer, that's more my cup of tea."

Picking up the book to examine it, I clarified, "It's in Greek, Mother. Oh, for goodness sake, would you credit it? It's only a Greek translation of the New World Translation."

"What's that when it's at home?"

"The Jehovah's Witnesses' Bible."

The irony wasn't lost on me that I had only been thinking about such nuisance door knockers earlier and all the while my mother had been hobnobbing with them on her doorstep. The three of us turned towards the door as a knock announced another caller.

"Don't worry, Mother, I'll get rid of them," I said, presuming the Jehovah's Witnesses were back for a repeat visit. They'd be wasting their time if they expected to make a doorstep convert of Violet Burke.

"Why would you want to get rid of my date, lad? Surely you don't begrudge your old mother a social life?"

Opening the door, I was relieved to see it was Panos, being in no mood to engage in a doorstop contretemps with a bunch of Greek speaking Witnesses. I barely recognised my old friend. Gone were the mucky wellies, replaced with a pair of scruffy old trainers which he'd paired with a dated suit stinking of mothballs.

"*Einai etoimi i Violeta?*" Panos asked if Violeta was ready.

"Tell him it's Violet, I'm not answering to any poncy Violeta," my mother yelled.

"*Pes tis na viasei, echo afisei to trakter na trechei,*" Panos said, telling me to tell her to hurry up as he'd left the tractor running. He certainly knew how to sweep a woman off her feet in style.

"*Pou pairneis ti mitera mou sto trakter?*" I said to Panos.

"What are you saying, Victor?"

"I asked Panos where he is taking you in the tractor."

"We're off to the taverna. I told him straight,

I wasn't walking there on these swollen feet. Tell him I'll be out in a jiffy, I just have to find something to cram my puffed up feet in."

"*Ena lepto*." One minute, I told Panos, watching as Violet Burke struggled to find suitable footwear.

"Oh, bugger it. I'll have to make do with these," she said, squeezing her swollen feet into a pair of fuzzy pink pig slippers. "You needn't look like that, lad. At least they're comfortable. They were a gift from Benjamin. I was tickled pink that he thought of his old granny."

"Mother, I'm curious how you managed to communicate enough to arrange a date with Panos," I said.

"It's not a date date, you daft apeth. I can't be thinking of romance with the state my coccyx is in. We're just going out for a plate of chips."

"But I thought you'd already eaten macaroni and meatballs," I said, pointedly looking at her too tight skirt.

"I could hardly say no when Maria had cooked them special for you," Vi said. "I know how you'd have forced them down to be polite even though you know they don't agree with you. I haven't forgotten how Maria's last batch of meatballs nearly finished you off. I was that worried when Marigold telephoned me and told me you'd been passed out on that bathroom floor and she had to find a strong fella to break the door down."

"So you ate them to spare me the ordeal of choking them down?"

"That I did, lad. I knew you'd be too polite to refuse them. It's high time I picked up a bit of this mothering lark, wouldn't you say?"

I was moved beyond words by Violet Burke's reasoning that she forced down Maria's meatballs to spare me another possible near death experience. I might be exaggerating just a tad but nevertheless I considered it a selfless and caring act.

"Now don't go waiting up for me, Victor. I don't want you worrying about me. I can handle myself if Panos gets it into his head to turn amorous," Vi assured me.

"I'm sure you can, Mother," I said, thinking that if my deft handling of Sherry earlier was anything to go by, I had likely inherited her knack of fighting off unwanted amorous advances.

Chapter 24

Telephone Talk

G roping my way back up the outside stone staircase in the darkness, I could hear the telephone ringing inside the house. My heart skipped a beat; it could well be Marigold calling from England. In my haste to reach the phone before it stopped ringing, I tripped over Pickles and ended up sprawled face down on the floor. Grabbing the cord, I yanked the phone to the floor, shouting at Pickles, "Stop licking my face."

"Really, Victor," Marigold trilled down the

phone. "I've only been gone five minutes and it sounds like you've turned the place into a brothel."

"I was talking to Pickles," I gasped, still trying to recover my breath.

"You're such a softie, darling. I can see right through your act when you pretend that the cats are a blasted nuisance. Now, are you managing all right without me?" Without waiting for me to reply, Marigold steamrollered on, launching into a complaint about the ghastly weather in Manchester. "I'd quite forgotten how damp it can be in November, it's playing havoc with my hair. And so bone-chillingly cold, I wish I'd sneaked one of Vi's hot water bottles over with me. I'm going to have to head straight to Marks and Sparks in the morning..."

"You should certainly be able to pick up a quality hot water bottle there. Just be careful not to select an inferior brand that hasn't been through a rigorous series of safety checks. I'd hate for you to scald yourself. You must ensure it comes with a BS 1970 mark to show it meets the safety standard for rubber," I advised.

"Marks and Spencer for warm winter dresses," Marigold clarified.

"No need to go mad," I cautioned,

wondering if it would be prudent to cancel the credit card. "You won't get much wear out of them over here in the sunshine."

"Must you rub it in about the glorious Greek weather? I expect you've been basking on the beach all day." I shook my head, wondering at the bizarre tangents my wife's mind travels. She certainly had a strange notion of how I might be spending my days since the only time I would likely be found basking on a beach was when Marigold dragged me to one. As a resident of Greece rather than a holidaymaker, I am usually much too busy to indulge in lounging around on the beach building sandcastles.

"I've been nowhere near the beach. I showed the Stranges around Leo's house and they put in an offer," I said before biting my tongue. Knowing Marigold, she would interpret my comment as an invitation to go on a reckless shopping spree in Manchester, splashing the cash from my hard-earned commission.

"Well, I hope that you didn't have your head turned by that model," Marigold said coldly, jealousy creeping into her tone.

"This will amuse you," I teased. "It turns out that Moira Stranges' modelling job isn't modelling in the conventional sense…"

"Do you mean to tell me she's one of those brazen Page 3 girls that flash off their breasts to a bunch of illiterate saddos who read the Sun?"

"Well, technically they wouldn't be classified as illiterate if they can read a newspaper..."

"Don't pick hairs, Victor."

"If you'd let me finish, I was about to tell you that Moira only models her ears," I said, belatedly realising that Violet Burke had already filled Marigold in on Moira's unusual job. I have always suspected that Marigold only lends half-an-ear to my mother's chatter and Marigold's ignorance to the true nature of Moira's job only confirmed it.

"Her ears?"

"Yes, apparently they are in demand for advertising such things as ear drops and hearing aids."

"So, she's not some great beauty with Page 3 breasts after all?" Marigold said in relief.

"I never even glanced at her assets," I reassured my wife.

"Ah well, that puts an entirely different complexion on the matter. I've had quite enough upset to cope with today without having to worry about you having your head turned by a glamour model."

"The only woman who turns my head is you, darling," I said honestly. "So, what upset have you had to endure?"

"Frank sweated all over the arm rest on the plane." I winced in sympathy. Since germ carriers are prone to shed their infected bacterium in their sweat, communal armrests are a health hazard waiting to happen if they are not thoroughly sanitised between flights. Even if Frank wasn't shedding germs in his sweat, it must have been particularly unpleasant for Marigold to be up close and personal with his dripping perspiration. I felt for her being squashed up next to someone sweating in unhygienic Lycra.

As if reading my mind, Marigold opined, "They really ought to introduce new legislation to ban people from flying in Lycra. It certainly lowers the tone of air travel. I was mortified in case anyone thought that Frank was my husband."

"So, I'm not such an embarrassment to you after all?" I smiled even though Marigold could not see me.

"Only when you insist on pairing your socks with sandals."

"It will be boat shoes all the way from now on," I promised my wife.

"How's your mother settling in? Tell me that she hasn't sent the *apothiki* up in flames with a chip pan fire," Marigold said, only half-joking.

"Nothing so drastic, though Cynthia has got it into her head that Violet Burke has somehow disposed of Kouneli. It hasn't shown its face since Mother hurled it out of the window."

"Good riddance to the vile creature," Marigold said, hastily adding, "I mean the mutant cat, not your mother."

"Surprisingly, my mother has been throwing herself into her new Greek life with enthusiasm. She has already landed herself a job at the taverna, cleaning the lavatory and peeling spuds, and she took to Cynthia's bicycle like a duck to water," I said, omitting to mention her unfortunate tumble. There was no point in Marigold worrying herself unduly about Violet Burke's bruised coccyx; there was nothing she could do about it in Manchester. "She's just gone out on a date with Panos."

"I knew it," Marigold exclaimed in a triumphant tone. "I told you that Panos was keen on your mother. Has he taken her somewhere romantic?"

"Apparently they were heading to the taverna to guzzle chips. He just called to collect her; he left the engine running outside…"

"I knew that Panos had the makings of a gentleman. A real gentleman always calls for his date in his car rather than expecting a lady to walk in her heels…"

"Panos came to collect her in his tractor and mother stuffed her swollen feet into some rather hideous fluffy pink slippers…"

"Did they at least have a kitten heel?" Marigold asked hopefully.

"No, they were those fuzzy pig ones with rubber soles, the sort that look like little old ladies' bootees," I winced.

"Has she no taste at all?"

"Apparently Benjamin bought them for her…"

"I'll have to have words with our son tomorrow or the next thing I know I'll be unwrapping an identical pair this Christmas. Anyway, at least I was right about Panos being keen on your mother. Now, what about you, dear? What did you do with your evening when you got back from sunning yourself on the beach?"

"I've barely had a moment of peace; it's been like Piccadilly Circus all evening with non-stop deliveries of Meals on Wheels…"

"Must you talk in riddles, Victor?"

"The village ladies took it upon themselves to bring me an assortment of home cooked meals, apparently mistaking me for the sort of helpless sap who is incapable of finding my way round the kitchen," I explained. "Sampaguita brought me some delicious pork adobo..."

"She's such a sweetheart. I'm so happy she is going to marry Spiros, they make such a lovely couple," the indefatigable matchmaker gushed.

"And Dina cooked me *dolmadkia avgolemono.*"

"Oh, I'm so jealous, Victor. I just love stuffed vine leaves in egg and lemon sauce. You are lucky, darling. Geraldine cooked up some rather uninspired cauliflower cheese slop. She hasn't got your knack for pulverising any lumps in the cheese sauce. It was a lumpy and curdled mess."

"For some reason the thought of curdled cauliflower cheese always puts me in mind of Ashley's sexually infected samples..."

"Well, I'm glad you didn't tell me that before I choked my curdled cauliflower down or it may have come straight back up again."

"Athena brought me some dodgy looking octopus. I don't think I'll risk it," I said, omitting to mention I planned to use Marigold's pampered felines to taste test it first.

"I hope you remembered to tell Athena that I won't be able to make it to the beautifying of the cemetery next Monday..."

"Sorry, I clean forgot. Athena was too concerned with frog-marching Sherry out of here to have time to stand round and chat."

"Sherry. What was she doing round at ours? Surely you haven't been inviting single women to pop round in my absence?" The note of unease in Marigold's voice led me to think there was perhaps just a grain of truth to Cynthia's theory about married women feeling a tad threatened by singles.

"The house has been chock full of single women all evening. Both Litsa and Kyria Kompogiannnopoulou stopped by," I said.

"Elderly Greek grannies don't count, Victor. What did Sherry want?" Marigold demanded, her tone veering on strident.

"I rather think she was on a mission to seduce me." I held the receiver at arm's length to avoid being deafened by Marigold's hysterical laughter.

Once she had recovered some semblance of control, my wife said, "You do come out with the most absurd things, Victor. Fancy imagining that Sherry has designs on you! I think you could be losing the plot."

Absurd it may be, but it also happened to be true. Whilst I had rather hoped the cringeworthy incident could be brushed under the carpet to spare future embarrassment all round, Athena's walking in and discovering me alone with Sherry done up like the dog's dinner meant that the cat was out of the bag. No doubt, it would be the talk of the village by the next day. The sensible thing was obviously to fess up to Marigold before the village gossips turned it into a full blown affair.

"Brace yourself, darling. You're not going to like this," I warned. "It appears that Despina has been spreading her unique brand of poisonous tittle-tattle…"

"Who has the old witch been spreading scurrilous rumours about now?" Marigold interrupted.

"You," I admitted.

"What? Don't tell me, I've eloped with Frank?" Marigold quipped.

"You might as well have. Despina put the word out that you've walked out on me. Not only that, you plan to divorce me and never return to Greece…"

"That's preposterous. How dare Despina stir up such lies? I swear she revels in being a scandalmonger," Marigold's outrage was palpable as she spoke. "It is such a nasty and poisonous thing to make up. You do know that I would never leave you, don't you, darling?"

"Of course I do."

"I hope that you gave that wart-faced old hag, Despina, a piece of your mind."

"I most certainly will when I see her. I only heard the rumour tonight when Sherry told me about it," I said.

"So that was why Sherry was with you. She came round to warn you there was a spiteful rumour going round that I have walked out on you…"

"Not exactly. She came round thinking that I was ripe for the picking now that I am apparently available. I'm afraid she made a bit of a fool of herself, flaunting her cleavage and throwing herself at my head," I said.

"Oh dear, she's more desperate than I thought. I knew that she was pretty keen to find a man but really… did she seriously imagine that you would give her a second glance?"

Making a thumbs up sign at the cats, I

resisted the urge to whoop. I was relieved beyond measure that Marigold didn't expect me to convince her that I had no interest in Sherry.

"It's a good job that I know that Sherry isn't your type, darling, otherwise I'd be giving you hell. I know how much her jolly-hockey-sticks manner grates on your nerves."

"I find the woman insufferable," I said with sincerity. "I couldn't help noticing that you sounded a tad annoyed earlier when I mentioned that Sherry had been here. I thought for a moment that you might be feeling jealous."

"Jealous. Don't be ridiculous, Victor. I was annoyed because I know how loathsome you find Sherry and I wasn't there to act as a buffer between you," Marigold explained. "But are you sure you didn't get the wrong end of the stick, Victor. I know that Sherry is pretty determined to catch herself a man but I think you could be a bit deluded if you think that she fancies you."

Whilst tempted to challenge Marigold's opinion that it was ludicrous to think that a member of the opposite sex may find me remotely attractive, I resisted the urge. I would likely only make a rod for my own back if I planted the seed in Marigold's mind that Sherry had discovered she had passionate feelings for this Bucket.

"I don't think she finds me attractive as such, but she definitely found the idea of my being available an attractive proposition," I clarified.

"Oh, you know how desperate Sherry is. She even made eyes at that smelly old garlic eater, Mathias," Marigold chuckled. "Now, I do hope that you let Sherry down gently when you rejected her advances rather than going full foot-in-mouth on her. I wouldn't like to think that you deliberately mocked her or hurt her feelings. I think she's a bit sensitive under that thick-skinned exterior. She's just lonely and deserves to find the same happiness that we have."

"She was pretty persistent. I wanted to make it crystal clear that I am not and never will be available...so I fed her a load of old cobblers about us renewing our vows."

"Oh, Victor, what a marvellous idea. After all these years, you can still surprise me with such a romantic gesture," Marigold screeched with glee down the long distance telephone wire.

"Marigold, I didn't mean it. It was just the first guff that came out of my mouth to convince

Sherry we are a committed couple and that I am in no danger of becoming an available bachelor," I said firmly.

My commanding tone made not an iota of difference: Marigold was already planning our imaginary vow renewal service.

"Don't try wriggling out of it now, Victor, it was your idea. You can't go promising me that we'll renew our vows and then back out when you've got me all excited." She certainly sounded giddy with excitement as she ploughed on, barely pausing for breath. "Now, should I splurge on an actual wedding dress or would that be a bit over the top as I won't be a blushing bride this time around. Perhaps something simple in silk, a silk pantsuit…or, do you think we should do it barefoot on the beach?"

"I don't think we should do it at all," I protested, sure my objections would be in vain. I really couldn't imagine how I was going to talk my way out of this one.

"Nonsense, darling, it's a perfectly splendid idea and so romantic of you to think of it. And of course it makes perfect sense as your mother missed out on our wedding."

"I don't think she minds, she's not overly sentimental…"

"True, but she never misses an opportunity to buy a new hat. Surely you wouldn't deprive Violet Burke of the chance to show off a new hat? Panos might even propose if her hat is jaunty enough," Marigold said, trying to guilt trip me into agreeing. "I expect it will be quite the dilemma for you to have to choose between Barry and Benjamin for your best man. They do have a best man at vow renewal ceremonies, don't they? Of course, Douglas' twins can be my bridesmaids and little Anastasia can be a flower girl. Can you imagine how thrilled little Ana will be?"

Desperate for my wife to put a sock in it, I adopted a firm tone, saying, "We'll talk about it when you get home, Marigold."

I realised that the likelihood of her having forgotten all about it by the time she returned to Greece was nigh on impossible. Marigold would never let it drop now the seed had been planted and I only had myself to blame for being the one to plant the seed.

"Whatever you say, dear," Marigold said with feigned meekness.

"So, how are things with Geraldine?" I asked, determined to change the subject.

"She's desperate to dump Ashley but he's

hanging around with all the persistence of a bad smell," Marigold sighed. "I'd no sooner got through baggage arrivals than he cornered me, suggesting we go ring shopping together. I've got my work cut out putting him off Geraldine before he proposes."

"You could always bring her back over here with you to put some distance between them," I suggested.

"No, I thought of that but Geraldine has used up all her annual leave already. Perhaps you could do some internet searches and see if there's any sexually transmitted infection conventions coming up that might appeal to Ashley. Something like that may get him out of her hair."

"Are there such things?" I asked, finding it hard to imagine.

"I expect so, dear. There are all sorts of conferences for things that are just too tedious to imagine. I remember you traipsing off to that one about diarrhoea in the kitchen. I couldn't imagine anything drearier."

"I think you are referring to the seminar I attended on 'New Hygiene Approaches to Fight Food Borne Pathogens in the Kitchen," I bristled. Marigold only ever listened with half-an-ear to anything to do with my glittering career in food safety standards.

"That's what I said," Marigold said in the absent-minded tone she tended to adopt whenever anything related to unhygienic microbes cropped up.

"Catastrophe, put that down at once or Marigold will skin you alive," I called out to the cat. The obese feline, having retrieved Marigold's notebook from behind the cushion, was engaged in using it as a scratching pad.

"Don't take that tone with the cat," Marigold chided. "I expect she is missing me."

"It's no skin off my nose if she rips your notebook to shreds," I snapped.

"My notebook?"

"Yes, some kind of diary. You left it lying round on the sofa."

"And you took it as an invitation to go snooping?" Marigold accused.

"Of course not. The very idea that I would invade your privacy."

"Then what made you say it was my diary?"

"That bit about Guzim flashing his privates." My hand flew to my mouth as I realised what I had inadvertently blurted out.

"Which you would only know if you've been reading it," Marigold astutely pointed out. "Anyway, if you must know, it isn't a diary. I've been jotting down a few notes in case I ever fancy writing a moving abroad book of my own."

"But I'm writing one," I said peevishly.

"Which I very much doubt will ever see the light of day. It won't magically get published from your sock drawer, you know."

"But I started mine first…"

"You aren't the only writer in this family, Victor, even though you may fancy you are."

The silence stretching between us felt interminable. As a devoted husband, I was the first to break it.

"I'm sorry I snooped in your notebook, darling," I said, full of remorse.

"And I shouldn't have wound you up about my writing. Of course I wouldn't do anything to steal your thunder, especially as you've made me so happy with your promise that we can renew our wedding vows," Marigold said. "Just pop the notebook in my bedside drawer to keep it safe from Catastrophe."

After another few minutes of chatter, we exchanged fond good-nights. Picking up Marigold's notebook, I carried it through to the bedroom. Whilst Marigold had rightly castigated me for invading her privacy by peeking inside, I recalled she had not been above doing the exact same thing herself. Marigold had not only pried by reading the first draft of my book but she gone too far by blackmailing Barry into shredding it because she didn't like the way I portrayed her. Unable to resist another peek, I flicked through Marigold's notebook again.

Such a lovely evening in the local taverna. The bank manager can be quite the charmer, so attentive!! I wish I could say the same about Victor. When we got home, I slipped into a new lacy negligee and Victor slipped into the kitchen!! He's been in there for over an hour disinfecting his rancid sponges!!!!! I wish he would show as much passion for me as he does for his obsession with hygiene!

Dropping the notebook like a hot potato, I realised that my unforgivable snooping proved one thing: there was truth in the old adage that one never reads anything good of oneself. It sounded as though Marigold was craving romance and I was too dunderheaded to see it.

All was not lost. Marigold would have the big romantic gesture she desired. I would drop all my arguments about renewing our vows and give Marigold a day to remember.

Chapter 25

Honorary Greeks

Throwing the French windows open, I stepped out onto the balcony with my coffee, bracing myself against the early morning chill as I sipped my aromatic brew. Bleak mist hovering over the sea on the horizon made for a foreboding vista and grey clouds skittering across the sky didn't bode well for the walk to the cave in Nektar. I hoped that we would be able to avoid a downpour. Shivering as the wind picked up, I reflected that at least a nice breeze would prevent us from getting overly sweaty on the walk.

Despite the early hour, the village was beginning to stir, olive pickers readying themselves for the work of the harvest. Nikos sped by on his moped, waving his olive combing rake to attract my attention because the sound of the moped's puttering drowned out his greeting. Tina had mentioned she may start opening the shop earlier than usual to cater to olive pickers fancying an early morning *raki* to warm their cockles before work. Personally, I was of the opinion that Tina should not be encouraging them to down strong alcohol before handling potentially lethal equipment such as chain saws and petrol powered olive shakers. The shopkeeper had simply brushed aside my well intentioned concerns about health and safety risks, demonstrating a very lax attitude towards such things.

Heading into the bathroom, the shower only managed to produce a stream of freezing cold water. Reluctant to shiver my timbers, I was forced to wait for the immersion heater to heat up the water in the tank. We had reached that time of year when sunshine was somewhat rationed and the solar panel didn't provide enough water for all our household needs: it was either a cold shower or hanging around in my pyjamas waiting on the immersion heater to do its thing. About to reach for my razor, I recalled my new resolve to grow a beard. The growth of day-old stubble struck me as so unsightly that I was tempted to lather up and scrape. The unkempt look wasn't really flattering on me, but with a bit of perseverance I hoped to have enough of a growth to keep my chin warm when I helped Dimitris with his olives. I must confess that going without a shave made me feel a tad daredevilish.

The untouched dishes my Greek neighbours had so generously delivered the previous evening reminded me it would be sensible to tuck into a hearty breakfast before engaging in a rigorous walk. Forgoing my usual muesli, I opted instead to breakfast on a large helping of Sampaguita's delicious pork adobo. Before I could heat it up, the cats started brushing up against my legs, their usual method of letting me know it was time to feed them. Instead of opening a tin, I spooned a generous measure of Athena's octopus and macaroni into their bowls, reflecting that if nothing happened to the cats, I could perhaps sample the dish myself at lunchtime. Whilst Catastrophe and Clawsome tucked in with apparent gusto, Pickles turned up his more discerning nose, holding out for a tin of sardines.

With the pampered cats catered to, my thoughts turned once again to my own repast. Fancying the Filipino dish would be rounded off nicely with the addition of a couple of fried eggs, I threw an overcoat over my pyjamas and headed down to the chicken coop to gather some newly laid eggs. Fortunately, Guzim was just emerging from the hen house holding a handful of eggs, the odd feather still clinging to their shells. I was relieved to be saved the bother of poking around beneath the chickens' bottoms.

"*Gia ti mitera sou.*" Handing the eggs over, Guzim said they were for my mother.

"*Gia mena,*" I contradicted, saying they were for me.

I couldn't help noting that Guzim looked even scruffier than usual, having apparently stopped shaving along with showering. Noticing that I was staring at his stubbly chin, Guzim ran a hand over the growth, commenting that we were both growing beards, "*Kai oi dyo mega-lonoume geneiades.*"

About to retort that at least I hadn't given

up on washing, I remembered I had yet to complete my own ablutions. I supposed that with my pyjamas trousers flapping around beneath my overcoat, I looked as dissolute as the Albanian shed dweller. At least Guzim was fully clothed. Sporting the brightly knitted Christmas pullover featuring the slogan 'Jingle', complete with immodestly placed bells, he would be hard to miss in the olive groves. Barry would no doubt be delighted that someone was finally getting some wear out of his rejected Christmas offering. The rather bizarre thought occurred to me that if Guzim actually jingled, any passing goats may confuse him with one of their own.

"*Pao sti douleia tora,*" Guzim said, telling me he was going to work now. Despite announcing he was off to work, Guzim demonstrated no great eagerness to be on his way, instead launching into a lengthy and guttural complaint about Nikos' slave driving tendencies. As best as I could follow, he complained that all day it was an endless litany of 'put the nets down, rake the tree, prune the branch, on and on': "*Oli mera. Valte ta dichtya kato, tsounkraste to dentro, kladepste to kladi, synechos.*" I was certainly glad that I had managed to avoid doing the harvest under such a hard taskmaster as Nikos, preferring to offer my services to Dimitris for a couple of hours. I certainly couldn't imagine Dimitris barking orders.

Finally, after seemingly venting all his complaints, Guzim repeated his assertion that he was off to work, "*Pao sti douleia tora*," before scuttling off through my garden. Returning inside, I discovered that a couple of fried eggs are indeed a satisfying accompaniment to pork adobo.

Arriving at the village square to meet Gordon, I was delighted to see that he was as punctilious about timekeeping as I am: I do so abhor tardiness. Gordon was equipped with a bulky rucksack which he assured me was packed with every essential for any emergency, a rather ridiculous precaution in my opinion since we were only walking to the outskirts of the next village. Breaking into a brisk stride, we set off on our walk. Our plan was to start off by following the road towards Nektar and then take a shortcut on a dirt track meandering through the hills.

We had only just turned onto the track leading to the cave when we ran into Litsa, the elderly widow being out and about collecting *horta*. Exchanging the usual greetings, I introduced Gordon, telling Litsa that he and his wife were buying Leo's house. With the pleasantries out of the way, Litsa adopted an accusatory tone, saying, *"Akousa sto katastima oti tha didaxeis Ellinki mageiriki."*

Not wanting Gordon to feel left out of the conversation, I duly told him that Litsa had heard in the shop that I was going to be teaching Greek cooking. Assuring Litsa that she had heard correctly, I was unprepared for the sweet old dear to take offence, apparently outraged that an Englishman should dare to presume to teach Greek cooking.

"Prepei na to didasko, ochi esy," Litsa said, telling me she should be teaching it, not me.

"Alla didasko Anglikous anthropous pou den katalavainoun Ellinka," I said in my own defence, telling her I was teaching English people who didn't understand Greek.

"Ematha na mageirevo apo tin Elliniki giagia mou. Boreis na peis to idio?" she said, telling me she learnt to cook from her Greek grandma before demanding to know if I could say the same.

"Den eicha Ellinida giagia." I admitted I didn't have a Greek granny. Litsa's anger faded as quickly as it had flared up, her wrinkled face

creasing in sympathy.

"*Esy ftocho agori,*" she said, calling me a poor boy, presumably because I had not been blessed with a Greek granny.

In faltering and ungrammatical Greek, I explained to Litsa that I only discovered cooking late in life, having not had the advantage of learning to cook at the knee of a Greek granny. I told her that moving to Meli had opened my eyes to the wonderful fresh ingredients available to me in Greece and how I had enjoyed experimenting with such fine produce as I learned to perfect authentic Greek dishes. Now, I hoped to pass on my love for Greek cooking to some fellow Brits who were somewhat challenged all round in the cooking department. Litsa openly gasped when I confided that many of them ate tinned food rather than fresh because they didn't know how to cook properly. "*Polloi apo aftous trone konservopolimena trofima kai ochi freska epeidi den xeroun na mageirevoun.*"

"*Sta alitheia?*" Lowering her voice to a whisper, Litsa asked me if it was true.

"*Nai, einai alitheia.*" I confirmed it was true before dropping a real shocker on the old lady, telling her some of them even ate pies out of tins, "*Merika apo afta trone pites apo metallika koutia.*"

Naturally I didn't admit that I had once been in the habit of indulging in such a deplorable practice myself; in fact I would have indulged only the day before if Marigold hadn't pre-empted me by hauling my stash of Fray Bentos downstairs and transplanting them into Violet Burke's daffodil cupboards.

Mention of my imminent cookery classes prompted Gordon to ask if he and Moira could join us, saying it would be a wonderful opportunity to meet some of the other expats in the village.

"I prefer to think of myself as a European citizen with Greek residency," I said.

"*Ti les*?" Maria asked what I was saying.

"*Eimai Evropaios politis me Elliniki katoikia*," I duly translated.

"*Esy kai Barry eisai Ellinas gia mena. Den tha xechaso pote pos irthes sto nosokomeio otan Imoun arrostos. Toso kala agoria, ta kalytera.*" I fumbled in my pocket for a clean handkerchief, Litsa's words bringing a sentimental tear to my eye.

"What did she say?" Gordon asked.

"She said that me and Barry are Greek to her. She will never forget how we went to the hospital when she was ill. She says we are such good boys, the best."

Litsa loved to regale everyone with tales of how two foreigners had visited her hospital bedside after her fall. No doubt she thought the mention of foreigners sounded more impressive when she recounted the tale, but between ourselves she saw us as honorary Greeks

After bidding good morning to Litsa, we continued on our way, maintaining a brisk pace since the wind was picking up. Gordon continually marvelled at anything that caught his eye. He stopped to appreciate the fuzzy smooth texture of a sage leaf on a wild bush and to admire the myriad colours of olives resembling a selection of glassy marbles, their hues ranging from palest to darkest green, from pink to red and purple to black. Whilst by no means an expert, I attempted to tutor Gordon in the difference between eating olives and the variety cultivated for oil. Clueless that olives were essentially inedible directly from the tree, he learned the hard way by eagerly biting into one, only to spit it out in disgust.

"It takes forty days of curing for an eating olive to become edible," I explained, while Gordon paused to ransack his rucksack.

"This should take the horrid taste away," he said, triumphantly brandishing a bar of Kendal

Mint Cake. "Fancy a bit?" he offered.

"I don't mind if I do."

We kept up a steady stream of chatter as we walked, Gordon eager to discuss his plans for the house once the pesky legal formalities were out of the way. Our speed increased when it began to spit: we hoped to reach the shelter of the cave before the heavens opened. Worried about the house being empty whilst he and Moira were back in England, Gordon was keen to fix security bars on the outside of the windows and install an alarm system. Fortunately he was willing to take my recommendation that Barry and his partner Vangelis would be up to the task, not that Barry deserved my putting work his way after pointedly excluding me from the romantic evening round at his place. My brother-in-law is well acquainted with my weakness for hot roasted chestnuts dipped in salt.

I talked Gordon through what to expect when we visited the lawyer and notary the following week to sort out the legalities, as well as giving him the lowdown on opening a Greek bank account and sorting out a residency permit, an essential requirement if they intended to purchase a car.

"Moira's main worry is ensuring that

Waffles is legal to travel?" Gordon said. His re-mark left me rather flummoxed until I recalled that Waffles was their goldendoodle.

"I'm afraid I can't offer any advice there," I admitted. "We brought cats over with us and I expect they may be a completely different kettle of fish to transport."

"How did you bring them over?"

"We drove through Europe and took the ferry to Patras."

"I don't think Waffles would enjoy being cooped up in a car for such a long journey. We'll probably fly him over," Gordon said. Being cooped up in a cage in the hold of a plane struck me as being a sight more traumatic than being cooped up in a car with an opportunity to stretch its legs at toilet stops, but I wisely kept my own counsel. "He'd certainly enjoy this walk, though. Waffles is really going to love ex-ploring the Greek countryside."

"I would think you'll discover all manner of tracks off the beaten path with a dog to walk," I said.

"You aren't tempted?" Gordon asked.

"I don't think the cats would tolerate living with a canine."

"I don't really see the attraction. Of cats, I

mean," Gordon said dismissively. "I suppose they're handy if there are mice about, keep them under control and all that. Have you found your cats are useful for that?"

"I'm afraid Marigold's pampered imported domestics are much too fat and lazy to chase after mice. I suppose they might manage to flatten one if they sat on it, but that's the most I could expect. I plugged some sonic devices in to keep any vermin away, mind you, the first lot I bought played havoc with my neighbour's hearing aid."

"And you can't even put them on a lead and take them for walks," Gordon commented.

"Sonic devices," I quipped.

"No, cats," Gordon chortled.

"Well, ours are too fat to manage any great distance," I pointed out.

"Moira would never give a cat houseroom, she isn't really a cat person," Gordon sighed. "They never used to bother her until she had a photo shoot with a Turkish Angora and it gave her a nasty dose of ringworm."

"Zoonotic dermatophytes can be very contagious," I said.

"What?"

"The fungi that cause ringworm. It can be a

rampant little mite," I explained.

"It gave Moira a really nasty rash. She had an outbreak on her neck, just under her ear: she had to cancel a modelling job on account of it. When the doctor diagnosed her with ringworm she nearly passed out, she thought she had actual worms. I think that's what gave her an unnatural fear of cats."

"Ailurophobia," I said, citing the specific phobia. "Still, a good anti-fungal topical cream should have cleared it up."

"No, she's still paranoid she'll pick it up again from any random cat," Gordon said.

"I meant that the cream should have cleared up the ringworm, not her fear of cats. Actual phobias are a tad harder to cure than a nasty rash."

"I suppose I'll have to keep a lookout for anything prickly in the undergrowth round here to make sure nothing gives Waffles a rash..." Gordon's sentence tailed off and he grabbed my arm. "Is that the mouth, there behind those trees?"

"I do believe it is," I said, catching sight of the cave.

Chapter 26

Victor has a Tippi Hedren Moment

Victor. Is that you?" The echo of Gordon's voice made it difficult to pinpoint his exact location within the cave. A note of revulsion crept into his voice as he asked, "Is that your shoulder?"

"Is what my shoulder?" I replied

"Whatever I've just put my hand on. It's quite firm and warm."

My hands shot up to my shoulders in an automatic reflex as though expecting to encounter a clammy hand. I couldn't feel anything except the beeswax finish of my waxed jacket.

"No hands on any part of my anatomy," I clarified, having hastily checked the rest of my person for Gordon's hands.

"Well, if it isn't you, what is it? Pufft, whatever it is doesn't half have bad breath."

"Mine's minty fresh from the Kendal Mint Cake," I pointed out.

I tried not to imagine what type of creature could be lurking in the dank darkness with a bad case of halitosis. "Try and make your way over to my voice," I advised.

"Hard to tell where it's coming from with that blasted echo," Gordon's voice echoed.

My walking companion had given me every assurance that he was prepared for any eventuality, having stuffed his rucksack with everything we could possibly need for a walk in the hills. However, he had neglected to ensure his flashlight was equipped with a battery with sufficient juice. Having reached the mouth of the cave, we had boldly ventured in, Gordon's torch illuminating the dark interior, allowing us to bravely go where no man had gone before. We had squelched through the rank mud underfoot, which I rather suspected may have been carpeted in cowpats, only for the flashlight to give up the ghost once we had ventured deep into the interior. In the ensuing panic, the two of us became separated, making me wish that we'd had the foresight to rope ourselves together or at least skip through the cave holding hands.

Aside from the dreadful smell which I again attributed to the multitude of cow pats, I could sense living creatures above us, most likely bats. No doubt the mess beneath our feet was deep in bat droppings in addition to cowpats. The torch, before it had died, had highlighted the wisdom of keeping our distance from the interior walls of the cave. They were thick with spiders of the enormous variety, the type of eight-legged arthropods one only expects to encounter in the props department of a low-budget horror film rather than in real life. Gordon had advised against shining the torch at the ceiling in case it disturbed any roosting bats hanging around upside down. Despite not having seen any evidence of bats, visual images of them flooded my mind, unnerving me.

"I'm not too keen on the thought of bats," I admitted in a tremulous voice. "It's one thing watching them put on a romantic display when they fly over Barry's ecological pond at dusk, it's quite another to be trapped in the dark with flying rats.

"Bats aren't related to rats. They're more likely related to flying lemurs..."

"Never heard of flying lemurs in Greece," I said.

"No, they're more commonly found in the Philippines..."

"I must ask Sampaguita if she's familiar with them."

Gordon's voice sounded a tad closer the next time he spoke but it may just have been wishful thinking on the part of my nerves. "I'm pretty sure that bats hibernate at this time of year."

"In a nice dark place like a cave," I suggested. "Suppose we've disturbed them. One moment we were enjoying a pleasant outing exploring a natural phenomenon and the next we're starring in an Alfred Hitchcock movie."

"Fancy yourself as Tippi Hedren in 'The Birds,' do you Victor? You haven't got the figure for it," Gordon chortled. "I don't think you need to worry about being attacked by gulls so far up from the coast."

"I'm not worried about gulls, I'm worried about bats," I admitted, attempting to control the hysteria creeping into my voice. Marigold had been onto something when she'd refused to venture into the cave, terrified that bats would try to mate with her hair. Whilst my own hair isn't nearly as thick and luscious as Marigold's, I still have enough of it for a handful of bats to get tangled up in.

"Do Greek bats carry rabies?" Gordon asked.

"I don't think we should hang around in here long enough to find out," I replied, recalling that I had read some dreary paper on the advisability of being vaccinated as a precaution against picking up rabies from infected bats if one intended to get up close and personal with the creatures in their natural habitat. Of course, I had never intended any such thing prior to Gordon's stupid suggestion that we go walkabouts in a bat infested cave.

"*Yparchei kaneis mesa*?" a hearty voice boomed through the darkness, asking if anyone was inside.

"*Edo. Voitheia parakalo*," I shouted back, saying "Here. Help please."

Gordon's voice joined mine, yelling, "Help, help."

A glimmer of light appeared, becoming brighter as the beam approached. A short stocky figure emerged from the gloom.

"*Voitheia. Den boroume na vroume ti diexodo, o fakos pethane,*" I cried, asking the figure for help and telling him we couldn't find our way out as the torch had died.

"You English?" the figure replied. "Speak English, you Greek not good."

Deciding this was not the moment to take offence at my competence in the Greek language being insulted, I swallowed my pride, begging, "Please show us the way out."

The man flashed his light around the cave, revealing Gordon to be less than six feet away from me, his hand resting on a cow lying down in the muck.

"I see you to come inside but not to come out," the stocky figure said.

"We couldn't find the way back to the mouth," Gordon explained, edging away from the mud-smeared bovine with halitosis.

"*Ela*, follow me," the man said, herding the cow at such a quick pace that the pair of us struggled to keep up with him.

It turned out that we didn't have far too squelch to reach the opening; in fact, if we had simply felt our way out by touching the spider infested wall we would have discovered we only needed to take about thirty paces. We had only been lost because the route we had taken curved away from the natural light. Still, if we had groped our way by feeling the wall we might have gone in the wrong direction and ended up stranded even further inside.

Although we had been desperate to find our way out of the dank, dung carpeted cave filled with bats ridden with rabies and spiders the size of saucers, we hesitated in the mouth, reluctant to step out into the torrential downpour and gale-force wind At least the weather explained why the cow had been lying down.

"I keep the cow inside." The man's explanation was self-evident.

"Well, thank you for guiding us out," I said. In the grey light of day, the man's weather-beaten face hinted he was long past pension age. I wondered if cow herder's had the same rugged hermit lifestyle as shepherds of yore, settling in a hut high in the mountains where they lived on a diet of bread, cheese and salt, tending the animals and rarely seeing another human face.

Peering at me intently beneath his flat cap, the cow herder said, "You the English with the wife leave you, yes."

"That will be me," I said, striding off in the

rain, marvelling at the distance Greek gossip could travel when a remote cow herder I had never set eyes on before apparently knew my business.

"Victor, slow down," Gordon called out. "There's a bat hanging off the back of your jacket."

I mentally composed a letter of complaint to the manufacturer of the supposedly waterproof waxed jacket as we made our way back to civilisation, soaked to the skin. The wind whipping my face made me wish I had started cultivating my beard a few days earlier, my paltry growth of stubble proving inadequate as a chin warmer. Traipsing past the field housing Giannis' colourful bee boxes, I remembered he had a pile of chopped wood waiting for me. I was in no mood to attempt to carry the equivalent of a wet tree all the way home.

Gordon appeared as downcast and dejected as I, but looks can be deceptive. "What an experience," he gushed as though it had been in some way enjoyable.

"Got any of that Kendal Mint Cake left?" I asked, my waterlogged walking boots making me flag.

"I think the rain's letting up," Gordon observed as we took a breather to munch on the mint cake. "Nice chap, that fellow with the cow. We could have been stuck in that cave for days if he hadn't come along."

"I'm sure they would have sent out a search party eventually," I said, sure of no such thing.

"The sun's coming out, it should help to dry us off," Gordon grinned. He really did appear to be the eternal optimist.

"It's a pity you didn't stuff a portable hairdryer in your rucksack," I said, thinking the sun would do little to dry my soggy socks.

"Would you look at that, Victor?" There was a note of awe in Gordon's voice. Presuming he'd been impressed with some sort of greenery he'd never encountered before, I reluctantly turned to follow his gaze, instantly wowed by the colourful display. A glorious rainbow arced from the shimmering sea in the distance, disappearing into the brooding greyness of Taygetos behind us, its radiance instantly thawing my grumpy mood.

"Wow."

"It's a sign, Victor."

"A sign of what?"

"The arch of a rainbow symbolises a portal.

It's a sign that buying that house represents a new opening in our lives."

I nodded sagely. Just because Gordon was spouting a load of superstitious twaddle didn't detract from the magnificence of nature's kaleidoscope.

Chapter 27

Beef and Olives

A bag of roasted chestnuts and a hot shower restored my good mood following the disastrous walk. Barry and Vangelis had popped up to town for some building supplies earlier and, thinking of me, Barry had snapped up a bag of the sweet flavourful nuts from a street vendor. I was quite touched by my brother-in-law's thoughtful gesture, knowing it was his way of apologising for excluding me from his romantic evening. By way of a thank you, I presented him with the pan of stinking tripe soup.

With my first cookery class about to commence at any moment, I surveyed the kitchen to check that everything was in readiness. I had placed sufficient chairs to seat all my pupils in a line facing a blackboard, temporarily concealed beneath a tablecloth. Whilst my initial thought had been to hide the food my neighbours had delivered the previous evening, perhaps stashing it under the bed in the guest bedroom, I instead decided to artfully display it in the hope it would convey the impression I was forever turning out classic Greek dishes. By leaving the selection of Greek meals lying around, I hoped my pupils would naturally assume, *'Here's one that Victor made earlier.'*

Since my students were all familiar with each other, it briefly crossed my mind to wonder if I had gone just a tad overboard in making them individual name badges. However, with Gordon and Moira as late sign-ups to the course, the badges would prove very handy since the Stranges were strangers to the others. I was particularly grateful that Gordon would be joining the ranks since Doreen had mentioned that Norman worried that he may stick out like a sore thumb, being the only man amidst a sea of aprons. I had assured Doreen that everyone would be in a pinny, no exceptions, aprons providing an essential barrier to prevent any contaminants from one's clothing jumping into the food.

Adjusting my hairnet, I answered the door, wondering which of my students was so eager that they felt the need to turn up ten minutes early. Surprised to find Dimitris on my doorstep, I considered my friend's arrival inconvenient since I would need to get rid of him in short order. I had no time to entertain random visitors with a class to conduct.

"Victor, I hear you are beginning classes," Dimitris said. "Can I join them?"

"I'm not running language classes, Dimitri, but cooking classes."

"Yes, I hear. But my cooking is not inspired. I cook most days the same pork *souvlaki*."

"That does sound a tad tedious," I agreed. Knowing that Dimitris rarely dined at the taverna, I imagined a continual diet of pork *souvlaki* must get very repetitive. "Surely you have something else in your repertoire?"

"Sometimes I cook the chicken *souvlaki* if the butcher has skewer it."

"I'm not sure I feel confident teaching Greek

cookery to a Greek," I prevaricated. "All of the people that have signed up are Brits."

"That is good, it will help me to improve my conversational English to mix with your British," Dimitris said.

I couldn't help but notice that Dimitris' skill in the English language had already come on in leaps and bounds in the almost two years we had been meeting to help each other out with the other's language. Not only had his mastery of English vocabulary grown extensively but he only peppered his sentences with occasional superfluous articles and rarely confused his genders. His proficiency in English far exceeded my own in Greek: I wasn't sure if that indicated I was the superior teacher of the more inept pupil.

Since Dimitris had the cash on him to pay for the class and didn't embarrass me by asking for credit, I welcomed him into the fold. This was after all a business venture and who knew, if it took off, I could perhaps market it as a franchise operation throughout Greece, or at least in the areas frequented by culinary challenged expats.

With Dimitris duly pinned up in a nice floral number, I took my place at the door, ticking my students off the register as they arrived: the Stranges, Doreen and Norman, Cynthia, Sherry and Milton. Standing there with my register attached to a clipboard reminded me of welcoming the holidaymakers as they tripped down the gangplank onto Pegasus. Smiling to myself at the comparison, I had to suppress the impulse to greet my pupils with a bombastic, "Beautiful towel."

"Edna is knee-deep in housework so she sent me along, what," Milton said, explaining why he had taken his wife's allotted place for the first class. "Got it in her head for some reason that the old house is filthy, what."

I imagined that my mother's words had hit home and Edna had been shamed into giving the house a good bottoming rather than her usual inadequate tickling with a feather duster. Still, it was most inconvenient since I hadn't made Milton a name badge.

"You'll have to wear Edna's name badge," I insisted.

"I can live with that, old chap." Lowering his voice, Milton whispered, "After all, I already answer to Scarlett."

As I introduced the Stranges to the others, I overheard a few muttered comments about them appearing perfectly normal with nothing apparently strange about them. All of my students engaged in a spot of juvenile humour, addressing Milton as Edna because of the name badge: still, Milton took it all in remarkable good humour. A couple of my students appeared a tad uneasy to find an actual Greek in our midst, apparently unfamiliar with Dimitris despite passing his doorway most days. There was an air of palpable relief when Dimitris told the British contingent that he was keen to practice his English, assuring them that they would be under no obligation to reciprocate with their non-existent Greek.

Sherry, as thick skinned as ever, sidled up to me, showing not a trace of embarrassment over throwing herself at me the previous evening. "Jolly good of you to round up a single fellow for me, Victor," Sherry brayed.

"What?"

"The Greek. He is single, isn't he?" Sherry said with a predatory gleam in her eye. Exposing her horsey dentures, she proclaimed, "He must be. No self-respecting wife would allow her husband out in public with that dated hairstyle. I can soon get him tidied up though."

Marching towards her prey, Sherry

adjusted her bosom before rudely elbowing Cynthia out of the way in order to bag the seat next to Dimitris. Noticing that my students were chattering between themselves, I utilised my repping whistle to bring the class to order.

"Welcome, one and all, to the first of my cookery classes where I will teach you the basics of Greek cooking, known in Greek as *Elliniki kouzina*. During each class, I will focus on an individual dish to ensure that you are competent enough to replicate it in your own kitchens. Since I am aware that you each have different levels of skill, ranging from complete novices in the kitchen..." I pointedly looked at Norman and Milton, aware that they found the simple task of boiling an egg a challenge too far..."whilst others amongst you are up on the basics but struggle to turn out anything resembling cordon bleu, I will initially focus on one pot dishes."

"I thought you were going to teach us how to make Greek food," Doreen piped up.

Irritated by the interruption, I responded, "Please raise your hand if you have any questions."

Sticking her arm in the air, Doreen repeated her question.

"And wait for me to call your name before speaking," I added. Subjecting Doreen to a withering look, I clarified, "I will be demonstrating one pot Greek dishes to start with. As the cold nights draw in, there is nothing more satisfying than a hearty Greek stew."

"It's such a jolly good idea to focus on one pot dishes. If the water goes off, there will only be one pot to wash in the water we have to bucket over from the village tap," Sherry said.

"I didn't see your hand go up, Sherry," I scolded.

"Oops, I forgot," she brayed, nudging Dimitris. The Greek man responded by edging away, leaving him precariously balanced on one buttock. I fancied his uncomfortable expression was a reaction to Sherry rather than anything to do with his awkward position.

"I thought it would be rather useful if I give the ingredients their Greek names to help you all become more familiar with the words when you head out with your shopping lists," I proposed. "Since we all live in Greece and are cooking Greek food, we really ought to make an effort to pick up a bit of the lingo."

"Spiffing idea, what," Milton said before belatedly raising his hand. Overlooking his interruption, I continued.

"And of course, now that Dimitris has joined our numbers, we can be confident that we will pronounce our *systatika* correctly."

"Sys what?" Norman interrupted.

"*Systatika*. It is the Greek word for ingredients," I clarified.

"Yes, Dimitris," I said in response to his raised hand.

"The accent go on the last syllable, not the first. It is pronounced *systatika*."

"Goes, the accent goes," I corrected Dimitris, smarting from his correction of my ingredients. I reflected that perchance I been had a tad rash allowing him to attend if he was going to deliberately undermine my authority.

"Now, I cannot overemphasise enough the importance of maintaining scrupulous standards of kitchen hygiene at all times," I continued with my well-rehearsed spiel. "I don't wish to see any cutting of corners: that means no skimping on thoroughly sanitising your sponges. Remember, bacterium love nothing more than the opportunity to breed on a soggy sponge; it is up to you to ensure there will no procreating bacteria under your watch."

My spiel was interrupted by Sherry giving

in to a fit of the giggles. Under my withering stare, she attempted to pull herself together.

"Sorry, Victor. It's just the thought of pro-creating bacteria," she hiccupped.

"Which is no laughing matter, Sherry," I scolded, resisting the urge to send her to stand in the dunce's corner.

"Now, to continue with the rules pertaining to hygiene. No using the tea towels to mop sweaty brows; paper towels are provided for that purpose. And absolutely no surreptitious use of any ingredients that have been dropped on the floor. It doesn't matter how quickly you retrieve it, the salmonella bug can attach itself in a jiffy and before you know it you'll be down with a nasty case of the vomiting trots."

"Yes, Edna," I said, acknowledging Milton's interruption since he had remembered to raise his hand. Since it appeared that Milton intended to make a regular nuisance of himself by inter-rupting with endless questions, I hoped that by addressing him with the name on his badge he might be shamed into shutting his trap. Despite happily answering to Scarlett, Milton decided to throw a strop.

"I say, old chap, you know full well that I'm Milton."

"Not according to your name badge," Doreen reminded him.

"I didn't see your hand go up, Doreen," I admonished.

"Sorry."

"Milton, you had a question," I reminded him.

"Is it okay to use any food we may have dropped in the sink, old chap, or is that as out of bounds as the floor?"

"Only if you like the taste of bleach," Cynthia interrupted. "I can't remember the amount of times that Victor has nagged me about the importance of always bleaching the sink after every use."

"Not everyone maintains such rigorous standards, Cynthia," I pointed out. "Milton could pick up something nasty from cross-contamination if he uses food he has dropped in an unbleached sink."

"Edna never bleaches ours because of the cats," Milton volunteered.

"If Edna is worried about using harsh chemicals around the cats, she could perhaps clean the sink with lemon juice and vinegar. Bicarbonate of soda is useful for stubborn stains," I advised.

"I'm so glad that we've decided to ask Violet Burke to do the cleaning," Moira said. "I never realised how many germs lurked in the kitchen."

"I used to believe that it would boost little Anastasia's immune system to expose her to the odd kitchen germ, but then Victor explained that there was no substantial evidence to back up the theory..." Cynthia said.

"Cynthia is referring to the scientifically debunked 'hygiene hypothesis,'" I explained. "Anastasia will be exposed to plenty of germs during everyday life without deliberately introducing her to the bacterial nasties that procreate in a filthy kitchen. Now, always clean up your work area as you go along, there's nothing worse than trying to work in a mess."

"I can't see Norman getting the hang of that, the kitchen looks like a bomb's hit if he so much as makes a sandwich..." Doreen interrupted.

"You can talk. Your idea of cleaning up after one of your dinner parties is giving the plates to the cat to lick," Norman retorted. I began to question the wisdom of allowing married couples to attend the classes together. I ought to have charged them extra if I was expected to monitor their petty bickering.

"I didn't see any hands shoot up," I chided.

"Sorry," Doreen and Norman said in unison.

"Keeping your work area clean naturally extends to immediately cleaning up any spills. This is not only an important rule for ensuring cleanliness but also as a safety precaution. One could easily go flying if a spillage of olive oil is not immediately mopped up."

As I spoke, I was gratified to notice that Gordon was hastily scribbling notes, clearly appreciative of my invaluable advice. It was not every day that mere laymen had the benefit of picking up vital tips shared by a retired public health inspector with a wealth of practical experience.

"Yes, Cynthia," I said, wishing she wouldn't roll her eyes so dramatically.

"Are we ever going to get round to the actual business of cooking?" she asked. Noticing several of my students looked a tad impatient, I decided to cut short my hygiene lecture and get down to brass tacks.

"Indeed. I am just about to begin demonstrating the dish of the day," I said.

"About time," Cynthia muttered impatiently.

"Today we will be learning how to prepare beef casserole with olives, or *vodino katsaroles me elies,* as it is referred to in Greek," I said.

"I say, old chap, that sounds awfully tasty," Milton enthused.

"It goes without saying that the two main ingredients are beef and olives, though there are other ingredients to include in the pot. Now, don't just select any old olives, use Kalamata olives..."

"Do we have to go all the way to Kalamata to get them? Bit tricky without a car, what," Milton interrupted.

"No, the name refers to the variety of olives grown throughout the region. You can buy Kalamata olives locally. I can recommend the ones that Tina stocks loose in barrels in the shop."

"We have an olive tree in the garden. Can I just pick the olives from that for this recipe?" Doreen asked.

"No, Doreen. The recipe requires cured olives..."

"Ours look healthy enough..." Norman interrupted.

"Curing refers to the process of turning olives edible. I learnt that from Victor this morning," Gordon piped up proudly. I got the distinct impression he was hoping to win the role of teacher's pet. Whilst I appreciated his enthusiasm, I was determined not to single out any favourites.

"Perhaps we could dedicate some time in a future class to the preparation of eating olives," I suggested. "For today though, we are concentrating on beef with olives. Now, when selecting the stewing beef for this dish, I recommend that you ask for *pontiki vodino*."

"But a *pontiki* is a mouse..." Cynthia gasped in horror.

"I'm not cooking any mice," Doreen screeched. "I don't care if the Greeks eat them, it's disgusting."

"We Greeks do not eat the mouse," Dimitris insisted, bristling with indignation at the very suggestion.

"*Pontiki* refers to the cut of beef, it has nothing to do with mice," I clarified to everyone's great relief. "The particular cut has a good marbling of fat which adds to the flavour when the meat is stewed."

"Sorry, Victor, I didn't realise," Cynthia apologised.

"I could hardly expect you to be familiar

with the different cuts since I know that you rarely cook from scratch," I said to my sister-in-law.

"I cook from scratch all the time," Cynthia objected. "Only the other day, I made toad-in-the-hole."

"And I have it on good authority that you used jars of mechanically processed wieners from Lidl. I very much doubt that an actual sausage went anywhere near your toad dish," I snapped.

"Says the man who isn't above throwing a Fray Bentos in the oven," Cynthia retorted, adding, "Barry and his big mouth. Is there anything he doesn't tell you?"

"Moving on," I hastily continued. "Before we commence cooking, we must assemble all our ingredients together to make sure we haven't overlooked anything. Only a disorganised cook has to dash to the shop for a forgotten ingredient in the middle of meal preparation. So, in addition to beef and olives, this particular recipe calls for quite a few other things."

Moving across the kitchen, I unveiled the blackboard. I couldn't help but notice my students collectively slumped at the sight of all the foreign words which I had chalked up earlier.

"I have written the full list of ingredients on this blackboard, with the Greek translation of each word next to it. Running down the list we have onions *kremmydia*, garlic *skordo*, olive oil *elaiolado*, canned tomatoes *konservopoilmenes ntomates*, a lemon *ena lemoni*...yes, Doreen."

"Can I use a lemon from my tree or does it need curing first? Doreen asked.

"A very pertinent question, Doreen. A lemon from your tree is perfectly fine and you may also use any of the herbs I will reference if you grow them in your garden. This recipe calls for bay leaves *fylla dafnis* and rosemary *dendrolivano*. Last but not least, a drop of red wine *krassi kokkino*, a dash of balsamic vinegar *valsamiko xydi*, and a seasoning of salt and pepper *alati kai piperi*. No need to write everything down, I have prepared a list of the ingredients for each of you to take home with you."

"You might have mentioned that in the first place," Gordon complained, shaking his cramped writing hand.

"Do me and Doreen get a list each or just one between us?" Norman queried.

"One each, of course," I confirmed. There was no need for me to scrimp on the photocopies since both Norman and his wife had paid their dues to attend, unlike Milton and Edna who were taking it in turns.

"Yes, Doreen," I said wearily, my efforts to ignore her raised hand futile when she started to flap it around.

"Could I have a quiet word please, Victor?"

"If you must," I said. Addressing the rest of my pupils, I advised them to try sounding out the Greek words, pointing out that I had written them in transliteration rather than using Greek lettering which would likely confuse them.

Dragging me out onto the balcony, Doreen hissed, "You promised you wouldn't put temptation in Norman's way but the recipe calls for wine."

"Well, it will be up to you to ensure he doesn't take a tipple from the bottle, Doreen, but I can assure you that the cooking process kills off any alcohol in the wine whilst adding flavour. Of course, you could always omit the wine entirely but the casserole will lose some of the rich flavour it adds."

"It should be okay if the cooking kills it," Doreen conceded.

"I can assure you that Norman won't get drunk from eating the casserole."

Returning to the kitchen, I continued the

lesson. "Now, let the cooking commence. Firstly, we need to sear the cubes of beef in olive oil…"

"I say, old chap, did the meat come ready cubed?" Milton interjected.

"Yes indeed, I asked Tina to cut it into pieces when I ordered it."

"I don't know how to ask for the meat to be cut up in Greek," Doreen complained.

"Tina understands English," I pointed out.

"Well, what if she's not in the shop? It might be that woman with the unpronounceable name who keeps dashing off to the loo. I fancy cooking this stew for our Sunday dinner."

"I will be manning the shop on Sunday," I said. Realising I had no desire to chop meat when next on duty, I added, "It will be good for your all round kitchen skills to practice cutting the meat yourself at home."

"I'd like to know how to ask for meat to be cut in Greek," Gordon piped up.

"Certainly. You would say *kopste to kreas, se parakalo*."

"And what does that mean?" Norman asked.

"Cut the meat, please." I replied, wondering if my pupils were collectively dense.

"Now, gather round whilst I sear the meat," I invited as I began to demonstrate the searing process. "Whilst the meat is browning, we need to slice the onions."

As I deftly peeled the onions and began slicing, I was interrupted by Violet Burke barging in, her intrusion reminding me that I had yet to have a discussion with her about establishing boundaries.

"Please excuse me while I speak to my mother…"

"Would you like me to take over slicing the onions?" Moira offered.

"That would be excellent, thank you," I accepted.

"Mother, I am in the middle of teaching a class. You can't just barge in like that," I said steering Violet Burke back towards the front door.

"I know you've got class, that's why I popped up. To see if any of them expats are in need of a cleaner," Vi replied, solidly resisting my attempt to steer her out.

"This is not a convenient time, Mother."

"Here, Victor, you've got a bit of bum fluff on your chin." Leaning in, my mother yanked out a couple of the hairs that I was painstakingly cultivating on my chin.

"It's called a beard, Mother."

"Oh, I can't see you with a beard, Victor. The scruffy look isn't you. You always have such a neat way of presenting yourself, nice and clean shaven. Now, how about I just put the kettle on…"

"I'm in the middle of teaching my class…"

"And make a nice cuppa. I'll sit quietly and you can send me a signal when you're having a break and then I'll bring up the cleaning."

"Very well, Mother," I reluctantly agreed as she followed me into the kitchen. "I think most of you are acquainted with my mother, Violet Burke. She's just going to be quietly observing."

"Unless you need a few tips on how to fry chips proper," Vi interrupted.

"We aren't cooking chips, Mother," I said with a withering look.

Amazingly, Violet Burke managed to sit quietly slurping her tea while I went through the next crucial steps of preparing the stew, though Milton's concentration had gone all to pot with my mother's arrival. Apart from Milton, everyone else appeared attentive as I combined all the ingredients in the casserole dish before popping it into the oven."

"You forgot the olives," Gordon said.

"We add the olives about half-an-hour before the casserole is ready. They'll turn a tad soggy if we add them too soon. Now, any more questions?"

Before any of my students had the chance to raise their hands, the telephone rang.

"Sorry about this, I'll try and get rid of whoever it is quickly," I assured my pupils as I answered the phone to *Kapetainos* Vasos. He was calling to see if I fancied a debauched night on the town, carousing and picking up women.

"*Ochi efcharisto, Vaso,*" I declined, adding debauched nights out weren't really my cup of tea.

"Is that the Captain? Victor, tell him to come round to mine one night and I'll cook him a nice spotted dick," Violet Burke shouted out, accompanying her words with a meaningful wink.

Struggling to keep a straight face, I proffered her invitation to Vasos, saying, "*Vaso, i mitera mou leei an tin episkeftheis tha sou mageirepsei chartopetsetes.*"

Vasos, delighted, confirmed he would visit soon. I duly sent my mother a thumbs up accompanied by a wink.

"Victor, really," Cynthia called out. "I know

you think that your Greek is passable but do you realise that you just told Vasos that your mother said if he visits her, she will cook him paper towels? Are you going to show her how to give paper towels a Greek twist? I don't know what the Greek for spotted dick is but it certainly isn't *chartopetsetes*."

"Victor got it just right, you dozy cow," Violet Burke shouted. "He knew I was winding the captain up with a bit of a joke. Vasos won't know what's hit him when he gets his gob round a real bit of spotted dick."

"My mother has been playing the esteemed captain for a fool by teaching him the incorrect meaning of English words," I explained to the group. "After all, the English he spouts is completely meaningless anyway. Can you imagine, he uses 'beautiful towel' as a greeting?"

"He certainly sounds a character," Gordon said.

"'Appen I'll save your Barry a bowl of spotted dick since he sorted me out with that old bike," Vi said to Cynthia.

"It's my bicycle, actually," Cynthia pointed out.

"How come you didn't bother to put a bit of padding on the saddle then, lass? It must have really dug in your arse. I'm thinking to knit a sort of tea cosy thing to put over it to give it a cushion like feel."

Although I could swear I could see Cynthia's mind boggling at the thought of her bicycle saddle being transformed with a knitted tea cosy, I was mistaken. She was actually working up the nerve to accost Violet Burke about the missing cat.

"Violet, are you sure that you haven't seen Kouneli? The last place anyone saw him was in your kitchen..."

"And I chucked it out of the window so there's no point going round accusing me of all sorts," Violet Burke retorted, looking every inch the bolshie harridan in her feigned outrage.

"I didn't accuse you..." Cynthia faltered. Staring at the floor in embarrassment, my sister-in-law missed the tell-tale look of guilt that flashed briefly across my mother's face. I began to suspect that Violet Burke was not as innocent of the cat's whereabouts as she liked to make out.

"Anyway, I can't be sitting round here all day, I've things to be getting on with," Vi declared. "I only popped up to see if any of you rich expats are in need of a cleaner."

"Oh, do you know of one?" Doreen asked. "I heard that Victor's Albanian gardener was in the market for extra work but he looks too grubby to engage as a cleaner."

"It's me what's after some cleaning work, you daft apeth," Violet Burke spat, hardly endearing herself to a potential future employer by firing insults in her direction. "Victor can vouch for my honesty. He'll tell you straight that I'm scrupulous about eradicating muck: I did birth a public health inspector, don't forget. My Victor likely inherited his hygiene obsession from me."

"Do say you'll come and work for me, Violet, once we get into the new house. Please say you will. I just know you'll be an absolute treasure," Moira begged.

"That would be grand, lass," Vi confirmed, a smile softening her features.

"And if Victor can vouch for you, then I'd be jolly happy to have you come and clean my house," Sherry said with her customary enthusiasm.

"You'd have to put a lid on all that jollity if I do," Vi replied. "I can't be doing with it, it grates on my nerves."

"I wish I could help you out, Violet, but we

haven't got two pennies to rub together to pay for a char," Milton said.

"'Appen feeding all them scabby cats leaves you a bit brassic," Vi retorted. "I can't say as how I'd be up for it anyway. I have my reputation to think of and what with you writing them mucky porn books...oops, have I let the cat out of the bag. I forgot that Victor says you don't want anyone knowing that you're Scarlett Bottom."

Chapter 28

Spawning Mutants in Distant Places

With no hope of restoring order to the cookery class after Violet Burke's shocking outburst, my students had been eager to scuttle away. Guessing they were keen to gossip amongst themselves as soon as the coast was clear, I was not too surprised to overhear Doreen whispering to Cynthia, asking where she could get her hands on a copy of Milton's porn. I hadn't seen Norman so perky for months, even though I had honoured my promise to Doreen and kept him well away from the cooking sherry. It seemed that Milton's secret life as a purveyor of porn had injected a bit of get up and go into Meli's resident couch potato.

I must confess to a sense of amusement when Sherry cornered Dimitris as they left, suggesting they do their class homework together. She was all over the poor fellow like a bad rash, Dimitris apparently having no say in the matter and seemingly unaware that I hadn't actually set any homework. Still, rather him than me.

As they took their leave, my students assured me that the class had been most educational and that they couldn't wait to get home and experiment with beef and olives. I was not so conceited to believe a word of it, convinced they were all desperate to rush home and plug themselves straight into the Internet to locate a copy of 'Delicious Desire'. Everyone promised they would most definitely return for a repeat performance the next week when I would be schooling them in the fine art of preparing the Greek dish of *revithia*, chickpea soup. Keen to ensure there would be no no-shows, I reminded them that they had paid for the classes in advance and that I didn't offer refunds.

"Not so fast, Mother," I said, putting a

restraining hand on her arm as she tried to sneak away after the others. "You may have fooled Cynthia, but I saw the look on your face when she accused you of doing something to her vile cat."

"Well, 'appen I do know something about it but it's not the sort of thing one goes blurting out in front of an audience of cat lovers."

"Just spit it out, Mother."

"If you must know, her horrible cat got inside again after your Marigold had cooked up that chicken dinner the other night," Vi admitted.

"Don't tell me you had a late night snack of fried cat and chips. Or did you put it in a toastie?" I was only half-joking.

"You need your head examining if you think I'd tuck into that scabby cat. Just 'cos they cook up some questionable things in some of them dodgy takeaways back home doesn't mean I've got an appetite for noshing on cats," Vi said. "While I've no time for meddling health inspectors in general, I'm all in favour of them clamping down on mucky places that cook up pets. It's a filthy practice and no mistake."

"Well, thanks for the vote of confidence in my previous profession," I said sarcastically.

"And don't go thinking you can wriggle out of it by changing the subject. Enough of the deflection, Mother. What did you do with Cynthia's cat?"

"Well, like I say, it snuck in when I got home so I grabbed hold of it to chuck it out the front door. It's hardly my fault that the thing just 'appened to land in the back of a passing pick-up..."

"I'd imagine your aim might have had something to do with it," I said, attempting to visualise how high off the ground the back of a pick-up actually was.

"That cat was nowt but a blasted nuisance. Good riddance to bad rubbish, I say. You've had plenty to say about it yourself, lad, and none of it good."

"Whilst I happen to agree it is a vile mutant, apparently little Anastasia is very fond of it," I said. "Not to mention Cynthia appears unnaturally attached to the thing."

"Well, give her one of Marigold's cats then to make up for it," Violet Burke barked. "You could cut down on all the filthy cat hairs littering the place if you got rid of one of them."

"Don't even think about it, Mother," I warned. "Marigold would drag me off to the divorce courts if she came back to discover one of her precious felines was missing. You know how she dotes on the creatures."

"I know that, lad. I was pulling your leg. I'm hardly going to go round deliberately upsetting that wife of yours when she was obliging enough to turn a blind eye to me moving in," Vi sighed. "I reckon it can't have been easy for Marigold, marrying an orphan then having a strange mother-in-law turning up like a bolt from the blue. I'll admit I'm not the easiest person to put up with, so credit where credit's due. Your Marigold deserves a medal for putting up with me."

"She's grown very fond of you too, Mother," I said, not voicing Marigold's usual disclaimer of 'in small doses.'

As my mother adjusted the spectacles on the end of her nose, I recognised the guileful gleam in her eye reflected in the lenses and I realised that I had been played.

"All that guff you just came out with was just your clever way of changing the subject. There's still the matter of Cynthia's missing cat to sort out," I challenged.

"Well, 'appen I did say some of it as a distraction, but it doesn't mean it wasn't true.

Anyway, there's nowt I can do about the cat now…"

"You could own up to Cynthia. We may be able to put the word out, see if anyone found a cat in the back of their pick-up."

Even to my own ears, my idea seemed lame. The passing pick-up could have been heading anywhere and Kouneli could well be raping its way through the local feline population of Patras or Athens by now, spawning a plethora of mutant kittens in distant places.

"All right, Victor, I'll come clean to the lass. I just hope she doesn't demand her bicycle back if I do," Vi grudgingly agreed.

"I'll buy you a new one if she does," I promised.

"I'll do it tomorrow, lad. Right now, I have to be making tracks. I've that mucky taverna to clean and a ton of spuds to peel."

Standing up to stretch, my mother groaned, pressing her hands into the small of her back.

"My coccyx isn't half giving me some gip," she complained.

"Perhaps you should give the taverna a miss until the bruising has settled down," I suggested.

"I've never pulled a sickie in my life, lad,

and I don't intend to start now. Besides, I need the money."

"I'll be happy to help you out with a bit of cash if you're short, Mother," I offered.

"Keep your cash, Victor. Being short is nowt new but I'm not a charity case."

"I appreciate that you have your pride, Mother, it's most commendable. I have to say though that I have never been able to understand why you insist on working your fingers to the bone at your age. Surely you are in receipt of the state pension, yet you're always broke."

"You'd be short too if you'd taken on the debts of that thieving bigamist, Arthur Burke. There's a lot of missing savings to make up what he fleeced from all them daft cows that couldn't see through him."

"You mean to say that you work like a navvy to replace the money that Arthur Burke stole from his victims."

"Aye, that I do, Victor. I can't abide dishonesty and I won't have people thinking I profited from his thievery. I'll put back every penny my dead husband fleeced from their post office accounts if it's the last thing I do."

Chapter 29

Victor's Wounded Dignity

Since Clawsome and Catastrophe demonstrated no ill-effects from breakfasting on Athena's *chtapodi me macaronia*, I decided to risk heating the rest of the octopus up for my supper. Popping a plate into the microwave to warm up on my return, I slipped down to the street and drove the Punto up the narrow track to old Leo's house, leaving it discreetly parked well away from prying eyes. Walking home in the fading light, I congratulated myself on my forward thinking. The absence of the

Punto outside the house would convey the impression that no one was home. I was quite prepared to dine on octopus in the dark if it meant I could avoid another fraught evening of Meals on Wheels deliveries.

The distinctive smell of burning olive wood pervaded the air, the olive farmers having set fires to burn the pruned offcuts. The odd cloud of smoke drifted across my path as I strolled home, causing my eyes to sting. Though most of the outdoor fires had already been doused, a red glow in the distance cast its light on the last of the olive pickers tending the embers.

Darkness had descended by the time I reached the village square, the rustle of leaves underfoot sounding like thunder cracks in the early evening silence. Walking past Spiros' house, I glanced up at the window, moved by the silhouetted figures of Spiros and his fiancée embracing. I was delighted that Sampaguita had overcome her reluctance to live in sin with the undertaker and that the sale of Leo's house meant that Spiros would be able to throw a big fat Greek wedding in the coming year.

The light from Barry's house across the square caught my eye but I wasn't tempted to intrude. Knowing what had happened to

Cynthia's vile mutant cat, I was in no mood to face her. I made a mental note to persuade Violet Burke that the best course of action would be to fess up to Barry and then leave my brother-in-law to handle his wife: the chances were that Cynthia would come over all hysterical.

Dimitris' front window was slightly ajar, the discordant sound of Sherry's braying laughter taking me by surprise. Since there was nothing remotely musical about Sherry's laugh, perchance it didn't grate on Dimitris' sensitive nerves. When Marigold telephoned, I would fill her on this latest development, knowing that my wife would welcome the opportunity to engage in some meddlesome matchmaking on her return. No doubt she would declare that she had known all along that Dimitris and Sherry would make a lovely couple even though they struck me as wildly incompatible.

"I say, old chap, you gave me a scare creeping round in the dark, what." I couldn't place the words at first until I spotted Milton bent over the meagre wood pile outside his front door, selecting a log to throw on the fire.

"I'm sorry that my mother let the cat out of the bag like that," I said.

"No harm done, old chap. I suppose it had

to come out sooner or later about my writing erotica. At least it gives me the chance to tell the world that Edna is my muse. Can't help thinking it may help with the old book sales too, what. I bet every expat for miles will be desperate to get their hands on a copy."

"I expect you're right," I conceded, wondering at what cost to Milton's privacy. I determined that if I ever unleashed my own up-sticks book on the reading public, I would preserve my own anonymity at all costs. There was no way I would allow my wife to become a laughing stock, a fate I predicted Edna would soon be experiencing now that Violet Burke had wilfully exposed Milton's identity as Scarlett Bottom.

"Do you need a hand with that log, Milton?"

"I'm fine, Victor. Good exercise for the old hip, what. Can I tempt you in for a glass of potato wine?"

"Not tonight, Milton. Another time perhaps." I appreciated his offer since it showed that Violet Burke's big mouth had failed to put a dent in our friendship.

Sauntering home, I smiled at the sight of a few random strays curled up dozing in doorways, oblivious to the chill in the air. I expected that with Kouneli off the scene, the strays would sleep much easier from now on.

Pausing outside the *apothiki*, the light indoors reassured me that Violet Burke had biked home safely from the taverna. No doubt, she would be enjoying a relaxing bath to ease the pain of her coccyx, perchance snacking on a Fray Bentos as she indulged in a pleasant soak. I don't mind admitting that I was envious, wishing that I'd tested out the bathtub in the *apothiki* before handing the key over to my mother. I really regretted being unable to persuade Marigold that we needed a tub in our bathroom since I often yearned for a bath. The cave walk coupled with the drenching I had received earlier left an ache in my bones. I decided another hot shower was in order after the octopus, even if my ruse that no one was home necessitated my showering by candlelight.

I had to admit that the octopus went down a treat, the cats eagerly pouncing on the leftovers. Marigold would be pleased to hear that I was feeding her pampered felines with such delectable treats. Alas, the shower didn't happen, the hose breaking away from the showerhead and flooding the bathroom the moment I turned it on: at least the flood demonstrated that the water pressure was operating on full throttle again. About to phone Barry to ask if he would pop over to fix it, I realised he wouldn't be able to sort it in the dark and any lights might act as a beacon to the Meals on Wheels brigade. The only company I really craved was that of my wife. When the telephone rang, my heart skipped a beat. I hoped to hear Marigold's dulcet tone.

"I haven't got long, darling. We're off to the Bhilai Bhaji for a curry as soon as Benjamin arrives. It seems forever since we had any of their deliciously piquant sour lemon pickle. Shall I try and smuggle some home for you, darling?" Marigold trilled. "Ashley invited himself along and is meeting us there so I've been busy making Geraldine look as repulsive as possible. Luckily she's thrown herself into it with gusto, though she had a terrible time trying to prise her middle-aged body into a skin-tight number designed for a street walker. There are bits of flab hanging out all over the place and she's rocking enough sequins to give her a nasty dose of glitter rash."

"It sounds horrible..."

"Well, it ought to do the trick and give Ashley second thoughts about proposing. I don't think he's planning to go down on one knee tonight because I deliberately stood him up at Argos where we were meant to be picking out a ring during his lunch break. I doubt he'll have gone ahead without me; he seemed very keen on a woman's opinion. I suppose if he does propose, Geraldine can feign a sudden dose of food poisoning to avoid giving him an answer..."

"I hardly think that's fair on the restaurant, dear. Such a deception could ruin the impeccable hygiene reputation of the Bhilai Bhaji," I scolded.

"Well, perhaps a sudden migraine then. Oh, you'll never guess who I ran into in Top Shop," Marigold teased. "Emily."

"Emily who?" The name didn't ring any bells.

"Emily, you know. From three doors down. The one with the heavy velvet curtains that made the place look like a funeral parlour..."

"The purple windows."

"That's the one. Well, it turns out that Emily and Bill..."

"Who's Bill?"

"Emily's husband, do keep up, darling. You remember Bill, he had that paunch and always wore braces..."

"I think I'd remember a fellow who flashed a mouth full of metal in my direction," I pointed out.

"Not those kind of braces, silly. The sort that held up his trousers."

"You mean suspenders," I corrected.

"Well, it turns out that Emily and Bill didn't have a clue that we'd moved to Greece. Anyway, before I could gather my wits about me, Emily had only gone and invited herself over to Greece to stay with us for a week. And Bill too, of course."

"Bother, Marigold. When will you learn to say no instead of handing out profligate invitations to people we barely know to go littering up our spare bedroom..."

"Must you take that tone, Victor? I'd like to have seen you try to wheedle your way out of it when put on the spot like that." Adroitly changing the subject, Marigold said, "What's been happening with you, dear? Anything exciting to report?"

"Not really. I walked to that cave in Nektar with Gordon and we had to be rescued from its bat ridden and spider infested interior by a random cow herder..."

"That's nice, dear," Marigold said, her absent

minded tone suggesting she was barely paying attention. "How was your cookery class? I'm sure it was a resounding success."

"I think it was rather well received. At least until my mother burst in and announced that Milton writes porn. Sherry left with Dimitris. I'm not sure if he had any say in the matter, she was all over him like a rash."

"Oh, that's wonderful news. I wouldn't have necessarily tried to pair them off but yes, now I think about it, it could work," Marigold said, the excitement evident in her tone.

"Just hold the line a moment, darling," I said, disturbed by the sound of banging doors and raised voices outside. "There seems to be a bit of a commotion coming from the *apothiki*. I could swear it sounds like *Kapetainos* Vasos."

"Don't be silly, dear. What on earth would that old reprobate be doing all the way up in Meli?" Marigold scoffed.

"Well, he did telephone earlier to extend an invitation for me to join him in an evening of carousing and debauchery..."

"And no doubt you were a killjoy and turned him down," Marigold correctly guessed. "I expect the noise you can hear is Panos arriving to take your mother out on another date,

Victor. Leave them be, she won't want you snooping on her, you know how much she values her independence."

"Perhaps you're right, dear," I conceded, resisting the urge to pop out on the balcony for a bird's eye view of what was going on. "It turns out that Violet Burke had a hand in the disappearance of Cynthia's cat..."

"Bravo for Vi. That vile cat is a menace. And apart from her love life looking up, how is your mother settling in otherwise?"

"Well, she managed to secure a couple of cleaning jobs from the expats at the cooking class," I said.

"On top of the job she landed at the taverna? I hope she isn't planning on overdoing it, she's hardly a spring chicken."

"I discovered the reason why my mother insists on working so much. She's determined to pay off all the debts that Arthur Burke left behind when he met his end under the number 47 bus. She's been working her fingers to the bone to pay back the women her bigamous husband fleeced."

For once Marigold was lost for words.

"Vi has just gone up in my estimation, Victor. That's probably the most noble thing I ever heard," Marigold said, emotion evident in her voice. "I think you should be proud to call her Mother."

With the key to the *apothiki* burning a hole in my pocket, I mulled the wisdom of Marigold's words. When my wife had heard that our shower was out of action, she proposed that I just simply pop downstairs for a bath whilst my mother was out on her date. I supposed that if I gave the tub a good scouring with Vim once I was done, Violet Burke would be none the wiser. It did seem a shame not to take advantage of the pristine new bath which I had, after all, paid for, when my aching bones were crying out for a long languorous soak.

Throwing caution to the wind, I embraced my recently discovered daredevil side and crept downstairs, surreptitiously letting myself into the *apothiki*. With the water pressure back to normal, the bath was filled with hot water perfumed with scented bubbles in no time at all. Slipping into the tub, I luxuriated in the water, the stress of the day slipping away. Relaxing in the bubbles, I admitted to myself how much I was missing Marigold. When I collected her at the airport next week, I would whisk her off her feet and romance her in five star luxury: well perhaps four star, there was no need to go overboard.

"I love you, beautiful towel."

"You daft apeth. Are you up for some spotted dick now? It will round the chips off nicely..."

"Suet dumpling..."

For one wistful moment, I imagined I was simply dreaming and then reality hit me in the face like a sharp slap from a wet washcloth. The blustering banter filtering through to the bathroom was not the stuff of dreams. I must have dozed off in the bathtub and Violet Burke had returned home with the carousing boat Captain in tow.

Hurriedly reaching out to grab a towel, I had no time to cover my embarrassment before *Kapetainos* Vasos burst into the bathroom without so much as by-your-leave: I instantly had a horrible flashback to the moment I had caught Guzim indulging in my outdoor spa. Fortunately the sight of my naked body covered in bubbles distracted Vasos from his intention of using the toilet. As he fell about laughing, I wished that I'd at least had the sense to follow the Albanian shed dweller's example and take a bath in my underpants.

"Hello, Victor," Vasos guffawed. "Mucky fat."

"Not so mucky if you don't mind. I've just had a bath," I retorted, wrapping the towel around my wounded dignity.

A Note from Victor

All Amazon reviews gratefully received, even a word or two is most welcome.

Please feel free to drop me a line if you would like information on the release date of future volumes in the Bucket to Greece series at vdbucket@gmail.com.

I am always delighted to hear from happy readers.

Printed in Great Britain
by Amazon